ART &
OF VALU

INVEST LIKE BILLIONAIRE WARREN BUFFETT

By
Scott Thompson, MBA

TEXTBOOK
ISBN# 9781300973959

WORKBOOK
ISBN# 9781304802804

Scan barcode for more info

SPECIAL THANKS!

Special Thanks to:	Peter Buffett (Foreword)
	Warren Buffett (Photo, back cover)
Front Cover Photo:	Trey Fortner, www.LastCallStudios.com
Back Cover Photo:	Jennifer Bintner
Graphic Design:	Trey Fortner, www.LastCallStudios.com
Stylist/Advisor:	Ebani Butler, www.EleganceBravery.com
Editors:	Scott Thompson www.ProValueSource.com
	Dr. Bud Labitan, Labitan Partners
	Bakul Lalla, MBA
	Dr. Kelly Johnson
Contributors:	Peter Buffett (Foreword)
	Dr. Bud Labitan, Labitan Partners
	Frank Betz, Carret/Zane Capital Management
	Paul Lountzis, Lountzis Asset Management
	Dr. Maulik Suthar, MD, Orange Holdings, India
	Bakul Lalla, MBA

TABLE OF CONTENTS

Readers of this book include: New York Times, CNBC, FOX Business News, and others. Universities across America are using this textbook and its accompanying workbook: Art & Science of Value Investing: WORKBOOK to teach the powerful skills of value investing. Volume discounts available at: info@ProValueSource.com

FOREWORD

By Peter Buffett

*Emmy Award winning musician, best-selling author, philanthropist,
son of billionaire investor Warren Buffett*

When I was in my twenties, I was home visiting my Dad in Omaha and he said to me – as he was heading off to the office one morning – "Pete, you know… you and I do the same thing. You create your music and I go off to Berkshire to paint on my canvas a little each day."

That is why I like the title of Scott's book. It's about the art *and* the science of investing. I always knew that my dad felt (and I would agree) that he is connected to the art of what he does. And this is a critical and often missed point of his success.

I know that I would create music no matter what the material outcome might be. Music has always flowed through me. Any other form of work – no matter what the financial outcome – could not replace the reward of creating a piece of music. And that is true for my father as well. He's not in it for the money. He would be doing what he's doing no matter how great the return on the investment. He's just wired for it.

He was born at a time and in a place that rewards what he's good at. Boy, does it! But as he sees it, that was dumb luck… or what he would call the "Ovarian Lottery." He didn't choose the factors of his birth. So every day he gets up grateful that he can live another day doing the thing he feels he was born to do. This feeling of gratitude – the polar opposite of entitlement – has made him the man he is today.

So now, instead of talking about what many would call the world's greatest investor, I'm writing about an artist who is grateful for every day he can paint on his canvas. I would imagine most people reading this would not have expected that.

What does that say about the importance he places on his wealth? It takes it from being the means to an end – which is usually consumption of material goods to help fill some psycho/emotional void or the external pressure of a "look at me" world – to the end itself. The money is a scorecard. It tells my dad that he is, indeed, good at what he does. It's like having a hit record, or a painting in the Met.

The question I hope this raises in the reader is – why am I interested in the methods of Warren Buffett's investment style? If it's to make sure your kids can afford college... or you can have a retirement nest egg... or maybe just have enough for fundamental needs, that's great! My concern is that too many folks are looking at my Dad's success and think that the money can lead them to happiness – a greater sense of one's self worth. It can't and it won't.

I hope that before you read this book you ask yourself – what does success mean to me? And if I'm good at following the investment principles in Scott's book and make a lot of money, what will I do with it? And – are the companies I'm investing in just creating a great return for me? Or are they also creating value for the world at large? And with that question, one must follow... what are the values I'm looking for in a company... just a good return, or something that puts people and the planet before profit?

Today's young investor has a lot more information than just the stock market at his or her fingertips. You can learn much more about the practices of the companies you're researching. As a young kid, I would see my dad reading these *huge* books – S&P and Moody's manuals. But they were just full of numbers – pretty boring to a six-year-old like me. It's a different world today. And I believe it's imperative for the young investor to take into account all of the parameters of a company's behavior... way beyond the P and L statement and balance sheet.

I will tell you my Dad's best investment advice – as predictable as this may be – *you* are your greatest investment. You and the people you surround yourself with. So before you read this book about value investing, I suggest you write out a list of your own values. What is your definition of success... of happiness... of enough? What would get you out of bed with a smile on your face and a spring in your step?

And, if you do end up with large numbers in your bank account and you've surpassed your definition of "enough," what will you do with the excess? As you will read in this book, Scott has given back in many ways.

And remember, philanthropy means "the love of people." So money is just one way of practicing it. Scott gives his time and expertise as well as his money. Everyone can practice philanthropy every day. But when there *is* money involved, making choices regarding where that particular investment should be made, can be as complex and time consuming as any other form of money management.

As with every choice in life – it's the motivation that moves you.

So I encourage you to check in with the motivation that attracted you to this book. Because if you're successful at value investing, the values you have will affect more than just your own future.

Peter Buffett

Peter Buffett, Scott Thompson, Warren Buffett
(Founder: Berkshire Hathaway)

INTRODUCTION

I'd like to thank Peter Buffett for his friendship and for contributing such an inspiring foreword to this book. This book is the result of decades of research into the field of value investing, gathered together and organized into a single convenient source. *(Also, check out the "Art & Science of Value Investing* WORKBOOK*" that accompanies this book: ISBN# 9781304802804).*

This book has guided students and investors around the world on a journey through the powerful value investing methods used by the most successful value investors. These include Ben Graham, Warren Buffett, Charlie Munger, and many more! Each valuation method is explained in a simple, easy-to-understand, step-by-step process.

Learning investing is similar to learning music. In music, the "science" refers to learning the notes, scales, chords, and practicing them. In music, "art" refers to the ability to create and compose music on your own after you've learned the science. As Warren would ask his musically gifted son, "Did you find your sound?" *(Indeed he has!)* Therefore, the goal of this book is to teach you both the "Art & Science of Value Investing."

Imagine for a moment, you were billionaire investor Warren Buffett. You possess decades of investing experience. You are not motivated by acquiring depreciating assets, new cars, homes, and yachts, etc. Instead you calmly sit reading thousands of annual reports, valuing businesses... waiting for "the right pitch."

When you find an investment you like, you decide quickly and definitively. You scribe hand-written notes throughout multiple pages of an annual report of a business in which you're considering investing. You estimate its total intrinsic value, and then its intrinsic value "per share."

You value this business at $100 per share. Later, you look up its stock price to discover it is trading at only $50 per share. A wide margin of safety! It's a high-quality business you understand, with sustainable competitive advantages, run by honest and trustworthy management. It's a rare and wonderful business. You decide to invest! And so it begins...

Wall Street scoffs and wonders why Warren would invest in such an unfavorable stock. Despite six decades of consistently outperforming the

S&P 500 market index, Wall Street does not understand Buffett's stock picks, nor can it match Buffett's outstanding value investing success!

How many speculators struggle, only to pour money into the wrong stocks again and again? Meanwhile, the world wonders, "How does Warren do it? How does Warren consistently outperform the market?" Fortunately, these answers are revealed in this comprehensive, easy-to-understand book: **ART & SCIENCE OF VALUE INVESTING**.

"There should be a course in business school that teaches how to value a business."
Warren Buffett

Now, you will learn to value businesses, stocks, bonds, and estimate intrinsic valuations like billionaire Warren Buffett and other investors! Discover how to use both qualitative and quantitative factors to identify high-quality undervalued businesses. Bonus: Includes charts, diagrams, and Web links to download free valuation models!
This book answers the most common value investing questions, such as:
- How do we identify high-quality undervalued businesses?
- What causes price to value opportunities?
- How can we profit from them?
- How do we estimate the intrinsic value of a business?
- What is the ideal "margin of safety" range?
- Which topics can we study to become better value investors?
- Why do value investors buy, when others are selling?

A common joke in our industry is… "What's the fastest way to end up with a million dollars in the stock market? Answer: Start with $2 million!" This witticism points out the importance of adhering to sound value investment principles. Question: Who is the wealthiest investor in the history of the world? Answer: Warren Buffett. Question: Which investment method does Warren Buffett use? Answer: Value Investing.

Other popular investment methods include: Modern Portfolio Theory (MPT), Capital Asset Pricing Model (CAPM), Efficient Market Hypothesis (EMH), day trading, options, momentum, chart reading, and other investment strategies. While all of these investment strategies may be popular, Warren Buffett simply adheres to his proven, successful, value investing strategies.

It is an honor to help perpetuate the investment strategies and legacies of some of the world's greatest value investors. Enjoy the book!

14

CHAPTER ONE

Forefathers

"The market is there to serve you, not instruct you." Benjamin Graham

"Rule #1: Never lose money. Rule #2: Never forget rule #1." Warren Buffett

"A great investment is not a bargain at any price." Scott Thompson

1.1 History and Evolution of Value Investing:

Phil Carret and Ben Graham were the first value investors. They influenced many investors. The most famous is Warren Buffett. Warren was born August 30th 1930 in Omaha, Nebraska. Warren's father was a stockbroker. Warren used to update the stock prices on the chalkboard in his father's office, as new stock quotes flowed in. During his early childhood, Warren discovered his fascination with numbers. By age 11, Warren had already read every book in the Omaha library about investing.

In 1949, when he was only 19, Warren read the "Intelligent Investor" by Benjamin Graham. (Graham, 1949) This was the time in Warren's life to choose a business school to earn his M.B.A. Warren interviewed at Harvard University hoping to become a student there, but was turned down by the Harvard alumnus who interviewed him. Fortunately, as he was browsing thru college brochures, Warren discovered that his value-investing hero Ben Graham was teaching at Columbia Business School. Warren applied close to the deadline at Columbia, but was accepted.

He earned the only A+ grade Ben Graham ever gave. After graduation, Warren applied for work at Ben Graham's business, "Graham Newman," but he was turned down. Warren even offered to work for free; to which Ben Graham replied that young Warren was overvaluing his talents.

Warren persisted, and after a while, Ben Graham eventually consented, and hired Warren Buffett as an investment analyst at "Graham Newman."

Warren eagerly applied his value investing knowledge, learned from his former professor and current employer, Ben Graham. Ben Graham, eventually retired and Warren moved back to Omaha, Nebraska. Ben Graham's investors asked him if he could recommend a good place for them to move their money. Ben Graham recommended Warren Buffett.

Warren Buffett began his first investment partnership in 1956, and he named it "The Buffett Partnership" in Omaha, Nebraska. (Buffett W., Buffett Partnership Letters, 1956-1969).

As Warren began his new partnership, he initially implemented Ben Graham's value investing strategies. These "deep bargain," or "cigar butt" strategies focused heavily on quantitative factors, and not on qualitative factors. Buffett's knowledge, experience, and philosophy evolved over time. You can witness the evolution of Buffett's value investing strategies from the beginning of his career into his later years:

- **Ben Graham's "Net Net" Stocks:** Benjamin Graham's quantitative "Net Net" process. This is where value investors invest only when a business's stock price trades at least 2/3rds below the business's Net Net Working Capital (NNWC). The (3) formulas are:

Net Working Capital = Current Assets − Current Liabilities

Graham's Net Working Capital = Current Assets − Total Liabilities

Net Net Working Capital = Cash + Short Term Marketable Investments + (Accounts Receivable x 75%) + (Inventory x 50%) − Total Liabilities

Net Working Capital can be divided by Total Shares Outstanding to determine "Net Working Capital per Share." The formula is:

Net Working Capital / Total Shares Outstanding = Net Working Capital per Share

Compare the business's current share price against the business's Net Working Capital per share. If the business's current share price were at least 2/3rds below its Net Working Capital per Share, then Graham would consider it to be a possible "Net Net" investment.

Since many investors are now aware of Graham's "Net Net" investment process, a much lower number of Net Net investments exist today, compared to during Ben Graham's day. However, they still appear from time-to-time, and savvy value investors know how to find them. This book will show you how to identify them.

- **NPV Analysis, or DCF Analysis:** Warren Buffett's investment process evolved into using the Net Present Value (NPV) and Discounted Cash Flow (DCF) analysis process developed in 1938 by John Burr Williams. See Williams' thesis and book called "The Theory of Investment Value." We will discuss this more in Chapter 9: Intrinsic Value.

This is where a business's Free Cash Flows (FCFs) are used to project or estimate future financial performance of a business using a Net Present Value (NPV) or Discounted Cash Flow (DCF) analysis. (See Chapter 9 for more detailed information about how to perform your own NPV or DCF analysis).

- **Four Filters Process**: Buffett's Four Filters Process added "qualitative" to the quantitative. This is when Warren's value investment philosophy evolved dramatically by the influence of Charlie Munger and Phil Fisher. By incorporating qualitative factors and adding them in front of the quantitative strategies, Buffett raised the probability of identifying high-quality businesses, with durable competitive advantages, run by honest and capable managers, selling for attractive prices. (Buffett's Annual Letter to the Shareholders of Berkshire Hathaway, Inc., 1977-2012).

- It's at this important stage when Buffett began to implement the Four Filters investment process, and greatly increased Berkshire Hathaway's investment success. Buffett first met his long-time friend and vice-chair of Berkshire Hathaway, Charlie Munger around 1960. In the words of Charlie Munger, "You have to understand the odds and have the discipline to bet only when the odds are in your favor." (Charlie Munger Talk at Harvard, 2001).

- **Buffett's Four Filters Investment Process:**
    1. Seek a Business you understand
    2. Find Durable Competitive Advantages
    3. Insist on Honest and Capable Managers
    4. Graham's "Margin of Safety" idea of buying cheap gives us an Attractive Price

We look forward to discussing more about Buffett and Munger's Four Filters investment process in Chapter 3.

- **Two-Column Method:** Presently, Warren Buffett uses what he refers to in his annual reports as the "Two-Column method," consisting of two primary components:

Column 1: The cumulative value of investments per share: stocks, bonds, cash, and cash equivalents.

Column 2: The cumulative value of pre-tax operating earnings per share. Then multiply these earnings by a multiple consistent with P/E multiples of other similar businesses within its sector and industry.

Add these two amounts together to arrive at a business's Intrinsic Value, as calculated by Warren Buffett's "Two-column method."

Warren Buffett rarely writes about his investment processes, but for the first time on page 6 of Berkshire Hathaway's 2010 Annual Report, Buffett surprised the world and revealed his previously confidential "Two-column method."

Warren republished his "Two-column method" again on page 99 of Berkshire Hathaway's 2011 Annual Report, and on page 104 of Berkshire Hathaway's 2012 Annual Report.

(See Chapter 9: for more detailed information about how Warren Buffett calculates his "Two-column Investment Method.")

This book will guide you on your journey toward becoming a value investor. You will learn what previously successful value investors like Warren Buffett, Ben Graham, Charlie Munger, Phil Fisher, and others look for while analyzing potential businesses in which to invest.

1.2 Warren Buffett:

Warren Buffett is the wealthiest investor in the history of the world with a net worth over $62 billion (US dollars) in 2007. Warren Buffett was born August 30, 1930 in Omaha Nebraska. In 1952, Warren married his first wife, Susan Thompson. They had 3 children: Howard Buffett, Suzie Buffett, Jr., and Peter Buffett.

Instead of living a "high-consumption lifestyle," Warren Buffett does exactly the opposite. Warren lives below his means and he says buying material goods do not make him happy. In fact, Warren still lives in the same home he purchased in 1958 for $31,500. His home is nice, but certainly modest compared with other homes owned by the world's wealthiest billionaires.

Warren is happy living a simple, somewhat frugal, lifestyle. He admits he's not much of a spender. By living in a modest home, especially during the early years, he has freed up more capital to buy more shares of undervalued businesses. These businesses significantly increased in value, and earned him billions.

To further demonstrate Warren's reluctance to spend: he drove an old Volkswagen Beetle for years while he was already worth several hundreds of millions. In the early days, many in Omaha remained in disbelief of Warren's massive wealth. When they saw Warren driving to work in his little VW Beetle, they skeptically wondered, "If he were really worth hundreds of millions, then why is he still driving a VW Beetle?" Many did not invest with Warren in the early days. However, those who did are now also worth millions. For one early investor named Franklin "Otis" Booth, Warren turned his $1 million investment into over $1 billion dollars.

When asked why Warren doesn't buy a new car, Warren referred to the "time value of money." (Net Present Value, or Discounted Cash Flows) Instead of buying a new $30,000 car today, Warren could invest the same money into shares of undervalued stocks. Over 30 years, the $30,000 invested could compound into $1,000,000 dollars, instead of buying a new car. And Buffett says, "$1,000,000 is too much to pay for a new car!"

Translation: instead of looking at only the price of the new car today, Buffett considered how much this same amount of money could be grown and compounded over several decades into a significant amount.

Therefore, by delaying or denying yourself the purchase of material goods today, you will free up more investment capital to invest that will compound over time to build your fortune.

Before spending money or investing, consider **opportunity cost.** This is when you consider outcomes of a range of potential choices. If you possess limited finite resources, which investment decision will offer the greatest security of principal and return on capital? Which is the value of the most lucrative alternative forgone (not chosen). In other words, if you only have $100, consider the potential consequences, risks, and gains of each opportunity, before you decide to allocate your capital.

"Live below your means and your wealth will multiply." Scott Thompson

"Why do people spend as much as they earn, no matter how much their incomes increase?" Scott Thompson

Warren Buffett loves valuing businesses. He says he loves his work so much, he "tap dances" to work everyday! Do you love your career? If you don't believe you work for the best business in the world, consider which business is the best, and apply to work for them. Or, if you're entrepreneurial, you may decide to start your own business.

Despite Warren's success and stunning wealth, it is important to understand that wealth was merely a by-product of working at a job he loved – investing! Money was never the primary goal. In fact, Warren Buffett's son Peter Buffett confirms, "For my dad, the money just followed, it never led."

Inspiring words from Peter Buffett, Warren Buffett's youngest son, who has an acclaimed career of his own, spanning over 30 years as an award-winning musician, composer, philanthropist, and author.

For Warren Buffett, no other investor in the history of the world has ever earned more money solely through value investing. Warren Buffett does not invest in real estate, or commodities (gold, precious metals, agriculture, etc.) Instead, Warren Buffett adheres to a strict value investing strategy.

"Allow your money to work for you, or you will always be working for your money." Scott Thompson

The intent of this book is to reveal and communicate Warren Buffett's powerful value investing strategies. We will not spend time detailing an in-depth biography of Warren Buffett's personal life, as numerous books on this subject already exist.

To better understand Warren Buffett, and his value investing strategies, we must mention Benjamin Graham. Benjamin Graham was Warren Buffett's MBA business school professor, mentor, former employer, and along with Phil Carret was one of the fathers of value investing.

1.3 Benjamin Graham:

Ben Graham was a famed value investor of his day, and one of the most successful investors on Wall Street. Warren Buffett first heard of Ben Graham after reading Ben Graham's books "Security Analysis" and "The Intelligent Investor."

Ben Graham wrote "Security Analysis" in 1934, and "The Intelligent Investor" in 1949. "The Intelligent Investor" was designed as a shorter and distilled version of his bigger book. In 1950, Warren Buffett was trying to enter Harvard University's MBA program. An alumnus of Harvard University interviewed Buffett and turned Warren down. Serendipitously, Warren Buffett found out that his investing hero, Ben Graham was teaching at Columbia University's MBA business school in New York. In the end, Harvard declined Buffett's application, and Columbia accepted.

At Columbia University, Ben Graham would use real world examples when teaching his investment classes. In fact, word of this spread and many Wall Street professionals began taking Ben Graham's courses just to be exposed to Graham's "hot stock tips" during class. Many other famous investors also took Ben Graham's class, including Bill Ruane, who managed the Sequoia Fund.

Students later interviewed from the class say financial sparks flew between Buffett and Graham. Buffett would always raise his hand and always have the correct answer. Warren Buffett earned the only A+ Ben Graham ever gave during his entire teaching history at Columbia University.

Ben Graham was more quantitative in his analysis, and did not implement much qualitative criteria in his security selection process. However, in his comparisons of two similar businesses, Graham would get students to look at the debt levels of the two similar businesses. Ben Graham would invest in a business if its market price were trading at or below 66% of "Net Net" Working Capital (NNWC) per share. Ben Graham was also an activist shareholder when he felt management was engaging in behavior that kept a stock price severely depressed.

What is Net Net Working Capital? Net Net Working Capital is the difference between Total Current Assets and Total Current Liabilities. Net Net Working Capital can be calculated by looking at a business's Balance Sheet. Find "Total Current Assets," and "Total Current Liabilities." The formula to calculate Net Working Capital is:

Total Current Assets − Total Current Liabilities = Net Working Capital.

If the business's total market capitalization were selling for 33% below Net working capital, Ben Graham would consider investing. For example, if a business's Total Current Assets are $500,000,000, and Total Current Liabilities are $200,000,000, the total Net Working Capital would be $300,000,000.

$$
\begin{array}{r}
\$500,000,000 \text{ Total Current Assets} \\
-\ \$200,000,000 \text{ Total Current Liabilities} \\
\hline
\$300,000,000 \text{ Net Working Capital}
\end{array}
$$

If the business's total Market Capitalization were to be $200,000,000, then the business's total Market Capitalization would be 33% below Net Working Capital, making it a potential business in which Ben Graham would invest. Market Capitalization is often listed next to the stock price quotes easily found on financial websites like:

Finance.yahoo.com
Morningstar.com
ValueLine.com
Scottrade.com and many others. Performing a simple search in your web browser will yield a multitude of other helpful financial websites.

Another way to calculate NNWC is to divide the Net Net Working Capital by the number of Total Shares Outstanding. Then divide the Market Capitalization by the number of Total Shares Outstanding. If the market price (per share) is 33% less than the business's Net Net Working Capital (per share), Ben Graham may choose to invest. As you can see, Ben Graham was more quantitative than qualitative.

For example, in the previous example we have $300,000,000 Net Working Capital and $200,000,000 Market Capitalization. If the business had 10,000,000 Total Shares Outstanding, we can use this to determine the Net Working Capital per share, and Market Price per share.

Net Working Capital per share:
$300,000,000 ÷ 10,000,000 = $30 Net Working Capital per share

Market Capitalization per share:
$200,000,000 ÷ 10,000,000 = $20 Market Capitalization per share (also known as Market Price per share)

$20 Market Price per share ÷ $30 Net Working Capital per share = 66%

Therefore, Ben Graham may decide to invest in this business, because Market Price is 33% below Net Working Capital. Remember the (3) formulas for "Net Net" Working Capital (NNWC) are:

1. Net Working Capital = Current Assets − Current Liabilities

2. Graham's Net Working Capital = Current Assets − Total Liabilities

3. Net Net Working Capital = Cash + Short Term Marketable Investments + (Accounts Receivable x 75%) + (Inventory x 50%) − Total Liabilities

Unfortunately, these types of businesses with Market Prices at least 33% below Net Working Capital are rare. There were more of these during Ben Graham's day, but they are now less common. However, they still exist. Graham's NNWC investing process is purely quantitative, and does not factor in qualitative criteria.

Warren Buffett started his investment career using Ben Graham's NNWC value investing process, but later incorporated qualitative factors, as a result of being influenced by Charlie Munger and Phil Fisher, that eventually became known as the "Four Filters Investment Process."

Warren Buffett would jokingly refer to Ben Graham's NNWC business investments as used "cigar butt" investments. Because it was like finding a used cigar butt in the street, that maybe had 1 or 2 puffs remaining in it.

Buffett initially used Ben Graham's purely quantitative value investing strategy, investing only in businesses where Market Prices traded 33% below Net Working Capital per share.

The transition towards seeking higher quality businesses occurred in the 1960's. During this period, Buffett and Munger invested in retail and textile businesses. These proved to have high operating costs, higher competitive pressures, and ultimately lower rates of return.

Then, Buffett began incorporating the powerful qualitative influences of Phil Fisher and Charlie Munger into his previously quantitative-only value investing strategy. Therefore, after 1965, Buffett invested in under-valued businesses that he understood, possessing enduring competitive advantages, giving us long term growth, run by good trustworthy management, available at attractive prices.

Instead of investing in Ben Graham's NNWC quantitative type investments, then selling them several months later, Warren Buffett began investing and holding "wonderful" businesses for decades. This is where Warren Buffett and Charlie Munger really began to multiply their wealth.

Munger described their system this way: "We came to this notion of finding a mispriced bet and loading up when we were very confident that we were right. So we're way less diversified. And I think our system is miles better." (Munger, A Lesson on Elementary, Worldly Wisdom As It Relates To Investment Management & Business, 1994)

1.4 Charlie Munger:

By: Paul Lountzis: Lountzis Asset Management
Scott Thompson: Ameritrust Group

Charlie Munger was born in Omaha, Nebraska, in 1924, and is best known as being Warren Buffett's Vice Chairman of Berkshire Hathaway. Charlie grew up five blocks away from Warren's current home. Warren and Charlie both worked at the same grocery store owned by Warren's grandfather, but did not know each other at that time.

Charlie met Warren during a dinner party in Omaha in 1959. Munger was practicing law in Southern California and Buffett was running his investment partnership. They immediately got along, and formed a lasting friendship that has evolved into an extraordinary partnership spanning over 54 years.

Value investors have benefited immensely from Charlie Munger's wisdom and incredible life experiences shared through his many books, speeches and interviews. Charlie's objective insights provide wonderful lessons on investments and life. His witty sense of humor permeates his books, interviews, and Berkshire's annual meetings.

Although Munger is less well known than Buffett, his investing acumen remains legendary. Like Buffett, Munger also managed his own investment partnership, from 1962–1975, and generated a compound annual return of 19.8%, dwarfing the 5% generated by the Dow Jones Industrial Average during that time.

Buffett credits Munger with broadening his investment philosophy to focus upon outstanding businesses, as well as providing in-depth investment insights. Warren stated, "Charlie has taught me a lot about valuing businesses and human nature."

Buffett influenced Munger as well, including convincing him to leave his law practice and become a full-time investment manager working with Buffett to build Berkshire Hathaway. On Berkshire's success Charlie says, "We both enjoy learning and we've improved over time." However, Munger credits Buffett as the key builder of Berkshire. "Warren is by far the most important person, and to a huge degree Berkshire Hathaway is the lengthened shadow of Warren Buffett."

In Munger's July 20, 1996 talk, "Practical Thought about Practical Thought," he shared many of his investing lessons, including:

- Focusing on the big "no-brainer" questions first
- Developing a circle of competence
- Becoming numerically fluent
- Understanding accounting, *(the language of business)*
- Always thinking in a multidisciplinary manner, *(utilizing basic concepts from a broad range of disciplines including, philosophy, mathematics, biology, history and psychology).*

Decision framing and solving problems requires a depth of understanding from a broad range of fundamental principles. Charlie states, "About 80 or 90 mental models across several disciplines will carry over 90% of the freight in making you a worldly-wise person." Once the key concepts are learned they can be utilized and adapted over time to provide solutions to ever changing problems for a lifetime.

Psychology is a particularly important discipline as he describes, a lot of people with high IQs are terrible investors because they've got terrible temperaments, and that is why we say that having a certain kind of temperament is more important than brains. You need to keep raw irrational emotion under control. You need patience and discipline and an ability to take losses and adversity without going crazy. You need an ability to not be driven crazy by extreme success. (For more info, see Chapter 11: Temperament)

Munger strongly believed in and implemented Albert Einstein's Four Principal Causes of Great Achievement in his own life:

- Self-criticism
- Curiosity
- Concentration
- Perseverance

Munger particularly enjoys admitting when he has made a mistake. This is a rare quality, and often provides an opportunity to learn painfully important lessons. He has stated, "There is no way you can live an adequate life without making many mistakes." The key is learning from them and moving on aggressively. He is never discouraged, as opportunities are always around.

In his University of Michigan interview with Becky Quick, he states, "There are two things one should never do, never ever feel sorry for yourself, and second never have envy. Envy is the only one of the deadly sins that you will never have fun with, so pick another one. The best way to get what you want in life is to deserve what you want."

Becoming a great investor requires a combination of patience and opportunism. One only needs a few great insights during their lifetime to achieve excellent investment success. Munger remarked, "The way to win is to work, work, work, work and hope to have a few insights... And you're probably not going to be smart enough to find thousands in a lifetime. And when you get a few, you really load up. It's just that simple."

On patience: "We have this investment discipline of waiting for a fat pitch. If I was offered the chance to go into business where people would measure me against benchmarks, force me to be fully invested, etc, I would hate it. I would regard it as putting me into shackles."

He quotes Mr. Buffett from business school lectures; "I could improve your ultimate financial welfare by giving you a ticket with only 20 slots in it, so that you had 20 punches representing all the investments that you could make in a lifetime. This limit should increase the analytical concentration and focus one places on their decisions." At Berkshire Hathaway, 15 key decisions account for the majority of Berkshire Hathaway's enormous out-performance of the S&P 500 Index.

Behaving ethically is one of the critical factors in leading a successful life, both personally and professionally. In describing unethical behavior Munger enjoyed the description given in congressional testimony, of robber barons Jay Gould and Russell Sage: "When they are talking they are lying, and when they are silent they are stealing."

He describes Buffett as a "learning machine," and goes on to say, "Warren is one of the best learning machines on this earth. The turtles who outrun the hares are learning machines. If you stop learning in this world, the world rushes right by you." Munger is also a learning machine, and believes that spending enormous amounts of time reading is critical to developing one's worldly-wisdom. Describing the importance of reading,

"In my whole life, I have known no wise people, over a broad subject matter area, who didn't read all the time. None. Zero. You'd be amazed at how much Warren reads - at how much I read. My children laugh at me. They think I'm a book with a couple of legs sticking out."

In developing our understanding of a business, read, study, look, listen, think, visualize, feel emotions, calculate profit, and learn. Charlie Munger brings a critical mind to the game. He advises us to build an understanding like a "latticework of mental models" based on facts with accurate and reality based impressions. (Munger, A Lesson on Elementary, Worldly Wisdom As It Relates To Investment Management & Business. A 1994 Speech, 1994)

I am looking forward to attending another Berkshire Hathaway Annual Meeting where I am sure Mr. Munger will frequently respond to Mr. Buffett's answers to questions as he has so often in the past, "I have nothing to add." Nothing could be further from the truth and we should all be grateful that Munger has shared so much of his life through philanthropy, as well as sharing his many insights and worldly-wisdom for all of us to learn and grow, both professionally, and even more importantly, personally; living higher quality lives.

1.5 Phil Fisher:

Phil Fisher was a very successful investor who incorporated qualitative factors into his investing style, and the author of the best-selling book "Common Stocks and Uncommon Profits." (Buffett W. , Phil Fisher, mentioned in the Berkshire Chairman's Letter to Shareholders, 1988)

In his book "Common Stocks and Uncommon Profits," Phil Fisher listed the following 15 qualitative investment criteria:

1. Does the business offer products or services with sufficient market potential to make possible a sizable increase in sales for at least several years? (Matter of fact, appraising the degree of sales growth).

2. Does the management have a determination to continue to develop products or processes that will further increase total sales

potential when the growth potential of currently attractive product lines have largely been exploited? (Measures management attitude toward growth strategies)

3. How effective is the business's research and development (R&D) efforts in relation to its size? Divide research dollars by total sales. What percentage of each revenue dollar goes to research? Compare against the industry average. Efficiency ratio, relative sales to relative research ratio, measured against industry standard. Some businesses get a 2-to-1 ratio out of every dollar spent on research. Others do not.

4. Does the business have an above-average sales organization? (It's the making of repeat sales to satisfied customers. This is the first benchmark of success. Outstanding production, sales, and research may be considered the three main columns upon which success is based. All are important.

5. Does the business have a worthwhile profit margin? Determine the percentage of each dollar of revenue that's brought down to operating profit. Not for single year, but for series of years.

6. What is the business doing to maintain or improve its profit margins?

7. Does the business have outstanding labor and personnel relations?

8. Does the business have outstanding executive relations?

9. Does the business have depth to its management? Capable management, not just in the power of a few top leaders, but also in lower-level management being trained to move up.

10. How good are cost analysis and accounting controls? Efficiency.

11. Are there other aspects of the business, somewhat peculiar to the industry involved, which will give the investor important clues as to how outstanding the business may be in relation to its competition? Patents are a source of additional strength, rather than basic strength. Allows businesses to enjoy wider profit

margins. Competitors must go a longer way around, giving the patent holder advantages.

12. Does the business have a short or long-range outlook in regard to profits? The investor wanting maximum results should favor businesses with a truly long-range outlook concerning profits.

13. In the foreseeable future, will the growth of the business require additional equity financing, requiring a larger number of shares outstanding that will largely cancel the existing stockholders' benefit from the anticipated growth? Intelligent investors should not buy common stocks simply because they are cheap, but only if they give promise of major gain to the investor.

14. Does the management talk freely to investors about its affairs when things are going well, but clam up when problems and disappointments occur?

15. Does the business have a management of unquestionable integrity?

As you can see, Fisher's list of 15-investment criteria contains qualitative elements, and differs greatly from Ben Graham's strictly quantitative investment process. Ben Graham was undoubtedly more quantitative, whereas Philip Fisher's investment strategy is more qualitative.

Charlie Munger believes in using checklist routines to help us avoid a lot of errors. These errors occur because our human brains are wired to find shortcuts, or what Munger calls, "shortcut types of approximations." Charlie Munger said: "The main antidotes to miscues from Availability-Misweighing Tendency often involve procedures, including the use of checklists, which are almost always helpful." (Kaufman, 2005)

Warren Buffett combined the quantitative value investment strategy of Ben Graham, with the qualitative investment strategy of Phil Fisher, and Berkshire Hathaway's vice-chairman, Charlie Munger. Warren Buffett's value investment strategy has evolved over the years into his current value investment strategy, which incorporates both the quantitative and qualitative factors.

In 1965, Warren Buffett said he's 15% Fisher and 85% Graham. However, as Buffett progressed through his amazing career, Buffett's value investing style evolved to be more like 50% Fisher/Munger, (qualitative, growth stocks) and 50% Graham, (quantitative, value stocks).

Buffett and Munger's "Four Filters" investment process will be discussed in Chapter 3. It combines elements of both quantitative and qualitative factors. This makes Buffett's "Four Filters" investment process one of the most significant developments in behavioral finance this century. (Labitan, The Four Filters Invention of Warren Buffett and Charlie Munger, 2010)

Warren Buffett's amazing multi-billion dollar career is a testament to the powerful results that can be achieved using his powerful value investing strategies. Warren certainly has done an excellent job expanding Ben Graham's original value investing process and evolving it into one of the most successful value investing models in the world. Now you can benefit from these powerful investment strategies that we will reveal in this book.

"It is better to invest in a wonderful business at a fair price, than a fair business at a wonderful price." Warren Buffett and Charlie Munger.

1.6 Bill Ruane:

By: Paul Lountzis: Lountzis Asset Management
Scott Thompson: Ameritrust Group

Bill Ruane and Warren Buffett initially met and became friends as college students together in Ben Graham's class at Columbia University in 1951. It was a wonderful relationship that lasted for 54 years until Bill's death in October 2005.

One of Warren's many gifts is his ability to identify great people. In Buffett's October 1969 letter advising his clients of his intention to liquidate his first Buffett Partnership, Warren recommended to his clients that, "Bill Ruane is the money manager within my knowledge who ranks the highest when combining the factors of integrity and ability. I have had considerable opportunity to observe his qualities of character, temperament and intellect. If Susie and I were to die, Bill is one of three trustees to have carte blanche on my investment matters."

While working together at Kidder Peabody, Bill Ruane and Rick Cunniff often thought about starting their own business. Over lunch in 1969, they decided to start their own firm, as Warren was folding his partnership and referring many of his clients to Bill and Rick. Buffett's referrals provided Bill and Rick with $20 million of client assets to start their firm. Today, Ruane, Cunniff and Goldfarb manages one of the most respected and successful investment firms in the world, the legendary Sequoia Fund, which now manages over $16 billion.

For Ruane, the early days were extremely difficult as Bill and Rick's timing could not have been worse and the firm struggled. They chose not to participate in the high valuations on the popular "Nifty Fifty" bull market stocks of 1969–1970. Then, they were severely impacted by the brutal bear market of 1973–1974, which resulted in the most challenging period in the firm's history. They remained committed to their process and principles in building a client-centered and research driven firm focused upon achieving excellent performance. This commitment saw Sequoia rise 60%–70% from 1975–1976.

In 1971, a year after the Sequoia Fund was started; Bob Goldfarb joined the firm and has been a key contributor for the past 42 years, leading terrific investment and administrative teams.

As Ralph Waldo Emerson once said, "An institution is the lengthened shadow of one man." Bob and the rest of the Sequoia team have continued as great stewards to preserve the unique culture at the firm begun by Bill Ruane and Rick Cunniff. As Bob Goldfarb said, "Bill Ruane loved the craft of investing." Bill's love of this craft will continue as the dominant culture driving the firm for decades to come.

Bill preferred to stay out of the limelight and few people outside the investment world knew him, which is exactly as he liked it. However, while his analytical and investment skills were well known to his partners, co-workers and many others in the investment industry, his personal side, including his soft touch and kind heart, were evident through his life, but visible to even fewer people, which again was fine with Bill.

I was fortunate enough to meet with Bob Goldfarb in the summer of 1990, which led to my joining the firm in September 1990. I spent almost a decade at the firm, becoming a partner after 4 years, and having the opportunity to study many industries and companies in-depth.

While I love to learn and the firm was a great analytical fit, what stands out above all is my special window into Bill Ruane, not the great investor, but the wonderful human being.

In my first interview with Bill, I was very nervous and he immediately made me feel at ease and totally comfortable. Bill's calming ways along with his great sense of humor made it a joy for people to be around him. I anticipated discussing several investment ideas that were held in the Sequoia portfolio. However, much to my surprise, Bill began asking about my family and specifically about our son Tyler, who needed open heart surgery at the tender age of 10 months.

Bill's primary focus during my interview was Tyler and we spent over a half hour discussing Tyler's condition and the many specifics relating to his surgery. Bill asked numerous questions about Tyler's diagnosis, surgeon, hospital and how much the operation would cost. Before I could even respond, Bill exclaimed, "Whatever Tyler's heart surgery costs, I will pay for everything." It was quite astounding to be interviewing for a job with one of the world's greatest investors, while his entire focus was on our family and specifically our son. I remember asking Bill, "I haven't even been hired yet." To which he replied, "I am looking forward to working with you."

Little did I realize in September 1990 that my interview with Bill Ruane would have such a profound impact on my life, far beyond investing. I am grateful for the opportunity to have worked alongside Bill, Rick, Bob, Greg, Carley, and the Sequoia Fund team to further develop my investment skills. Bill's uniquely human approach demonstrated his core values, and what a truly remarkable human being! My interview with Bill is permanently etched in my memory and it has served as a guide in my own life to try to make a difference in as many other lives as I can.

Bill Ruane did pay for everything regarding Tyler's open-heart surgery. Bill was an honorable man, and lived by his word. Tyler's surgery was a complete success. In 2013, Tyler is now 23 years old, and starting his first year of college after serving 4 years in the U.S. Army in Korea and Iraq.

While Bill preferred a low profile, he remains recognized as one of the world's most successful investors and an even greater human being. His philanthropic devotion in his later years equaled his investment acumen and he applied the same talents he used toward investing to being an outstanding philanthropist. Bill strongly believed in education, and funded the Accelerated Reader program, which helps children learn to read and develop a love for books. The program has already helped over 20,000 children. Bill also provided 90 scholarships.

In closing, Bill Ruane was among the most towering individuals in the history of the American investment industry, as measured by any metric. He exemplified a lifelong commitment of caring for people that extended far beyond those within his immediate circle. Bill left a profound impact on me, and on many others who had the privilege to have known him.

1.7 Phil Carret:

By: Frank Betz: Carret/Zane Capital Management
Scott Thompson: Ameritrust Group

Phil Carret was born in 1896, and was a third generation Harvard graduate in 1917. In 1928, he founded the Pioneer Fund, which is now the 3rd oldest mutual fund in the United States. A $10,000 investment into his fund at the start would have grown to be worth over $8 million dollars during the 55 years Carret managed his fund.

Phil began his career as a bond salesman, who in due course, introduced himself to Howard Buffett, Warren Buffett's Omaha stockbroker father, while killing time awaiting a train connection to his Seattle territory. Later on, Phil and the younger Buffett became and remained warm friends until Phil's death in 1998. Warren considered Phil one of his investing heroes, and often praised Phil as having one of the best long-term investment performance records ever. Like Buffett, Phil was a voracious reader of a wide variety of daily newspapers, trade publications, annual reports, and SEC filings, and often found his best investing information hidden within the footnotes of annual reports most readers find too boring to study.

Carret's investment strategy was like Warren's, focused on businesses with strong balance sheets, low debt, predictable free cash flow, consistent earnings growth, and capable managements who personally held significant holdings in their own companies.

Early on, Phil published his "12 Commandments of Investing," which became widely accepted by industry professionals and individuals alike. Originally, they were:

1. Never hold fewer than 10 different securities covering five different fields of business;

2. At least once every six months, reappraise every security held;

3. Keep at least half the total fund in income producing securities;

4. Consider (dividend) yield the least important factor in analyzing any stock;

5. Be quick to take losses and reluctant to take profits;

6. Never put more than 25% of a given fund into securities about which detailed information is not readily and regularly available;

7. Avoid inside information as you would the plague;

8. Seek facts diligently, advice never;

9. Ignore mechanical formulas for value in securities;

10. When stocks are high, money rates rising and business prosperous, at least half a given fund should be placed in short-term bonds;

11. Borrow money sparingly and only when stocks are low, money rates low and falling, and business depressed;

12. Set aside a moderate proportion of available funds for the purchase of long-term options on stocks in promising companies whenever available.

In later years, Phil viewed his "12 commandments" as generally sound guidelines, but he was not at all arbitrary or doctrinaire in their implementation. He came to view numbers 3, 10 and 12 as rather archaic, and did not arbitrarily adhere to these.

Phil's name rarely appeared in media without being preceded by the word "legendary," which he had surely become, well before I became his personal assistant, sharing a partners desk with him from 1985 until his death at age 101 fifteen years later.

Phil had a healthy enough ego, but utterly no sense of personal aggrandizement, as so many investment industry "rock stars" have exhibited in recent years. As a result of the extraordinary success of his Pioneer Fund, he earned near universal recognition and ongoing admiration of his investing industry peers. Warren Buffett's high esteem for Phil was widely shared by other industry gurus: Jack Bogle, Michael Holland, Bill Ruane, Byron Wien, Jim Rogers, Charles Ellis, and others.

Andy Kilpatrick, author of a series of books titled "Of Permanent Value," detailing everything Berkshire over the past twenty some years, paid homage to Phil (and to Benjamin Graham) by designating Phil as having been "the grandfather of value investing." Phil had essentially defined the entire "value" concept in his best selling "The Art of Speculation" book (still in print), published four years before the two investing classics by Benjamin Graham: "Security Analysis" (1934) and "The Intelligent Investor" (1939).

Phil's first job on Wall Street was working for Hugh Bancroft, founder of The Wall Street Journal, when they both were working for Clarence Barron. While he was stationed at a desk outside of Mr. Barron's office, he overheard a conversation, which gave him the idea to establish his Pioneer Mutual Fund, which he did in 1928 - not the most propitious time in history! It is a little known fact that Carret initially named it "Fidelity Fund," but within a year or so he decided he liked "Pioneer Fund" better, and changed the name. Pioneer Fund went on with unprecedented success until Phil thought the fund's clients deserved a younger owner/manager when he reached age 66. So he sold the entire package to a young associate in 1962, and set up his own private "boutique" advisory firm, Carret and Company. He continued to commute most days from Scarsdale to the firm's mid-town office where he actively and intelligently participated in the management of client accounts until his death in 1998.

Phil had the most extraordinary intellect I ever came across on Wall Street over my 50 years there. He was a visionary, a pragmatist, had an awesome analytical capability, but always eschewed defined formulaic processes or "systems" in predicting future successes of the companies in which he invested his clients' funds.

What can today's investors learn from studying Phil Carret and his investment process and strategies? Plenty, if one pays attention and recognizes that most of his biggest successes were the result of disarmingly simplistic ideas. He made an early killing after he first arrived in New York City and learned that unlimited amounts of free water were available to all residents. He figured that situation wasn't going to last indefinitely, and that the city would soon harness that potential revenue source. So he researched and bought shares in every meter manufacturer he was able to locate, and that simple idea turned into an early killing when the city metered every address.

Fifty years later, while attending a Pioneer board meeting in Boston, he very much liked the unusual glycerin-based soap he found in his Ritz Carleton Hotel bath. It was Neutrogena, and he made a significant investment into the obscure manufacturer, which resulted in a handsome payoff when Johnson & Johnson later acquired the maker. Early on he fell in love with the rather boring municipal bond insurer MBIA. The financials looked just fine, and Phil surmised there was minimal downside risk to insuring municipal underwritings issued by authorities who had taxing power to make good any bond defaults. When they built the Detroit International Bridge to Windsor, Ontario, he loved it and invested heavily. He correctly assumed the company owning it had authority to charge whatever tolls they saw fit; wonderful insurance against downside risk. He later became a director there, as did Charles Munger.

Another idea from which Carret profited significantly was Handy & Harman, a precious metals marketing company. Phil surmised that major, and generally unrecognized, gold, silver and platinum inventory valuations carried on company books at cost were worth substantially more, offering shareholders protection from downside risk. Later he and Warren Buffett served together on their board for years, and the Carret and Company management of the company's pension fund was so extravagantly successful the company was taken over by a buyout firm, more for the value of its dramatically overfunded pension account than for its operations.

Perhaps his favorite investment of all time was Greif Bros., an Ohio container manufacturer, an idea he attributed to Howard Buffett. He originally paid about $15 a share, and by 1994 after many stock splits, each share had become forty shares. When I joined Phil at Carret and Company he owned 400 shares of Berkshire Hathaway, having received these at a cost valuation of $235 per share in exchange for his holdings in Warren Buffett's Blue Chip Stamp Company.

Carret wrote several books on investing, including his most famous book titled, "The Art of Speculation." He chose that name because in those days "investing" referred to buying bonds, and "speculation" referred to buying and selling common and preferred stocks. Phil flatly rejected and disdained the many faddish investment styles based on computer modeling or charting.

Carret once claimed that successful speculation ("investing") requires capital, courage, and judgment. But he later said the single most important characteristic of a successful investor is <u>patience</u>. Warren respected Carret immensely, and even introduced Phil at a Berkshire stockholders' meeting and joked to the thousands attending that investors could learn more from Carret in 15 minutes than by listening to Buffett all day.

A reporter once asked Phil who the hardest clients to serve were. Phil's immediate response was doctors, worse than all others. Later he explained why, and his reply made perfect sense: Doctors too often believe in their own omnipotence, resulting from the fact that they must deliver performance that is right about 97% of the time. "In our business," he replied, "if we succeed in making good investment decisions 65% of the time, we will be the equivalent of rock stars to our clients."

Personally, Phil was always a joy to be around. He was a gentle person with a lovely sense of humor and a ready smile for all. Around the time he was about 97 he was asked about his dietary preferences. He explained that several times a week he enjoyed thick cuts of rare prime rib and other red meats, lots of potatoes, and desserts that would curl the hair of a nutritionist. And what did his doctors think of his dietary regimen? "They're all dead," he replied.

Phil disdained arrogance, pretensions, excessive self-assurance, and sarcasm, and was himself modest in every way. He never gave a thought to exploiting or even considering the potential marketing value of his own name or his investment successes, either at his Pioneer Fund or later at Carret and Company. In spite of the wide recognition he had gained, he was never driven by a desire to accumulate great wealth, or to promote himself, and never drew a salary more than $100,000 annually from his company, and gave generously to his favored beneficiaries, mainly Harvard, Wellesley, the Congregational Church of Scarsdale, and many other charities every year.

Value investors would discover much relevant contemporary significance in reading Carret's two books, and seek out more information about Phil's impressive investment record and how it was earned.

CHAPTER TWO

Key Concepts

"Invest in businesses so wonderful even a fool could run them. Because sooner or later one will!" Warren Buffett

2.1 Value Traps:

"Some, believing they are investing, may be unintentionally donating." Scott Thompson

"Rule #1, never lose money. Rule #2, never forget Rule #1." Warren Buffett

One of the most common mistakes in value investing is when investors invest in businesses selling at cheap prices, but the stock price never appreciates after the investor invests. These are referred to as "value traps," which we will now explore.

What are value traps? Value traps are businesses that appear to be under valued, but are actually suffering from long-term unsolvable problems deeply rooted in their underlying fundamentals. These problems will keep their stock price from rising appreciably. As value investors, we must identify and avoid "value traps." Value traps are businesses appearing attractive on the surface as being undervalued, but will not significantly rise in value after the investor invests. Developing a rigorous due diligence process before you invest is important, since discovering a value trap after you invest is too late.

Financial Statement analysis is often a helpful component of a rigorous due diligence process, as can be reading the business's quarterly reports, annual reports, and SEC filings (Securities Exchange Commission) at http://www.SEC.gov

Value traps may have exorbitant amounts of debt (balance sheet), high interest payments (income statement), high capital expenditures (cash flow statement), and other problems. This book will guide you through the maze of financial statements, ratios, metrics, and other important factors, to help you become a skilled value investor, and help you choose the best value investments for you.

We will discuss what factors to look for in financial statements (Income Statement, Balance Sheet, and Cash Flow Statement) in Chapter 4. We will also show you how to identify the kinds of wonderful businesses in which Warren Buffett invests.

Think about value investing as owning a piece of a business, and not as buying stocks. Can you accurately value what the underlying business is worth? We will show you how to value businesses using various valuation strategies, which will empower you to possess advantages over other investors who lack these fundamental valuation skills.

2.2 Overvalued, Fairly Valued, or Undervalued?

"There are three ways to invest: When a business is overvalued, fairly valued, or undervalued. Value investors prefer undervalued." Scott Thompson

Value investors want to invest when the business is undervalued, and sell when business is fairly valued or overvalued. Some investors, like Warren Buffett, prefer to hold stocks "forever." Therefore, before investing, determine, "Is the business overvalued, fairly valued, or undervalued?"

Valuations are important in value investing. Ben Graham was very quantitative, and would only invest when stocks of businesses met very specific valuation criteria. Buffett learned from Graham, but over time Warren evolved adding qualitative components to his value investing process, as influenced by Phil Fisher and Charlie Munger.

Value investing is not just about buying stocks with low prices. Instead, value investing is about buying pieces of wonderful businesses earning consistent amounts of free cash flows (FCF) that steadily increase over many years, even decades. Both quantitative and qualitative factors are important to consider before investing. In other words, don't just look at the stock price. Also consider if it is a business you understand, with a sustainable competitive advantage, run by honest and capable managers.

How do we identify these wonderful businesses? This book reveals several different strategies used by the most successful value investors. You will learn to seek high-quality undervalued businesses possessing strong underlying fundamentals, while avoiding value traps.

2.3 Intrinsic Value:

"Intrinsic Value" is a term used by the value investing community, originally coined by Benjamin Graham, the father of value investing. Ben Graham first referred to intrinsic value in his book, "Security Analysis" published in 1934. Intrinsic value refers to the present value of all future cash flows a business will generate over its remaining lifetime, discounted back to the present according to a discount rate. We will show you how to calculate intrinsic value in Chapter 9. First, we must show you some necessary information you will need with which to better understand intrinsic value.

If the asset in which you want to invest is a publicly traded business, divide its total intrinsic value by the number of "shares outstanding" to determine its "intrinsic value per share." We will reveal how to calculate intrinsic value in Chapter 9: Intrinsic Value.

After intrinsic value "per share" is calculated, we can then compare the intrinsic value per share, against the business's current market price per share.

If the business's current market price per share is significantly below the business's intrinsic value per share, by an adequate **margin of safety**, the investor may consider the business a potentially attractive investment, to which further due diligence must be applied.

Calculating intrinsic value is only one step of many steps in the security selection process. Value investors must analyze the business's financial statements, SEC filings, annual reports, etc., to determine why the business' stock price appears to be undervalued, and perform a rigorous due diligence process. Both quantitative and qualitative factors must be considered.

2.4 Price to Value:

Benjamin Graham invented the "Price to Value" (P/V) ratio and the "Margin of Safety" (MOS) ratio. Ben Graham was Warren Buffett's college professor, mentor, and employer. Warren Buffett often refers to the phrases: margin of safety, price to value, and intrinsic value in his annual letter to Berkshire Hathaway shareholders. These concepts are very helpful in determining how undervalued a particular asset actually is.

Businesses showing higher price to value ratios, means the business is closer to being fairly valued. Businesses showing lower price to value ratios, means the business is closer to being undervalued.

Lower price to value ratios are better when acquiring new shares. Higher "margins of safety" are better when acquiring new shares. As you can see, the price to value ratio and "margin of safety" (MOS) are inversely proportional to each other. When one goes up, the other goes down. For example, a 30% margin of safety (MOS) equals a .70 price to value ratio. A 40% margin of safety (MOS) equals a .60 price to value ratio. A 50% margin of safety (MOS) equals a .50 price to value ratio.

Price to Value Ratio is calculated as:
Current market price ÷ intrinsic value = Price to Value ratio

Margin of Safety is calculated as:
((Intrinsic Value) − (Market Price)) ÷ (Absolute value (Intrinsic Value))

Or, an easier way to calculate "Margin of Safety" is:
(1 − Price to Value Ratio)

2.5 Margin of Safety:

Margin of Safety (MOS) is the difference between Market Price and Intrinsic Value. Some investors will invest if there is a 25% margin of safety. Some investors will invest if there is a 33% margin of safety. Others will invest if a 40% MOS is present, and others may require a 50% MOS, or more. Each investor must determine his own acceptable "margin of safety."

Many value investors use 30% as their minimum acceptable margin of safety. In the early days of Berkshire Hathaway, Warren Buffett used 50% as his minimum acceptable margin of safety. Benjamin Graham used 33%. Now, Berkshire Hathaway manages billions of dollars instead of millions, very few 50% margin of safety opportunities exist at the billion-dollar level, if any. Therefore, it is believed Berkshire Hathaway now uses a 30% margin of safety, instead of 50%, in its investment selection criteria.

It's important to point out that a larger quantity of investment opportunities are usually available at only a 30% MOS than at a 50% MOS. The deeper the margin of safety the more undervalued the asset may be. Therefore, opportunities with a 50% MOS tend to be less common than opportunities with only a 30% MOS. Therefore, the deeper the margin of safety is, the fewer the number of available investment opportunities from which to consider.

When these 50% "margin of safety" opportunities occur, it is important NOT to make an immediate knee-jerk reaction to automatically invest in these businesses for just the 50% MOS reason only. The most successful value investors understand the importance of a rigorous due diligence process consisting of both quantitative and qualitative research.

A common question asked is, "How often do assets sell for LESS than their intrinsic value?" The answer is, "Actually, quite often!" You may have shopped at a discount store and found an item whose value you know is worth far higher than the current sales price. Maybe the item is an article of clothing, or another item selling at an attractive discount to intrinsic value! Maybe it is selling for a price at which there is a 50% margin of safety, between market price and the item's intrinsic value.

"I buy dollars for 50 cents." Warren Buffett

For example, an item is worth $100 at Macy's, but one day you see this exact same item is selling at a discount store for only $50. You do not immediately make a knee-jerk reaction to buy the item based on low price only. Instead, you begin your rigorous due diligence process…

Current market price ($50) ÷ intrinsic value ($100) = Price to Value Ratio of .50

You also calculate your margin of safety. It is 50%. A 50% MOS is good. Your due diligence process continues: Is there something wrong with the item? Why is it selling for 50% less than what it is worth? Is this a good deal or a value trap? Great questions to ask!

For instance, if the item is a retail item or an article of clothing; you begin your due diligence process: Are any buttons missing? Hmmm... all buttons are intact. Are there any rips in material? No rips, all material is intact. "Well what's wrong with it?" you ask. Your due diligence process continues: Are any stitches missing? All stitches are in place. Are there any visible stains? No stains. The item is in great condition, but just has a low price! So you decide to purchase it. Congratulations! You've just purchased an undervalued asset for 50% below its intrinsic value! If you can do it for a retail item, you can do it in the stock market!

This is what successful value investors do. They invest in businesses at 50% discounts below intrinsic value. Value investors search for these undervalued investment opportunities. When they are found, a rigorous analysis, research, and due diligence process must be implemented to eliminate bad investments and value traps discussed earlier in this chapter.

2.6 Mr. Market:

Benjamin Graham often used the term "Mr. Market" to describe the stock market as if it were a manic person suffering from wide unpredictable mood swings. Everyday, Mr. Market would arrive at your door to offer you an opportunity to either buy or sell shares of any business. Some days Mr. Market would be wildly excited offering to buy or sell shares of businesses to you at high prices. The next day Mr. Market would arrive at your doorstep depressed, offering to buy or sell shares to you of businesses for low prices. You never know which mood "Mr. Market" will be in when he arrives.

Benjamin Graham was wise, and taught the young Warren Buffett **not to focus on market prices, but instead focus on the underlying intrinsic value of the business.** If you could accurately assign a valuation to a business, then divide that valuation by the number of shares outstanding, you could determine the per share intrinsic value of a business!

Graham's teachings were ground-breaking for Buffett, and many others in the class. Graham stated that some businesses could be valued more easily than others. However, if a business proved too difficult to value, Graham instructed Warren Buffett to move on, and find another business to value where he could be more certain. Warren Buffett now invests based on the principle of "certainty" not "probability."

Over the years much has changed, but Mr. Market has not. Mr. Market still shows up every day at your door with wildly unpredictable mood swings offering to buy or sell shares of businesses to you. Some days you take Mr. Market up on his offer, and other days you tell Mr. Market that you are not interested. Either way, Mr. Market will return the next day with another quote.

"Many say, 'Buy low and sell high,' but few actually possess the rational temperament to achieve it." Scott Thompson

"The market is there to serve you, not instruct you." Ben Graham

2.7 Inefficient vs. Efficient Markets:

Value investing is the act of investing in an asset at a price lower than its intrinsic value, then selling the asset later at a higher price, at or close to its intrinsic value. Value investors profit from the difference between the original (lower) purchase price and the final (higher) sales price. Any volatility that occurs in the middle does not matter to the original buy price or the final sell price.

In order for value investing to work, markets must be inefficient. Efficient Market Hypothesis (EMH) erroneously teaches us that markets are always efficient. By "efficient" we mean always "accurately priced." However, history and the facts prove Efficient Market Hypothesis (EMH) to be simply untrue. Multibillionaire value investor Warren Buffett confirms this, and says Efficient Market Hypothesis is a waste of time. Unfortunately, Efficient Market Hypothesis (EMH) and Modern Portfolio Theory (MPT) are investment theories being taught in business schools, and are being implemented by the majority of Wall Street professionals.

Value investors, like Warren Buffett, profit from price dislocations in financial markets caused by other financial professionals who tend to be more "short-term" focused, instead of "long-term" focused like billionaire value investor Warren Buffett.

"Markets are inefficient in the short-term, and efficient over the long-term." Scott Thompson

Warren Buffett's success confirms market prices can become mispriced and inefficient during the short term, and efficient over the long-term. In other words, "intrinsic value and market price may remain apart, sometimes for extended periods, but intrinsic value and market price eventually converge." This confirms markets are not always efficient (accurately priced) during the short-term. This is the first premise of understanding value investing.

"Efficient Market Hypothesis (EMH) and Modern Portfolio Theory (MPT) are beautiful equations that do not necessarily equate to the real world." Scott Thompson

2.8 Economic Moats:

Warren Buffett often describes highly profitable businesses as castles surrounded by "moats." When potential attackers try to attack the castle, they're unable to reach the castle, due to the large protective "moat" surrounding the castle. Successful businesses like Coca-Cola possess economic moats. Economic moats are synonymous with Buffett and Munger's "Filter #2: Durable Competitive Advantage" that we will explore further in Chapter 3: Four Filters Investment Process.

Economic moats can be non-existent, narrow, or wide. Businesses possessing wide economic moats can be identified many ways, including through their financial statements. High gross margins above 40% are often signs of a wide moat business. Conversely, businesses whose income statements show gross margins below 20% may be operating in highly competitive industries.

In Chapters 4, 5, and 6, we will reveal which financial statements, financial data, financial ratios, and screening criteria you can use to identify these wide-moat businesses in which Warren Buffett invests.

On the subject of Coca-Cola, during the 2011 Berkshire Hathaway shareholders' meeting, Warren Buffett hinted Coca-Cola was a wide moat business. Buffett went on to say that even if a new competitor emerged loaded with $10 billion of new capital to spend in order to try to dethrone Coca-Cola as the world's #1 selling soft drink, it would fail.

Coca-Cola is one of the most widely recognized brands in the world. Coca-Cola also possesses one of the largest, most established global distribution networks in the world. It would take a new soft-drink competitor years, even decades, to accomplish an equivalent distribution network. The new competitor would likely run out of money and fail before it could ever overcome Coca-Cola's wide economic moat, and durable competitive advantages.

Conversely, a business possesses no economic moat and no durable competitive advantage if it can be duplicated by competitors. This causes the business to lose money. Eventually this may cause the firm to go out of business. The best businesses possess wide economic moats competitors cannot duplicate.

How does Warren Buffett identify businesses with economic moats? Warren reads all the annual reports and financial statements of each business within an industry, and compares them to each other.

Businesses possessing economic moats can charge higher prices for their products, which gives them "pricing power." This shows up on their financial statements. Therefore, seek businesses with the highest gross margins, operating margins, net margins, return on equity (ROE), return on invested capital (ROIC), and lowest debt, within their industry.

Businesses holding patents also possess competitive advantages over their competitors, until their patents expire. This occurs frequently in the pharmaceuticals sector, after businesses enjoy years of prosperity only to watch their profit margins erode by "generic" drug manufacturers aggressively taking away market share after patents expire.

What's your competitive advantage? What can you do to create competitive advantages? How can you widen your moat, and increase the competitive advantages you already possess?

2.9 Introduction to Value Investing:

This simple example will help you understand the basic concept underlying how value investor Warren Buffett invests and became a billionaire.

Imagine a 24-pack case of beverage cans that costs $24.

Each can in the 24-pack is worth $1/each. *(Think of cans as shares).*

Now, imagine if the 24-pack were a business, and each can were 1 share of the company's stock. Each share of stock is $1, and the 24-pack is $24.

What if you could buy 1 can (1 share) for only 50 cents, instead of $1? You would have a 50% Margin Of Safety, between the 50 cents you paid, and the underlying "intrinsic value" of $1 per can (share).

After buying shares at a discount, Buffett holds the shares until the share price rises upward toward its "intrinsic value" of $1 per can ($1 per share).

Using this same example, imagine if the 24-pack were a business worth $24,000,000. If it has 24,000,000 Total Shares Outstanding, each share is worth $1 each. However, what if you could buy 1 share of this business for only 50 cents, instead of $1 each? You would have a 50% Margin Of Safety. In other words, focus on value, not price!

Warren first values the underlying business. Then divides by Total Shares Outstanding to find "intrinsic value per share." Then compares this amount against "market price per share." Is it overvalued or undervalued?

The same is true if you could buy a $20 gift card for only $10. In other words, buy high-quality assets for less then they are worth. Note: Comparing "Price vs. Value" is only one filter of Buffett's "Four-Filters" Investment Process. We will discuss this now.

CHAPTER THREE

Four Filters Investment Process

Of Warren Buffett and Charlie Munger

"Invest in businesses so wonderful even a fool could run them. Because sooner or later one will!" Warren Buffett

3.1 Overview:

Billionaires Warren Buffett and Charlie Munger of Berkshire Hathaway make their investment decisions based on the "Four Filters Investment Process" they developed over several decades. I agree with Bud Labitan who asserts that the Four Filters Investment Process may be one of the greatest developments in investment decision-framing and behavioral finance since Ben Graham's "margin of safety" and John Burr Williams' "intrinsic value" principles were described.

On the surface, the Four Filters decision-framework appears rather simple, but possesses the power to help investors make significantly better value investment decisions. The Four Filters Investment Process is:

1. Understandable businesses
2. Durable competitive advantages
3. Able and trustworthy managers
4. Attractive price to value, via Graham's concept of margin of safety

3.2 Filter #1: Seek Understandable Businesses:

Warren Buffett's "Circle of Competence" is his holistic knowledge base about a business and its competitive position in its industry. Think of

Buffett and Munger's Circles of Competence as their basic understanding about a business and its competitive position within its industry. Munger refers to this as a Latticework of Mental Models that gives them a better understanding of the business's products and services, and how that individual business can thrive within its own competitive ecosystem.

When we start out studying an investment prospect, we have a small latticework of memories about a business and its products and services. However, as we grow our latticework of mental models, we develop a better sense of how strong a business is. And, we begin to better understand its competitors and its competitive position within its industry.

Warren Buffett's Circle of Competence has led him to seek out businesses that appear to be simple and stable. He reasons that, if a business is too complex and too prone to constant change, then he will not be able to predict future cash flows of such a complex business. He bases his investment decisions upon the certainty (not the probability) with which the long-term economic characteristics of that individual business can be evaluated. Simple and stable businesses with competitive advantages having relatively predictable increasing cash flows pass his first filter.

Warren Buffett and Charlie Munger only invest in businesses they understand. So should you. They do not invest in technology businesses, because technology businesses are not businesses they can predict what the business and competitive landscape will look like in 10-20 years.

For example, Buffett never invested in "dot com" tech stocks during the tech bubble of 1999 and 2000. Instead, Buffett invested in Allstate Insurance. Compared with "dot com" tech stocks, an insurance business may appear boring, but extremely profitable! During the "dot com" craze, the Wall Street press called Buffett "outdated," and a "dinosaur." However, Buffett quietly stuck to his sound value investing principles he learned from his mentor Ben Graham, and time proved him right... again.

Buffett would rather invest in simple businesses he understands like, Gillette, See's Candies, and Wrigley gum. Buffett says that the Internet won't change how people chew gum 10–20 years from now.

"If principles change, they are not principles." Scott Thompson

Buffett never invested in "dot com" tech stocks, because the valuations simply did not make sense. Furthermore, their business models were "untested by time." Wall Street investment banking firms were releasing IPOs (Initial Public Offerings) of tech start-up businesses into the stock market, even though the new tech start-up had little or no earnings, no operations. In many cases, these were just an entrepreneurial idea with a business plan and no sales staff.

Buffett wisely avoided this folly. When the "dot com" bubble finally popped and the stock market crashed, Buffett looked like a genius because he literally held no "dot com" stocks. In retrospect, Buffett's investment into an insurance business, a business sector he understands, was a very profitable decision for Buffett and Berkshire Hathaway shareholders.

Don't get caught up in stock market bubbles and the frenzy of valueless speculation. Just because everyone is investing into a certain sector, with stock prices escalating higher and higher, just don't do it. During the dot com craze, an announcement was made that the rules of valuation no longer apply. This was a warning sign that IPO (Initial Public Offering) valuations from investment bankers were not based in reality.

If a sector you don't understand is in a bubble, don't get caught up in the folly of Wall Street. Instead, stick to the businesses, industries, and sectors you understand, perform your valuations, seek your adequate margin of safety. And, like Buffett, you will do well.

Stay within your circle of competence, and areas of expertise.

"To get rich, you don't have to do too many things right, you just need to avoid doing the stupid things." Warren Buffett

"If you only have a 120 IQ, don't act like you have a 150 IQ. You can do more smart things within your circle of competence." Warren Buffett

3.3 Filter #2: Durable Competitive Advantage:

Successful businesses with durable competitive advantages possess what's known as "pricing power." Some businesses possess pricing power because loyal customers continue to pay more for their special products or services. One of the best ways to identify businesses with durable competitive advantages is to find businesses possessing signs of pricing power. What is pricing power?

Pricing Power is a business's ability to charge higher prices for their products and services higher than its competitors. Meanwhile, customers continue to buy the products and services from the business possessing pricing power at the higher prices.

Pricing Power reflects a business's ability to earn income above the firm's cost of capital, or above their Net Asset Value (NAV). The difference between Net Asset Value (NAV) and Earnings Power Value (EPV) is called Franchise Value (FV). We will discuss these concepts in greater detail in Chapters 7 and 8.

However, for now, suffice it to say that Franchise Value (FV) is created when a business generates greater than $1 in earnings power for every $1 it invests into its assets. In other words, every dollar invested into a business's Net Asset Value (NAV) generates greater than a dollar in Earnings Power Value (EPV).

In later chapters, we will show you how to how to calculate:

• Net Asset Value (NAV) from the Balance Sheet
• Earnings Power Value (EPV) from the Income Statement
• Discounted Cash Flow (DCF) analysis from the Cash Flow Statement

For now, it is important we lay a basic foundation of understanding about durable competitive advantages and pricing power. How do we identify businesses with durable competitive advantages and pricing power? One way is to look at the business's income statement.

What are its gross margins?
What are its operating margins?
What are its net profit margins?

How do the business's gross margins, operating margins, and net profit margins, compare with those of competing businesses within the same sector and industry? A business showing 40% gross margins, 30%

operating margins, and 20% net margins may likely be a business exhibiting durable competitive advantages. This business may also possess pricing power over its competitors who exhibit only 20% gross margins, 15% operating margins, and 10% net profit margins.

Note: It's best to compare businesses within the same industry, as anomalies can occur if comparing financial statements across different sectors and industries.

Businesses with durable competitive advantages and pricing power simply create more value, and this will be shown in their financial statements, annual reports, and SEC filings (Securities and Exchange Commission) http://www.SEC.gov

An obvious example of pricing power is a talented concert violinist (Person A). If "Person B" were to try to compete with her, and earn their living solely through playing the violin, then the professional violinist's financial statements would show higher profit margins and higher earnings, Whereas Person B's financial statements would show lower profit margins and lower earnings at the end of the year.

The same is true when businesses compete against each another. By examining and comparing businesses' financial statements, SEC filings, and annual reports, it becomes clear which businesses are the leaders within their industries.

Businesses unable to earn more than their cost of assets usually go out of business. Whereas, with the professional violinist, she pays for the asset (the violin) once, and will continue generating high earnings power because of her ability to employ the asset to its highest and best use.

"Anyone can buy an asset, but to optimally allocate the asset to its highest and best use requires more talent than luck." Scott Thompson

It takes a little detective work, but in what other profession can a few hours of work remunerate thousands, millions, billions, or even tens of billions (in Warren Buffett's case)? While we're hunting for undervalued businesses it is important to enjoy the journey as much as the destination. In other words, enjoy the process of finding undervalued investments, as much or more than enjoying the financial results.

3.4 Filter #3: Able and Trustworthy Managers:

Seek businesses you understand, run by competent and trustworthy managers. The ability of the management team to optimally allocate capital is one of the greatest factors determining the profitability of the business. Therefore, if the management team effectively allocates capital, the business will likely be more profitable. Conversely, if the management team does not allocate capital effectively, the business is likely to be less profitable.

"Before allocating capital, always consider opportunity cost." Scott Thompson

The Enron debacle is an excellent example of untrustworthy management. The dishonesty of Enron's management team caused shareholders to lose significant amounts of money – in many cases their life savings, due to the price of their Enron shares plummeting downward.

"You can't make a good deal with a bad person." Warren Buffett

Businesses with competent management teams often possess little or no debt. Unfortunately, it is common for managers to borrow large sums of money and incur debt onto their Balance Sheets in order to increase their Return On Equity (ROE). However, if a business has a high Return On Equity (ROE), and also possesses little to no debt, these are often businesses run by better management teams.

"Invest in a businesses so wonderful that even an idiot could run it, because sooner or later one will!" Warren Buffett and Charlie Munger

Capital is finite. Managers must become skilled at wisely allocating capital toward investments that will earn greater than each dollar invested. Net Present Value (NPV) analysis is a financial analysis process managers can use to analyze all available investment opportunities. Then investment opportunities can be ranked in order from best to worst. This allows managers to choose the most optimal investments, while ignoring the suboptimal ones. Net Present Value (NPV) analysis is explained in Chapter 9: Intrinsic Value.

Businesses with honest and trustworthy management often show steady increases to their Retained Earnings, year after year, on their Balance Sheets. Value investors are wise to consider a 5-year, 7-year or 10-year history of Retained Earnings before investing. Investors can find Retained Earnings listed toward the bottom of a business's Balance Sheet.

Honest, trustworthy managers will begin with the amount of finite capital. Then, they begin analyzing potential investments into which to potentially invest their capital. Does the investment have a positive Net Present Value, or a negative Net Present Value? Investments with positive Net Present Values are often the best investments, whereas negative Net Present Values tend to be investments to avoid. See Chapter 9, for more information about how to calculate Net Present Value (NPV) and Discounted Cash Flows (DCF).

Managers unable to allocate capital wisely will unwisely invest finite capital into investments that earn less than each dollar invested. In these businesses with underperforming managers, Balance Sheets tend to show Retained Earnings that decrease year over year, instead of increase year over year.

Managers who are unwise stewards of their business's limited capital still require large sums of money to run their businesses, even after they've misallocated previous sums of limited capital. Unwise managers in these situations tend to focus on short-term fixes to the problem, such as borrowing large sums of money (debt), or issuing more shares of their stocks (equity). This action dilutes the value of all shares outstanding, lowers earnings per share, increases the Price-to-Earnings ratio, and devalues the value of shares held by previous investors.

Businesses show short-term debt and long-term debt on their Balance Sheets. Interest paid on their debt is shown on their Income Statement. Successful value investors like Warren Buffett prefer to see businesses with little to no debt on the Balance Sheet, and little to no interest on their Income Statement. Businesses with high costs of capital pay high interest rates. Therefore, if a business is paying large amounts of interest just to service its debt, there is less money available for Net Income, which decreases earnings-per-share (EPS). This, in turn, puts downward pressure on the stock price. Businesses like these should be avoided.

In summary, you can begin to identify businesses with able and trustworthy management by examining a business's financial statements. These quantitative factors can help reveal important qualitative factors about how well, or how poorly management is running the business.

Follow these steps and you will possess advantages over other investors. You'll learn more about how to use quantitative factors to reveal qualitative aspects about businesses in Chapter 5: Financial Ratios.

"Use the quantitative to help reveal the qualitative." Scott Thompson

3.5 Filter #4: Attractive Price:

After Filters #1, #2, and #3 have been satisfied, we seek to identify businesses selling at prices below their intrinsic value, offering a satisfactory margin of safety. Ben Graham's "margin of safety" principle shows us how to look for businesses possessing an adequate margin of safety. Earlier in his career, Warren Buffett and the author preferred to invest in businesses offering 50% margins of safety or higher. However, Warren Buffett says, "You can't run billions as efficiently as millions. Size is an anchor to performance."

Therefore, many younger readers will be pleased to know they possess an advantage by managing smaller amounts of money, as only a few potential investment opportunities exist costing billions, whereas thousands of investment opportunities exist when you only run a few million.

As previously stated, opportunities offering extremely wide margins of safety are rare. Conversely, investment opportunities with margins of safety less than 30% tend to be more common. Businesses with higher market capitalizations seldom offer wider margins of safety. Conversely, businesses with smaller market capitalizations may offer wider margins of safety more often, due to their increased level of price volatility.

In other words, investment opportunities offering margins of safety of 50% or greater tend to be more common for businesses in the small cap and mid cap market capitalization range, $50 billion and below. These 50% margins of safety almost never occur in large cap businesses.

Filter #4 represents the bargain, or Margin of Safety in a value investing moment. Once you have an estimated intrinsic value, subtract the market price from the intrinsic value. Your result is the bargain in dollars.

If you wish to know your margin of safety percentage, do this: Think of estimated intrinsic value as the "true value," and the market price as the price quoted by the manic Mr. Market, described by Benjamin Graham. So, pretend you invested in something worth an intrinsic value of $4, but paid only $3. Your bargain is $4 − $3 = $1. Your percent bargain is 25% where the denominator is the true value.

Your resulting percent bargain is calculated like this: 1 − .75 = .25 or 25% bargain. On the other hand, if someone asks you your Price to Value (P/V) ratio, say you bought it at a .75 price to value ratio.

While some investors rely on Filter #4 (price to value) only, Warren Buffett relies on all Four Filters. When we identify a business possessing all Four Filters, we begin a rigorous due diligence process on their fundamentals, financial statements, annual reports, SEC filings, and performance ratios before investing.

"Wall Street is more concerned with correlation than valuation." Scott Thompson

3.6 Three Ways to Invest:

- Overvalued
- Fairly valued
- Undervalued

Question: When is the best time to invest?
Answer: When the business is undervalued!

If you invest when the business is <u>overvalued,</u> this is the worst time to invest, because the value of the business is less likely to keep rising higher.

If you invest when the business is <u>fairly valued,</u> this is not as bad as buying in when the business is overvalued, but still, there is a better alternative; investing when the business is undervalued.

If you invest when the business is <u>undervalued,</u> this is the best time to invest! Because investing in a business when it is undervalued is like a buoy on the bottom of a lake that wants to spring back up to the surface of the lake. Avoid value traps, and do not invest based on price only (Filter #4), because it can be dangerous to ignore qualitative factors such as Filter #1, Filter #2, and Filter #3.

As this chapter demonstrates, qualitative factors (Filters #1, #2, and #3) must be considered along with considering quantitative factors, such as price (Filter #4). However, in order to explain the significance of Filter #4, it is important to make sure to invest only when the business is undervalued, and only when qualitative factors such as Filters #1, #2, and #3 have also been satisfied.

Unfortunately, the majority of investors have no idea how to value a business, or how to evaluate qualitative factors about a business. After you learn how to value a business, you will possess an advantage over other investors who cannot. Warren Buffett compounded billions of dollars throughout his career correctly evaluating qualitative and quantitative factors, and valuing businesses.

How do you value a business?
When do you invest in a business or stock?
Do you overpay or underpay?

Obviously, your goal is to underpay and invest only when the business is undervalued, so you do not overpay. This way, value investors can profit as stock prices appreciate over time and rise closer toward underlying intrinsic value.

Always understand how much "margin of safety" exists between the current market price and the intrinsic value of the business before you invest. Define for yourself in advance what your minimum "margin of safety" is. Develop your own investment policy and stick to it. Know what you will decline, and what you will accept.

Similar to that of Warren Buffett during his investments during the 1970's, the author prefers a minimum margin of safety of 50%. Develop your own minimum acceptable margin of safety and stick to it, most likely between 25% and 50%. Remember, most unsophisticated investors lose money because they lack the ability to value a business which causes them to overpay, and as a result, they lose money.

Fifty percent margins of safety occur more frequently in small-cap and mid-cap stocks (market capitalizations less than $10 billion). Whereas, large-cap stocks rarely trade at 50% margins of safety. Warren Buffett now manages billions of dollars. As a result, he must invest primarily in large cap businesses due to Berkshire's large financial size. This forces him to reduce his minimum margin of safety to something closer to 25%, since 50% margins of safety tend not to exist in large cap stocks.

"Size is an anchor to performance." Warren Buffett

Warren Buffett says that you cannot run $100 billion the same way you run $1 million. Why? Because, there are abundantly more businesses to invest in if you only have $1 million, vs. if you're trying to intelligently allocate $100 billion.

For example, if a business has a market capitalization of $100 million, but is believed to be worth $150 million, savvy value investors believe they can earn a 50% gain by investing in this $100 million business. However, if you're Warren Buffett and manage $100 billion, it is not possible to invest $100 billion into a $100 million business. This would be like trying to fit an ocean into a drinking glass. In other words, if the business is only worth $100 million, you cannot invest $100 billion into only a small $100 million market-cap business. Make sense?

This is why Warren Buffett must now seek larger businesses in which to invest. Because, now he manages billions instead of millions. Presently the 50% gains Warren enjoyed earlier in his career, while only managing millions, have decreased. Because now he's managing billions, and 50% margins of safety just don't happen as often when you manage billions.

This is the reason many mutual funds stop accepting new money, because they understand they can earn higher rates of returns by staying small and managing millions instead of billions. There are simply a higher number of lucrative investment opportunities at the million-dollar level, than at the billion-dollar level.

Buffett accepts this as a challenge and enjoys seeking higher-return investment opportunities for his shareholders. Just like successful baseball hitter Ted Williams, you should <u>not</u> swing at every pitch. Instead, wait for the right pitch. When it comes, take a big swing.

We will teach you how to identify undervalued businesses, quantify the margin of safety, understand and apply Buffett and Munger's Four Filters investment process, and select only those investments possessing higher certainty to earn you more money over the long term.

3.7 Catalyst:

Warren Buffett confidently states that a business's market price and intrinsic value eventually converge. This usually occurs over the long-term, and it rarely occurs quickly. After you make an investment into an undervalued business, a catalyst is necessary to occur before the share price rises again. Catalysts can be major events, or manifest themselves as only gradual changes occurring slowly over time.

Examples of catalysts may include: legislation, regulation, interest rate changes, fed rate changes, investor sentiment, macroeconomic events, geo-political events, environmental disasters, wars beginning, wars ending, corporate mergers, acquisitions, fraud, adjudication, and other events. These all may serve as catalysts that can affect investor sentiment and market prices, either positively or negatively

Catalysts can be highly probable events in the middle of the bell curve predicted to occur in advance. Or, catalysts can be highly improbable events that unexpectedly occur from out on the far tails of the bell curve. The events of Sept 11th 2001 are an example of highly improbable events that negatively impacted the world, lives, and global financial markets.

The best investors are the ones who can see around corners. In other words, the best investors are those who develop a "feel" or innate quality to know where a market, sector, industry, or business is headed. Successful investors must have their research done in advance before market events occur, to remain prepared to invest when opportunity presents itself.

For instance, Warren Buffett invested in American Express (AXP) back in the 1950's during a period when AXP's stock price was negatively impacted by highly publicized lawsuits caused by a vegetable oil receipt scandal. Investors began selling. AXP's stock price plummeted. Warren began buying. Warren seized this rare opportunity, and invested big into

American Express. Warren's investment earned 300% over the next few years.

"Be greedy when others are fearful, and fearful when others are greedy." Ben Graham

Warren knew the lawsuits would eventually fade into the past, and AXP would recover to generate high returns on equity and on invested capital. As this AXP example shows, catalysts can sink market prices lower in the short-term. Similarly, catalysts can also raise market prices higher over the long-term. Value investing requires patience, and Warren is patient... to the tune of $43 billion.

Buffett wrote about his colleagues' success in the article entitled, "The Super investors of Graham-and-Doddsville." These super investors seem to do a better job in looking and finding discrepancies between the value of a business and the price of small pieces of that business in the market. (Buffett W. E., 1984)

Value investors must develop solid understandings of the businesses into which they invest. If an investor is right, the results can be wonderful. However, if the investor is wrong, markets often do not give 2nd chances. Do your research, valuations, and due diligence before you invest.

3.8 Annual Reports:

Annual Reports contain important information about a business's performance, along with its financial statements for the past year. They also contain important information about business risks, such as the competitive environment. Warren Buffett reads (10-K) Annual Reports, (10-Q) Quarterly Reports, and other important documents businesses publicly release. Although Buffett reads these reports on paper, you can view and download them online at: http://www.SEC.gov

In Buffett's office, there is no computer. He does all his calculations in his head or by hand. At annual meetings, Warren claims he makes most of his investing decisions just by reading annual reports. Mr. Buffett has said annual reports are the main source of the study material needed for understanding. (Buffett W., From a talk given at the University of Florida, quoted in the Miami Herald (December 27, 1998), 1998) He rarely contacts management, or visits the business.

Buffett likes to read annual reports first, and perform valuations on businesses without looking at the stock price. After his valuations are complete, then Warren looks at the stock price. If the business meets Buffett's Four Filters investment criteria, and its stock is selling at a discount to intrinsic value with a satisfactory "margin-of-safety" (MOS), Buffett invests in the business.

"Some guys read Playboy. I read Annual Reports." Warren Buffett

A clever technique Warren uses to evaluate the effectiveness of management teams is, he reads old annual reports of a business from the past several years. For instance, let's say Buffett reads a 5-year old annual report of a business where management announces plans to cut costs by 15%. Buffett can then read the annual reports from the past several years, up to the present, to determine if management actually accomplished the goal they announced several years ago. This is one effective method to help gauge the effective stewardship of the management team.

Warren has read so many reports, he has a mental file on hundreds of businesses he can recall and cross-reference at will. Warren can see through the veil of overly rosy annual reports that gloss over the truth of what's really occurring to the underlying business. Remember, Warren possesses decades of investing experience. This is impossible to replicate with a computer model. As of 2013, Warren is 83 years young, at the top of his game, and better than ever!

As you read annual reports, stay focused on identifying details about the underlying business. Don't be duped by superfluous language. Stay focused on what is important, and what makes the business poor, good, or great. If the business does not meet your Four Filters investment criteria, move on, and find another one that does. There are thousands of businesses, so don't waste your time on those where you cannot be certain of their future. Warren Buffett puts weight on certainty, not probability. Think about the difference.

Read Warren Buffett's letters to shareholders from 1959 – present at: www.ProValueSource.com

Like Buffett, the more annual reports you read the more skilled you will become at identifying poor, good, and great businesses.

"Invest in a business so wonderful that even an idiot can run it, because sooner or later one will." Warren Buffett and Charlie Munger

3.9 Summary:

Buffett and Munger's Four Filters process and catalyst are simple in concept, but difficult for most Wall Street investors to adhere to over the long-term. Unfortunately, many Wall Street investors are so focused on the short-term; they often overlook wonderful undervalued businesses likely to outperform the market over the long-term.

Instead of investing in undervalued businesses, many money managers seek short-term gains at any cost: using momentum strategies, options derivatives, Modern Portfolio Theory (MPT), etc. Avoid investment theories measuring risk as volatility, instead of studying individual businesses based on underlying fundamentals, common sense, financial statements, and intrinsic valuations.

I recently met with a friend working for a large Wall Street firm. We discussed a few undervalued businesses, and we both agreed these businesses were wonderful businesses and undervalued. Surprisingly, he informed me he would not be allocating any of his clients' capital into these wonderful undervalued businesses, because they may not perform well over the next quarter. I reminded him:

Filter 1: It is a business he understands.
Filter 2: The business has honest and capable management.
Filter 3: It possesses strong durable competitive advantages.
Filter 4: The business is trading at a share price significantly below its intrinsic value.

Catalyst: A "catalyst" event was publicly announced to occur later in the year likely to improve the stock price.

He agreed with me, but reminded me if his portfolios did not perform well each quarter, his clients would transfer their money away from him. Then he would not be able to afford the high-consumption, high-debt life-style he enjoyed. Several months later, the "catalyst" event occurred as previously announced, and the stock price shot upward rapidly. However, since my friend neglected to invest into this undervalued business, he and his clients did not enjoy the financial gain from this undervalued investment.

Instead, he invested his clients' money into over-valued businesses that did not perform well. Where did he receive the "buy" recommendation to invest in those businesses? – From his Wall Street firm's "brilliant" investment analysts who use mathematical models based on Modern Portfolio Theory (MPT).

"Wall Street is more concerned with correlation, than valuation." Scott Thompson

It turns out his large Wall Street company's investment bank also underwrote many IPOs for these overvalued businesses. His firm needed buyers for shares of these IPOs, so the firm's investment analysts rated them a "Buy." Can't happen on Wall Street? Do your own research. Don't rely on the research of others.

This is a great lesson, to do your own research and due diligence before you invest. Warren Buffett performs all his own investment research. Warren does not need to look at "buy, sell, or hold" stock recommendations from large Wall Street firms.

Warren Buffett bought General Re Reinsurance Company during the 1990's. At that time, General Re employed a team of 150 investment experts to allocate the billions of dollars of General Re's insurance "float." After Warren Buffett purchased General Re, Warren dissolved the team of 150 investment experts and replaced the team of 150 with... himself. Now that is efficiency!

Bottom line: Use the Four Filters Investment Process and search for catalysts. Learn how to value businesses, and perform your own research.

CHAPTER FOUR:

Financial Statements

"Use the quantitative to help reveal the qualitative." Scott Thompson

4.1 Overview:

Financial statements are written reports of businesses' financial information. They are usually released quarterly and annually. They quantitatively illustrate the financial status of the business. Financial statements can help us determine if the business is healthy or unhealthy, and headed in a positive or negative direction.

Before we begin, each financial statement offers valuable information the value investor can use to gain a clearer picture of the underlying business. Financial statements help the value investor decide if this is a good business in which to invest, or a bad business in which to not invest. Therefore, each financial statement offers a unique glimpse into the underlying fundamentals of the business. There are three major financial statements. The three major financial statements are:

Income Statement
Balance Sheet
Cash Flow Statement

Each financial statement tells a story. Like detectives pursuing a trail of evidence, value investors examine data contained within financial statements to determine if a business is worth investing in, or not. Remember most analysts decline over 95% of investments they analyze. Like the famous successful baseball hitter, Ted Williams, you do not have to swing at every pitch. Create your set of investment criteria of what you will and will not invest in. Focus on the intrinsic value of the business, not market price.

Financial statements help investors answer questions, such as:

- How much debt does the business currently carry?
- Is the debt decreasing or increasing?
- How many years will it take to pay off all the debt?
- How profitable is this business?
- How does this business compare to others within its sector/industry? *(Perform sector comparisons)*
- Is the number of total shares outstanding decreasing or increasing?

These are just a few of the questions value investors ask when analyzing financial statements.

Warren Buffett prefers businesses with little to no debt, and high returns on equity (ROE). The average return on equity is about 12, so businesses showing returns on equity (ROE) of 15 or higher, and have little to no debt, can be worth exploring.

Investors must also consider "opportunity cost." In other words, is this investment the most optimal investment? Or, are there better alternatives from competitors that may be better investment alternatives.

Remember "Opportunity Cost." When you say, "Yes" to one investment, you inadvertently say, "No" to another. Do your research before you invest. Investment capital is finite. Allocate it wisely.

Ultimately, it is up to the investor to determine which businesses will return the highest return on investment. Remember Buffett's and Munger's Four Filters investment process as you examine each business's financial statements. Over time, you will become better and better at identifying businesses that will outperform others. Just like anything else, it just takes a little practice and determination to succeed.

Eventually, you may sharpen your financial analysis skills to the point where you can quickly glance at a business's financial statements and within just a few seconds determine if it is a business worth exploring further, or not.

Here are the fundamentals of each financial statement, and an explanation of the helpful information contained on each. Now, we'll take a look at each of the (3) major financial statements, beginning with the Income Statement.

4.2 Income Statement:

The income statement is a profit and loss statement revealing valuable information about a business's total sales revenues, cost of goods sold, gross profit, operating expenses, interest expenses, taxes paid, net income, and number of total shares outstanding.

- **Total Revenue**: The amount of gross sales of products and services sold by the business over a specified time, such as a quarter (3 months) or 1 year.

- **Cost of Revenue**: The cost to produce the products and services, which the business sells.

- **Gross Profit**: The formula to determine Gross Profit is: Total Revenue minus Cost of Revenue = Gross Profit. The business with the highest Gross Profit in their sector or industry may be a sign of "Pricing Power," which is the ability to charge more than competitors for their products and services.

- **Operating Expenses**: The expenses businesses incur to run their business, such as "Sales, General, and Administrative (SGA)" costs, or "Research and Development (R&D)" costs. These expenses must be subtracted from Gross Profit, to determine the amount of Operating Earnings.

- **Operating Earnings**: Operating Earnings are the amount of earnings after Cost of Revenue and Operating Expenses have been subtracted. Operating earnings are also commonly referred to as EBIT, or Earnings Before Interest and Taxes (pronounced ee-bit). Warren Buffett often uses Operating Earnings in his calculations to determine the valuation of businesses in which he's considering investing. Buffett's "2-column process" uses Operating Earnings. (We'll show you how you can calculate Buffett's "2-column process" in Chapter 9: Intrinsic Value).

- **Interest Expense**: The amount of interest a business pays its creditors for debt previously borrowed. Interest Expense is on the Income Statement, but the "Short-term debt" and "Long-term debt" owed by a business is shown on the Balance Sheet. Businesses with higher debt pay higher amounts of interest payments. Businesses with little to no debt pay much smaller or no interest payments. Warren prefers businesses with little to no debt, because more of the profit can be used for reinvestment purposes instead of making high interest payments. Businesses with little to no debt, compared to others within their sector or industry, may also be a sign of better management.

- **Taxes**: Are the amount of taxes paid to the government of the country of domicile in which the business in located. This is based on the amount of taxable income the business earned over a specified period, such as the past quarter (3 months) or 1 year. Tax rates vary per country.

- **Net Income**: Is the net amount of earnings a business earns after all other expenses have been deducted. Net income is an important metric used by investors and financial analysts in many of their calculations on the financial health of businesses. A business with negative Net Income means the business is not profitable, and it is losing money. A business with positive Net Income means the business is profitable.

- **Total Shares Outstanding**: Think of a share of stock as owning a small piece of the business. How much is the underlying business worth? (Chapter 9) After you determine the valuation of the business, divide the overall value of the business by the number of (diluted) Total Shares Outstanding. This gives you the Per Share Amount to estimate what the business is worth.

When investing, investors earn money based on the percentage gain of the total return earned, not by the number of shares owned. For instance, investors will earn more money investing into 10 shares at \$10/share (\$100 original investment), that increases by 25%, so now the investor owns 10 shares at \$12.50/share = \$125.

Conversely, for some reason, many investors decline these opportunities to instead invest in 100 shares of a business at $1 share ($100 original investment), but it only increases 5%, so now the investor owns 100 shares at 1.05/share = $105. These shortsighted "share based" investors erroneously misperceive that they own a higher number of shares. They feel as if they own something more valuable. Remember, the goal is achieving percentage gains on total returns by investing in the highest-quality businesses, and not to own the highest number of shares of penny stocks.

Note: *Use "diluted" total shares outstanding instead of "Basic" total shares outstanding, because "diluted" already contains stock option grants and other items, and makes your estimates more conservative. It is better to be surprised on the upside, than the downside.*

Net Income and Total Shares Outstanding are important items on the Income Statement, and work together. For instance, Net Income divided by Total Shares Outstanding = Earnings per Share (EPS). Earnings per Share is an important metric used by many financial professionals.

Similarly... Stock Price divided by Earnings per Share = P/E Ratio

Another way to express this is... Earnings per Share x P/E Ratio = Stock Price

Net Income vs. Earnings per Share:

When analyzing the income statement, Net Income tells a more complete story about the actual net earnings of the underlying business than Earnings per Share (EPS). Be aware, "Earnings Per Share (EPS)" data can be manipulated by managers either upward (by buying more shares) or downward (by selling more stock).

For instance, let's assume a business earned the same Net Income amount during the current year as it did the prior year, but initiated a stock buyback program. This would cause Earnings Per Share (EPS) to be higher, even if net income stayed the same as the prior year. This is because the same net income amount is simply divided by a lower number of total shares outstanding, which results in a higher Earnings Per Share (EPS) amount.

Conversely, if this business earned the same Net Income as the prior year, but a company issues more total shares outstanding, this would result in Earnings Per Share (EPS) being lower. This dilution effect occurs because the same net income amount is being divided by a higher number of total shares outstanding. This results in a lower Earnings Per Share (EPS) amount. Make sense?

Therefore, Net Income is the better, more accurate indicator of the profitability of a business than Earnings Per Share (EPS). This reveals why Warren Buffett places more weight on Net Income than Earnings Per Share (EPS), because Earnings Per Share (EPS) can be manipulated by changing the number of Total Shares Outstanding. Conversely, Net Income is calculated BEFORE Earnings Per Share (EPS).

The point here is Earnings Per Share (EPS) is a function of the number of total shares outstanding. If the number of total shares outstanding is higher, the EPS will be lower. Conversely, if the number of total shares outstanding is lower, the EPS will be higher. The number of total shares outstanding may go up or down, depending on whether management issues more shares, or implements a share buyback program.

So, as you can see, the Income statement can be very useful in uncovering insightful information about a business, and can help you make better investment decisions. Here's an example Income Statement:

Income Statement: Coca Cola (KO): 2012

USD in millions except per share data

Revenue	$48,017
Cost of revenue	$19,053
Gross Profit	$28,964
Operating expenses:	
Sales, General, and administrative	$17,738
Other operating expenses	$ 447
Total operating expenses	**$18,185**
Operating income	$10,779
Interest Expense	$ 397 ·
Other income (expense)	$ 1,427
Income before taxes	$11,809
Provision for income taxes	$ 2,723
Other income	0
Net income from continuing operations	$ 9,086
Other	($67)
Net income	$ 9,019
Net income available to common shareholders	$ 9,019
Earnings per share:	
Basic	$ 2.00
Diluted	$ 1.97
Weighted average total shares outstanding:	
Basic	4,504 shares outstanding
Diluted	4,584 shares outstanding

Income Statements are often shown "in millions." Therefore, Coca-Cola's Revenue shown on the top line of the Income Statement of: $48,017 is actually $48,017,000,000. As you can see, Coca-Cola's Net Income in 2012 was $9,019,000,000. If we divide $9,019,000,000 by 4,584,000,000 (diluted) Total Shares Outstanding, then Coca-Cola's 2012 Earnings per Share (EPS) is: $1.97 per share.

Net Income divided by Total Shares Outstanding = Earnings per Share

If you were to multiply Coca-Cola's EPS of $1.97/share by its P/E ratio, the result is its current stock market price. For instance, if Coca-Cola has a P/E ratio of 10, then $1.97 x 10 = stock market price of $19.70/share.

Similarly, if Coca-Cola has a P/E ratio of 20, then $1.97 x 20 = stock market price of: $39.40/share.

From this example, you can clearly see it is best to invest when P/E ratios are low, and to sell when P/E ratios are high. However, there is much more to selecting quality investments than using the P/E ratio alone. Never rely on any single financial metric to make an investment decision. Instead, be sure to consider all available quantitative and qualitative information, and perform your due diligence before you invest.

Think of your valuation process as a combination of your qualitative observations plus your quantitative observations. Like a good family doctor, you can make a better diagnosis on the quality of your business investment prospect. Warren Buffett always advises us to look at each potential investment as an individual business.

Regarding the Interest Expense shown on Coca-Cola's Income Statement of $397 (expressed "in millions," so the actual amount is $397,000,000). This means Coca-Cola is paying interest of $397,000,000 on debt it has borrowed. The Income Statement shows the amount of interest paid on debt, but the Balance Sheet shows the actual amount of debt the business had borrowed. Next, we examine the Balance Sheet.

4.3 Balance Sheet:

The balance sheet describes the business' assets, liabilities, and stockholders' equity. Equity is also referred to as "shareholders' equity," or the business' "net worth." The business' net worth is determined by: simply subtracting Total Liabilities from Total Assets. The formula is:

$$\text{Total Assets} - \text{Total Liabilities} = \text{Shareholders' Equity}$$

Current Assets: Current assets are assets realized by the business within a 12-month period. Examples of current assets are: cash, cash equivalents, short-term investments, receivables, inventories, prepaid expenses, etc. Current assets are to be received within a shorter-term 12-month period, which is why they are called "current" assets.

Non-current Assets: are assets owned by a business that creates value and positively impacts the balance sheet for periods longer than 12 months. Examples of non-current assets are: property plant and equipment (PP&E), equity long-term investments, goodwill, intangible assets, and other long-term assets for periods longer than 12 months.

Current Liabilities: Current liabilities are debts and obligations owed by the business negatively impacting the balance sheet, and must be paid within the next 12 months. Examples of current liabilities are: short-term debt, accounts payable, taxes payable, accrued liabilities, etc. Current liabilities are due to be paid within the next 12 months, which is why they are called "current" liabilities.

Non-current Liabilities: are debts and obligations owed by the business negatively impacting the balance sheet, which are owed by the business for periods longer than the next 12 months. Examples of non-current liabilities are: long-term debt, deferred taxes, capital leases, minority interest, etc. Non-current liabilities are due to be paid over a period longer than 12 months, which is why they are called "non-current" liabilities.

Stockholders' Equity: is the "net worth" of a business. A net worth calculation can be simply performed by subtracting "total liabilities" from "total assets." The formula to calculate Stockholders' Equity is:

Total Assets − Total Liabilities = Stockholders' Equity

For example, Coca-Cola's Balance Sheet shows Total Assets of: $86,174, and Total Liabilities of: $53,384. If we subtract $53,384 from $86,174, the difference is: $32,790. Remember, numbers are shown "in millions" so $32,790 actually represents: $32,790,000,000 or $32.79 billion. This exactly matches the amount of "Stockholders' Equity" toward the bottom of Cola-Cola's Balance Sheet.

Another way to look at this is, add Total Liabilities of: $53,384 (million) and Stockholders' Equity of: $32,790 (million) together, and you arrive at: $86,174 (million). This exactly matches the amount of Total Assets, making the Balance Sheet "balance," which is why it is called a Balance Sheet. Here's an example Balance Sheet:

Balance Sheet: Coca Cola (KO): 2012

USD in millions except per share data

Current Assets:

Cash and cash equivalents	$ 8,442
Short-term investments	$ 8,109
Total cash	**$16,551**
Receivables	$ 4,759
Inventories	$ 3,264
Prepaid expenses	$ 2,781
Other current assets	$ 2,973
Total current assets	**$30,328**

Non-current Assets:

Gross property, plant and equipment	$23,486
Accumulated Depreciation	($9,010)
Net property, plant and equipment	$14,476
Equity and other investments	$10,448
Goodwill	$12,255
Intangible assets	$15,082
Other long-term assets	$ 3,585
Total non-current assets	$55,846
TOTAL ASSETS:	**$86,174**

Current Liabilities:

Short-term debt	$17,874
Accounts payable	$ 1,969
Taxes payable	$ 471
Accrued liabilities	$ 6,711
Other current liabilities	$ 796
Total current liabilities	**$27,821**

Non-Current Liabilities:

Long-term debt	$14,736
Deferred taxes liabilities	$ 4,981
Minority interest	$ 378
Other long-term liabilities	$ 5,468
Total non-current liabilities	$25,563
TOTAL LIABILITIES:	**$53,384**

Stockholders' Equity:

Common stock	$ 1,760
Additional paid-in capital	$11,379
Retained earnings	$58,045
Treasury stock	($35,009)
Accumulated other comprehensive income	($3,385)
Total stockholders' equity	$32,790

TOTAL LIABILITIES & STOCKHOLDERS' EQUITY: $86,174

An important item to consider during your Balance Sheet analysis is **Retained Earnings**. Retained Earnings are the portion of net income retained by the business not distributed to shareholders as dividends. If the business experiences a gain, this gain is shown as a positive amount of its Balance Sheet. Conversely, if the business experiences a loss, then the loss is retained and shown as a negative amount on its Balance Sheet.

Warren Buffett prefers to invest in healthy businesses whose Balance Sheets show a long-term history of steadily increasing Retained Earnings. For example, on Coca-Cola's Balance Sheet notice the generally increasing amount of Retained Earnings over this 10-year period:

2003: $26,687 (in millions)
2004: $29,105 (in millions)
2005: $31,299 (in millions)
2006: $33,468 (in millions)
2007: $36,235 (in millions)
2008: $38,513 (in millions)
2009: $41,537 (in millions)
2010: $49,278 (in millions)
2011: $53,550 (in millions)
2012: $58,045 (in millions)

Graph shows Coca-Cola's 10-year Retained Earnings from 2003 through 2012.

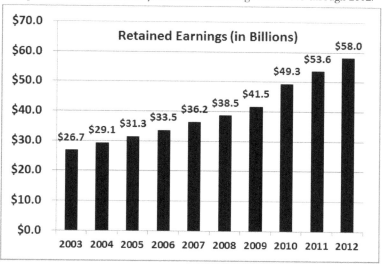

When we find Balance Sheets showing a long-term history of steadily increasing Retained Earnings, it may be a sign of a healthy business run by honest and capable managers.

Treasury Stock: Shares of stock owned or bought back by the original issuing corporation. When a business buys back their own stock, it reduces the number of total shares outstanding. Treasury stock may be either held for reissue, or cancelled. Treasury stock does not pay a dividend and has no voting rights.

Stock Repurchases: Warren Buffett likes businesses engaging in Stock Repurchases, because it can be a more tax-efficient way to increase the value per share owned by shareholders, instead of paying a dividend.

Dividend distributions are taxable events, if held in taxable accounts, whereas stock repurchases are a non-taxable way to increase the value of remaining shares outstanding after a stock buyback. To illustrate this point, Coca-Cola's Treasury Stock on their Balance Sheet shows a long-term 10-year history of consistently engaging in stock buybacks. The parentheses around the Treasury Stock at the bottom of Coca-Cola's Balance Sheet reflect stock buybacks being a negative number, since the business is spending money to buyback its stock.

Now let's reveal how financial statements work together in harmony like a symphony:

The fact that Coca-Cola engages in stock buybacks is also shown on their Income Statement. See "Weighted Average Shares," which is another name for "Total Shares Outstanding." You can see Coca-Cola's long-term 10-year history of "Total Shares Outstanding" steadily decreasing over time.

Question: How do stock buybacks decrease "Total Shares Outstanding" and increase shareholder value?

Answer: Simple. Coca-Cola's Income Statement shows their 2012 Net Income (available to shareholders) was $9,019 (million), with 2012 (diluted) "Total Shares Outstanding" of 4,584 (million). Notice in the previous year of 2011, Coca-Cola had 4,646 (million) "Total Shares

Outstanding." Therefore, from 2011 to 2012, Coca-Cola repurchased 62 (million) "Total Shares Outstanding." The Earnings per Share (EPS) formula is:

(Net Income / Total Shares Outstanding) = Earnings per Share

EXAMPLE #1: Apply this EPS formula to Coca-Cola's 2012 Net Income of $9,019 (million) and their 2012 Total Shares Outstanding of 4,584:

$$\$9,019 \div \underline{4,584} = \$1.97 \text{ EPS}$$

EXAMPLE #2: Next, apply this EPS formula to Coca-Cola's 2012 Net Income of $9,019 (million) and their 2011 Total Shares Outstanding of 4,646:

$$\$9,019 \div \underline{4,646} = \$1.94 \text{ EPS}$$

As you can see, Coca-Cola's 2012 Earnings per Share (EPS) are $1.97, instead of $1.94 because Coca-Cola bought back 62 million shares of its stock during 2012. This effectively decreased the number of Total Shares Outstanding from 4,646 to 4,584 shown on Coca-Cola's Income Statement, and also on Coca-Cola's Balance Sheet shown by a negative value of "Treasury Stock" repurchased.

Therefore, because Coca-Cola's amount of Total Shares Outstanding decreased, the denominator is smaller in the EPS calculation, and this makes Earnings per Share increase! Higher EPS values increase shareholder value, and help the stock price rise higher– all without creating a taxable event. Only after the investor sells their shares is there a taxable event, and we all know Warren Buffett's favorite holding time is… forever!

Note: In 2006 Warren Buffett began transferring shares of his Berkshire Hathaway stock into charitable foundations, in stock form, without selling the shares. Then, after the tax-exempt foundations own the stock, they can choose to sell the stock, and the entire stock sale owned by these tax-exempt organizations is tax-free.

Accounting (Book) Value vs. Liquidation Value:

Balance Sheets show accounting value or book value, but do not show the tangible book value or liquidation value. For instance, a business may carry a $25 million building on its balance sheet at its original $5 million acquisition price, less accumulated depreciation, instead of its current market value of $25 million. Conversely, a business may have purchased a building at the top of the real estate market, and its current market value may be well below the original acquisition price.

The point here, is accounting "book values" shown on the balance sheet may not always reflect the true underlying valuation of business assets, and adjustments may be necessary in order to more accurately determine a valuation of underlying business assets.

Warren Buffett's mentor, Benjamin Graham was an expert at identifying businesses trading for less than their Net Working Capital, also known as Net Current Assets.

Remember the formula:

Net Working Capital = Total Current Assets – Total Current Liabilities

Ben Graham would buy shares in businesses whose stock prices were trading less than their liquidation value per share. Remember, assets on the balance sheet only show accounting book values, and they often do not represent the true tangible value of the business. This is why we make adjustments on the balance sheets – sometimes called the "haircut method" – to identify liquidation value, in the following manner:

Total Cash: Count 100% of all total cash. In a liquidation sale, cash on the balance sheet retains 100% of its value.

Receivables: Remove 25%, so 75% is remaining. In a liquidation sale, if customers learn a business is going out of business, 15%–25% of customers will likely not pay their balances due, so we remove 25% and retain 50% liquidation value.

Inventories: Remove 50%, so 50% is remaining. In a liquidation sale, inventories are often sold quickly, discounting these assets at 30%, 40%, or even 50%. We conservatively remove 50% from the balance sheet amount, so 50% value is remaining.

Deferred Income Taxes: Remove 100%, so 0% is remaining. In a liquidation sale, taxes the business has not yet paid do not generate value for investors seeking to selectively acquire remaining assets of a business under liquidation. Selective investors would rather acquire inventories at 50% of value, than sign up to pay remaining deferred taxes, so we remove 100% of deferred income taxes, so 0% remains.

(Net) Plant Property and Equipment (PP&E): Remove 55%, so 45% is remaining. Use Net PP&E, not Gross PP&E. In a liquidation sale, net PP&E assets are usually expensive and highly specialized, making the pool of buyers for these types of assets small. For these reasons, we remove 55% and retain 45%.

Goodwill: Remove 100%, so 0% is remaining. In a liquidation sale, we seek tangible assets only. Goodwill is not a tangible asset. Remove 100%, and retain 0% for liquidation value.

Intangible Assets: Remove 100%, so 0% is remaining. In a liquidation sale, we seek tangible assets only. Intangible assets are not tangible assets. Remove 100%, and retain 0% for liquidation value.

Total up all items on the balance sheet, including these adjusted amounts, to find a quick "back of envelope" liquidation value. There are experts who make their living valuing corporate assets in liquidation sales, so remember this is just an approximate method to determine liquidation value.

After you've arrived at your total "liquidation value," divide by total shares outstanding, to arrive at your liquidation value per share. If today's share price is below liquidation value per share, you may be able to buy shares of businesses trading for less than their liquidation value!

It's important to understand how money flows in and out of various categories on the balance sheet. For example, "Cash" buys "Inventory." Inventory, after being sold becomes "Accounts Receivable." After payment is received from customers, "Accounts Receivable" becomes "Cash," and the cycle repeats. Next we examine Cash Flow Statements.

4.4 Cash Flow Statement:

The cash flow statement reveals information to investors about the firm's flows of cash between the business and the outside world. The first line of the Cash Flow Statement is Net Income. The bottom of the Cash Flow Statement usually shows: Cash at beginning of period, Cash at end of period, and Free Cash Flows.

Cash Flow Statements are often divided into three segments:

- Cash Flows from <u>Operating</u> Activities
- Cash Flows from <u>Investing</u> Activities
- Cash Flows from <u>Financing</u> Activities.

Cash Flow from Operating Activities pertains to the flow of cash in order to support the normal operations of the business. For instance, components of Net Cash from Operating Activities may include: depreciation and amortization, deferred income taxes, stock based compensation, accounts receivable, inventory, prepaid expenses, accrued liabilities, other working capital, and non-cash items, etc.

Cash Flow from Investing Activities shows how the businesses invested its cash in and out of various investing activities over the period. For example, components of Net Cash from Investing Activities may include: investments in property plant and equipment, acquisitions, purchases of investments, sales/maturities of investments, and other investing activities, etc.

Cash Flow from Financing Activities indicates how cash flowed through the various financing activities of the business. For instance, components of Net Cash from Financing Activities may include: debt issues, debt repayment, common stock issues, common stock repurchased, dividend paid, and other financing activities, etc.

Toward the bottom of the Cash Flow Statement, you may see a section titled, "Free Cash Flow (FCF)." Free Cash Flow (FCF) is one of the most important items on the Cash Flow Statement to which value investors pay the most attention. As a value investor, you should pay attention to Free Cash Flow too.

Free Cash Flow (FCF) is a measure of how much cash a business generates after paying all necessary expenses required sustaining and growing business operations. Free Cash Flow reveals a clearer picture to investors of the business' ability (or lack thereof) to generate cash. Free Cash Flows are important, as this is the money businesses can use to make acquisitions, pay dividends to shareholders, engage in stock repurchases, etc. All of these activities create value for investors, so as value investors we pay close attention to the ability of businesses to generate Free Cash Flows (FCF). Furthermore, this metric tends to be more difficult for management to manipulate.

The formula for calculating Free Cash Flow (FCF) is:

Operating Cash Flow – Capital Expenditures = Free Cash Flow

Or, look at it this way:

(Operating Income x (1 – Tax Rate)) + (Depreciation and Amortization) – (Changes in Working Capital) – Capital Expenditures = Free Cash Flow

Remember:

- Operating Income is also referred to as EBIT or Earnings Before Interest and Taxes, shown on the Income Statement.
- Working Capital is: (Current Assets) minus (Current Liabilities), shown on the Balance Sheet.

Businesses lacking Free Cash Flows (FCF) are businesses that should be left to other investors. Although, no single financial metric can be used to make any investment decision, Free Cash Flow (FCF) is an important financial metric to which value investors pay attention.

Warren Buffett prefers to see a long-term history of steadily increasing amounts of Free Cash Flows (FCF), as shown at the bottom of the Cash Flow Statement. As you develop your value investing and analytical skills, soon you may be able to glance at a Cash Flow Statement and determine in a few moments whether the business is worth digging-in and spending more time analyzing, or not. Here's an example Cash Flow Statement:

Cash Flow Statement: Coca Cola (KO): 2012

USD in millions except per share data

Cash Flows from Operations:

Net Income	$ 9,086
Depreciation and Amortization	$ 1,982
Deferred income taxes	$ 632
Stock based compensation	$ 259
Accounts receivable	($ 33)
Inventory	($ 286)
Prepaid expenses	($ 29)
Accrued liabilities	$ 770
Other working capital	($1,502)
Other non-cash items	($ 234)
Net Cash provided by operating activities	**$10,645**

Cash Flows from Investments:

Investments in plant, property and equipment	($ 2,780)
Plant, property and equipment deductions	$ 143
Acquisitions, net	$ 2,189
Purchases of investments	($16,391)
Sales/Maturities of investments	$ 5,622
Other investing activities	($ 187)
Net cash used for investing activities	**($11,404)**

Cash Flows from Financing Activities:

Debt issued	$42,791
Debt repayment	($38,573)
Common stock issued	$ 1,489
Common stock repurchased	($ 4,559)
Dividend paid	($ 4,559)
Other financing activities	$ 100
Net cash used for investing activities	**($3,347)**

Effect of exchange rates	($ 255)
Net change in cash	($ 4,361)
Cash at beginning of period	$12,803
Cash at end of period	$ 8,442

Free Cash Flow:

Operating cash flow	$10,645
Capital expenditures	($ 2,780)
Free Cash Flow (FCF)	$ 7,865

Here are a couple more examples revealing how financial statements work together in harmony like a symphony:

"Cash at end of period" on the Cash Flow Statement is equal to "Cash and cash equivalents" on the Balance Sheet.

Another example is: Net income shown in the middle of the Income Statement, is equal to Net Income located at the top of the Cash Flow Statement.

Now that you have developed a stronger understanding of financial statements, you ask, "What information does Warren Buffett look for on financial statements?" Or, "What types of businesses does Warren Buffett seek to acquire?" Next, we disclose Warren Buffett's Acquisition Criteria from Berkshire Hathaway's 2010 Letter to Shareholders.

4.5 BERKSHIRE HATHAWAY INC. ACQUISITION CRITERIA

We are eager to hear *from principals or their representatives* about businesses that meet all of the following criteria:

- (1) Large purchases (at least $75 million of pre-tax earnings unless the business will fit into one of our existing units),

- (2) Demonstrated consistent earning power (future projections are of no interest to us, nor are "turnaround" situations),

- (3) Businesses earning good returns on equity while employing little or no debt,

- (4) Management in place (we can't supply it),

- (5) Simple businesses (if there is lots of technology, we won't understand it),

- (6) An offering price (we don't want to waste our time or that of the seller by talking, even preliminarily, about a transaction when price is unknown).

The larger the business, the greater will be our interest. We would like to make an acquisition in the $5 billion to $20 billion range.

We are not interested, however, in receiving suggestions about purchases we might make in the general stock market.

We will not engage in unfriendly takeovers. We can promise complete confidentiality and a very fast answer – customarily within five minutes – as to whether we're interested. We prefer to buy for cash, but will consider issuing stock when we receive as much in intrinsic business value as we give. *We don't participate in auctions.*

Charlie and I frequently get approached about acquisitions that don't come close to meeting our tests. We've found if you advertise an interest in buying collies, a lot of people will call hoping to sell you their cocker spaniels. A line from a country song expresses our feeling about new ventures, turnarounds, or auction-like sales. "When the phone don't ring, you'll know it's me."

4.6 Exercise:

Can you locate each of Warren Buffett's Berkshire Hathaway acquisition criteria in each of the (3) financial statements? We will show you now:

Item #1: Operating Income: Also known as EBIT (Earnings Before Interest and Taxes), operating income is shown on the Income Statement. Warren Buffett clearly states, he seeks Operating Earnings of $75,000,000 USD or more. The $75,000,000 operating income just sets a minimum requirement threshold the acquiree's business' size must meet or exceed in order to be considered for acquisition. This is due to the fact Berkshire Hathaway is so large financially, it must acquire larger prospective businesses (at least $75 million in EBIT) in order to impact Berkshire Hathaway's immense multi-billion dollar bottom line.

Item #2: Earnings Power: For now, refer to Net Income on the Income Statement to determine if the business's Net Income earnings show a consistent long-term history of growth, decline, or erratic earnings. Warren Buffett likes businesses showing consistent long-term earnings growth. Businesses exhibiting Earnings Power often possess a durable competitive advantage. This is Warren Buffett and Charlie Munger's second investment Filter.

Another way to determine the level of earnings a business returns on its assets, refer to the "Return on Assets (ROA)" ratio. Furthermore, we'll explore Earnings Power Value (EPV) in detail in Chapter 8.

Item #3: <u>Return On Equity (ROE)</u>: Return on Equity is a financial ratio calculated by dividing Net Income (after tax) from the Income Statement by Stockholders' Equity from the Balance Sheet. The industry average ROE is 12%. Businesses showing Returns on Equity (ROE) above 15% are generally considered good, and worth a closer look. We explore Return on Equity in the next chapter: Chapter 5: Financial Ratios.

Warren Buffett likes businesses showing high Returns on Equity (ROE). Businesses exhibiting Earnings Power often possess a durable competitive advantage. This is Warren Buffett and Charlie Munger's second investment filter.

Item #4: <u>Management</u>: This is Warren Buffett and Charlie Munger's investment Filter #3. The business must come with its own management team. Berkshire Hathaway wants to buy businesses with honest and capable managers. Berkshire Hathaway does not provide managers for businesses. The business must come with its own managers.

Item #5: <u>Simple Business</u>: This is Warren Buffett and Charlie Munger's investment Filter #1. Warren Buffett prefers simple businesses he can understand. Over the past 6 decades of Warren's investment career, he has preferred simple businesses such as Coca-Cola, Gillette, Proctor & Gamble, Wrigley's, etc.

Warren Buffett has never invested in technology businesses because he cannot predict what the business or competitive landscape will look like in 10 years. However, undervalued businesses within the Consumer Defensive sector are simple businesses Warren understands, and it is easier to predict what these types of businesses will look like 10 years in the future. When Buffett bought Wrigley's he said, "The internet is not going to change the way people chew gum."

Item #6: <u>Price</u>: This is Warren Buffett and Charlie Munger's fourth investment filter. Berkshire Hathaway buys businesses when they are selling at discounts below their intrinsic value, and provide an adequate margin of safety (MOS). We explore Intrinsic Value in greater detail in Chapter 9: Intrinsic Value.

4.7 Summary:

Financial statements help us determine the past and present financial condition of the underlying business. Financial statements can also help us determine the future of the business. Do the business's financial statements show a long-term consistent upward trend in net income and free cash flows? Or, do the financial statements reveal another story, with erratic unpredictable earnings, little or no Free Cash Flows, and no consistent upward trend?

Examining financial statements is like detective work. It is an art as much as it is a science. As value investors, we must examine both the quantitative (science) and the qualitative (art) aspects of businesses, to determine if a particular business is worth investing in, or not.

Even after you identify a business you believe may be suitable for investment, consider analyzing other similar competing businesses within its same industry / sector, so you identify the best business within each sector / industry. Just because you suddenly identify a "good" business, do not just "knee-jerk" and reflexively buy it. Although, it may be a "good" business, it may not be a "great" business. In other words, it may not be the best, most optimal business within its sector or industry.

Being a successful value investor requires patience and a willingness to examine lots of businesses. Now that you understand financial statements, let's explore how financial statements work together to form "financial ratios."

"If a business does well, the stock price eventually follows." Warren Buffett

CHAPTER FIVE:

Financial Ratios

5.1 Overview:

Financial ratios can be useful to help us form a clearer understanding about the underlying business. One of the most common financial ratios is the price to earnings ratio, or P/E Ratio. The P/E Ratio is a commonly used financial ratio, but it only tells part of the story. The P/E Ratio is determined by dividing the market price (per share), by the net Earnings (per share). The result is the P/E Ratio.

For example, if a business has a market price of $20 per share, and earnings-per-share of $2 per share, if we simply divide $20 (market price per share) by $2 (earnings per share), the resulting P/E Ratio is 10. ($20 ÷ 2 = 10). Therefore, a business with a market price of $20 per share, and earnings of $2 dollars per share, has a P/E ratio of 10.

Note: In Benjamin Graham's book "Security Analysis" written in 1938, Ben Graham wrote he preferred investing in businesses with P/E Ratios less than 16.

No one single financial ratio should be used to make any investment decision. Instead, use multiple financial ratios, and use data over a longer 5, 7, or 10-year history. Historical data tends to produce better results.

Expand your research across a wider range of information and sources. Then, you will obtain a deeper, richer understanding of the underlying business. Remember to consider both quantitative and qualitative factors, as per the Four Filters Process of Warren Buffett and his partner Charlie Munger (Chapter 3).

Financial ratios can often help us identify businesses with durable competitive advantages, because they can quantitatively reveal the qualitative. In other words, if a business possesses a high quality management team, nuances of this may be found on the business's financial statements. Look for factors like: Low or no debt, low or no interest payments, low SGA expenses, low operating expenses, share repurchases, decreasing number of total shares outstanding, high free cash flows (FCFs), increasing retained earnings, low capital expenditures, etc.

Remember, it is helpful to have a solid understanding of financial statements, as this will help you understand financial ratios more clearly, how to use them, and how they can assist you in selecting better businesses in which to invest. To review your understanding of financial statements, see Chapter 4: Financial Statements.

As you can imagine, there are many financial ratios in existence. Some are more important than others. Now that you've developed a good foundational understanding of financial statements, let's explore some of the main financial ratios used by billionaire investor Warren Buffett and other successful value investors.

5.2 FINANCIAL RATIOS:

In this chapter, we will explore the following financial ratios:

Price / Earnings (P/E)
Price / Book (P/B)
Price / Free Cash Flow (P/FCF)
Price / Sales (P/S)
Free Cash Flow / Sales (FCF/S)
Sales / Net Receivables (S/NR)
Sales / Employee (S/E)
Debt / Equity (D/E)
Dividend Yield
Payout Ratio

Research & Development / Gross Profit (R&D/GP)
Sales, General, & Administrative / Gross Profit (SGA/GP)
Total Operating Expenses / Gross Profit (TOE/GP)
Depreciation & Amortization / Gross Profit (DA/GP)
Interest / Operating Income (Interest / EBIT)

Capital Expenditures / Operating Income (CapEx/EBIT)
Capital Expenditures / Net Income (CapEx/NI)
Long-term debt / Net Income (LTD/NI)
(Long-term debt + Capital Expenditures) / Net Income

Current Ratio
Quick Ratio (Acid Test)
Inventory Turnover

Return On Assets (ROA)
Return On Equity (ROE)
Debt-Adjusted Return On Equity (DA-ROE)
Return On Invested Capital (ROIC)

Net Net (Benjamin Graham)

Price / Earnings (P/E):

Price-to-Earnings ratio is used by investors to help determine if a business is undervalued or overvalued. The P/E ratio is calculated by simply dividing the current market price (CMP) by the Earnings Per Share (EPS). This is commonly known in the financial industry as the "P/E Ratio" or P/E." Lower P/E ratios can indicate a particular business may be undervalued, and higher P/E ratios can indicate a business may be overvalued. Bear in mind, the P/E Ratio is only one financial ratio, and cannot be relied on solely. It can be manipulated. The formula is:

$$\frac{\text{Market Price}}{\text{Net Earnings (per share)}}$$

The P/E Ratio tells us the multiple the price is trading at, relative to its underlying Earnings Per Share (EPS). If a business' Income Statement shows Earnings Per Share (EPS) of $2 per share, and a market price of $10 per share, the business is said to have a P/E Ratio of 5. Because, Market Price ($10) divided by ($2) Earnings Per Share, equals a P/E Ratio of 5.

A second example is a business with Earnings Per Share of $8, and a Market Price of $80, is said to have a P/E Ratio of 10. Because, Market Price ($80) divided by ($8) Earnings Per Share, equals a P/E Ratio of 10.

Again, no single metric should be used solely to determine an investment decision. Some ratios can be manipulated more than others.

Ben Graham, Warren Buffett's teacher and mentor, wrote that he would not invest in businesses with P/E ratios higher than 16. During the late 1990's, many of the high-tech "dot.com" businesses that IPO-ed had P/E ratios above 100, and some with P/E ratios above 200. Most of them have since crashed, out of business, and investors have lost their money.

During the 1990's, many dot.com companies had no earnings. The "E" part of the P/E ratio was negative, meaning these companies operated at a loss with high cash consumption "burn-rates." Therefore, valuations were conveniently changed to use multiples of revenues, instead of P/E.

The P/E ratio can be used as a general guide, but again it is important to consider many financial ratios and information before making any investment decision. We will explain many other financial ratios here for you now.

Price / Book:

The Price / Book ratio, (also known as the P/B ratio), informs investors how much a business may be worth today if it were to cease operating, sell of all its tangible assets, and pay off all its debt. The Price / Book ratio can be calculated a number of different ways. One of the simplest ways is to use the following formula, which is more difficult to manipulate. The formula is:

$$\frac{\text{Share Price}}{(\text{Total Tangible Assets} - \text{Total Liabilities}) / \text{Total Shares Outstanding}}$$

Total Tangible Assets are all the Assets on the business's balance sheet that can be sold in a liquidation sale. Items such as "Intangible Assets" and "Goodwill" are often left out of this calculation.

Although, the Price / Book ratio does not tell the entire story, it does reveal a general picture of how the business's share price compares with its net tangible assets on its balance sheet. Book value is also known as "accounting value."

In 2012, Warren Buffett initiated a rare stock buyback announcement, buying back shares of his Berkshire Hathaway. Buffett announced that if shares of Berkshire Hathaway dipped within the range of 10% above book value, then he'd begin buying shares back. However, months later, Warren announced he was buying back Berkshire shares when the share price dipped below the range of 20% above book value.

When the share price is 10% above its book value, the business is said to have a price-to-book ratio of 1.1. When share price is 20% above book value, the business is said to have a price-to-book ratio of 1.2.

If the business is trading below book value, you have a P/B ratio less than 1.0. Lower price-to-book ratios imply a better time to invest in the business. Higher price-to-book ratios imply the stock price may be too high at the moment.. Value investors obviously seek to buy shares of businesses when their stock prices are temporarily depressed. Therefore lower price-to-book ratios may appear more attractive to value investors. Conversely, higher price-to-book ratios may appear less attractive to value investors.

Buffett likes to see a long-term consistent history of book value growth.

Price / Free Cash Flow:

The Price / FCF Ratio is another financial ratio measuring the multiple at which the current Market Price is trading relative to its underlying fundamentals, in this case Price to Free Cash Flow, instead of Price to Earnings. (P/E).

To calculate the Price / FCF Ratio, locate the business's Free Cash Flow (FCF) located toward the bottom right of the business's Cash Flow statement. Divide this amount by the (diluted) Total Shares Outstanding, located on the bottom right of the Income Statement. This shows you the business's Free Cash Flow (FCF) per share.

After you calculate the business's Free Cash Flow (FCF) per share, locate the business's current market price (CMP). Divide the business's current market price (CMP) by the Free Cash Flow (FCF) per share. This is the "Price to Free Cash Flow (FCF) ratio." The formula is:

$$\frac{\text{Market Price}}{\text{Free Cash Flow (per share)}}$$

The Price / Free Cash Flow (FCF) ratio is a valuation metric to help investors compare and contrast a particular business's market price against its amount of Free Cash Flows (FCF). While it may tell us something about the relationship between price and free cash production, it does not really tell us much about the true nature of the business. So, we must consider this ratio within its context of use.

The Price/FCF Ratio functions similar to the P/E Ratio, but the Price / FCF Ratio is a better indicator because it is based on the firm's Free Cash Flows (FCFs) instead of Earnings Per Share (EPS).

The Price / FCF ratio can also be calculated by taking the business's market capitalization rate, and dividing it by its total Free Cash Flow (FCF). Remember, market capitalization is easily calculated by multiplying the business's current market price by the number of Total Shares Outstanding. Many financial websites conveniently show the business's market capitalization rate (along with other financial ratios) when you type in a ticker symbol. The formula is:

$$\frac{\text{Market Capitalization}}{\text{Free Cash Flow}}$$

Remember, Free Cash Flow (FCF) differs from Operating Cash Flow, in that Free Cash Flow (FCF) is a stricter financial metric, because Free Cash Flow (FCF) is Operating Cash Flow after Capital Expenditures have been subtracted out. Since it is a stricter metric, learn to look more towards Free Cash Flow and "trends in Free Cash Flow" as useful information, rather than other metrics.

Many businesses are dependent on continually reinvesting large amounts of Capital Expenditures back into the business. Buffett looks for businesses with lower capital expenditures since these businesses have more capital to invest back into their business. This way, there is more capital remaining at the bottom of the Cash Flow Statement, called Free Cash Flow (FCF). Businesses with higher Free Cash Flow (FCF) tend to perform better over the long term, than businesses with little, zero, or negative Free Cash Flow (FCF).

Therefore, use this Price / Free Cash Flow (FCF) Ratio to identify healthy businesses when they temporarily trade at low Price/FCF multiples. Capitalize on these rare investment opportunities to own a piece of wonderful businesses that generate abundant amounts of Free Cash Flow (FCF). Invest in them when the ratio of price/FCF is temporarily low. Again, do not to rely on any single financial ratio.

The Price/FCF Ratio is most useful in comparing business within a particular sector, or industry. For example, if you were comparing publicly traded businesses within the Communication Services sector, and Telecom Services Industry, you would find a wide range of businesses showing Price/FCF Ratios from 2 up to 200.

Question: If you were an investor investing with your own money, would you rather pay a multiple of two times Free Cash Flow, or 200 times Free Cash Flow to own part of a business?

Answer: Obviously you would rather pay two times Free Cash Flows, because you will be buying in at a much lower price relative to the business's Free Cash Flows, instead of paying 200 times Free Cash Flows.

On rare occasions, you may discover businesses trading with market prices below their Free Cash Flow per share. In these rare cases, the business may be terminally sick and its stock price will remain depressed for an extended period. Or, the business is going through a temporary phase, has strong fundamentals, will experience a "catalyst" event soon that may cause its stock price to rise upward to levels reflecting its underlying Intrinsic Value. Seek healthy businesses. Avoid value traps.

Examine financial statements, financial ratios, research SEC filings at http://www.SEC.gov , read annual reports, perform your due diligence, and you will identify those rare and wonderful businesses.

Price / Sales:

The price to sales ratio can be calculated by starting with the business's total revenues found at the top of its income statement. Then divide revenues by the number of total shares outstanding. The result is the price to sales ratio. The formula is:

$$\frac{\text{Market Price}}{\text{Revenue (per share)}}$$

The price to sales ratio is helpful in showing us how the business's market price compares with its total annual revenues. Lower price-to-sales ratios suggest the business's stock price may be temporarily depressed. Conversely, higher price-to-sales ratios suggest the business's stock price is trading at a higher multiple of total sales.

Since value investors seek undervalued businesses, known investors prefer to invest in businesses with lower price-to-sales ratios, instead of when the price-to-sales ratio is higher.

After all, the whole point of value investing is buy low sell high, right? Again, it is important to take a comprehensive approach to value investing, and never rely on any single ratio or factor when making any investment decision.

Free Cash Flow (FCF) / Sales:

This is an important ratio revealing the percentage of each revenue dollar that gets converted directly into Free Cash Flow (FCF). Higher values are better because this means a higher percentage of each revenue dollar is converted straight into the business's bottom line. The formula is:

$$\frac{\text{Free Cash Flow}}{\text{Revenue}}$$

A higher FCF/Sales Ratio can be very beneficial to shareholders. Because, Free Cash Flow (FCF) can be:

-   Returned back to investors in the form of dividends

-   Allocated to making additional strategic acquisitions

-   Reinvested back into the business

-   Allocated toward share buyback programs to reduce the number of Total Shares Outstanding, which in turn increase earnings per share (EPS), which in turn increase the business' stock price

Free Cash Flow (FCF) is located at the bottom of the business's Cash Flow Statement. Revenue (also sometimes shown as Sales) is shown at the top of the business's Income Statement. Free Cash Flow (FCF) is the remaining net operating cash flow of the business after capital expenditures have been subtracted out.

In short, look for businesses with higher FCF / Sales ratios. Identify which businesses have the highest FCF / Sales ratio in each sector or industry.

Sales / Net Receivables:

The Sales / Net Receivables (S/NR) ratio informs the investor the number of times the business's accounts receivable turns over during a particular period, usually over 1 year. The formula is:

$$\frac{Sales}{Net\ Receivables}$$

For example, if a business's income statement shows Revenues of $10,000,000, and their balance sheet shows Net Receivables of $1,200,000, we simply divide revenues of $10,000,000 by net receivables of $1,200,000, which equals 8.33.

$$\frac{\$10,000,000}{\$1,200,000} = 8.33$$

The 8.33 result indicates the business turns over receivables into cash 8.33 times/year. So, 8.33 into 365 (days) results in receivables turning into cash about every 44 days.

If the management team at this business were to arbitrarily establish a targeted "Sales / Net Receivables ratio" of 10, the accounting dept. could achieve this target by lowering the amount of Net Receivables. How are Net Receivables amounts lower? By spending more time collecting past due receivable balances from customers.

Higher values for this ratio suggest a business is doing a better job collecting money due from its customers, in a timely manner. Conversely, lower values for this ratio suggest a business is not collecting money due from its customers in a timely manner. A receivables turnover of 10 implies the business turns receivables into cash much sooner, because 10 into 365 (days) results in receivables turning into cash in about 37 days.

Identify the best businesses within each sector / industry by comparing these ratios against other competing businesses within the same sector / industry. As a general rule, higher values of 10 or higher, are good.

Sales / Employee:

The Sales/Employee ratio, (also known as the Revenue/Employee ratio), is calculated by starting with the amount of the business's total annual revenue for the current year, then dividing it by the total number of employees. This ratio reveals how much revenue is generated per employee. After this ratio is calculated, compare it against the Sales/Employee ratios of similar businesses within its same competitive sector / industry. The formula is:

$$\frac{\text{Revenue}}{\text{\# of Employees}}$$

Businesses showing higher Sales/Employee ratios tend to be more efficient because they generate greater amounts of Revenue per employee. Businesses showing lower Sales/Employee ratios may be less efficient, and generate lower amounts of Revenue per employee. These less efficient businesses can improve their Sales/Employee ratio by decreasing their work force, as long as the work force reductions do not negatively affect revenue generation.

Debt to Equity (D/E):

The Debt / Equity (D/E) Ratio is calculated by dividing <u>Total Liabilities</u> by <u>Total Shareholders Equity</u> located on the Balance Sheet. The average Debt to Equity Ratio is .5. A business with Debt to Equity Ratios of .51 or more, indicates the business carries a higher amount of debt relative the amount of equity owned by shareholders. The formula is:

$$\frac{\text{Total Liabilities}}{\text{Total Shareholders Equity}}$$

Warren Buffett seeks businesses with low Debt to Equity Ratios, because if interest rates suddenly rose, businesses with low Debt to Equity Ratios would remain in stronger, healthier financial positions. These businesses would be more likely to weather through unexpected financial storms. Whereas, businesses with higher amounts of debt on their Balance Sheets, would be like a ship without a rudder, at the whim of interest rate moves of volatile markets.

Dividend Yield:

Dividend yield reveals the percentage of each share price the business pays out annually to investors. In other words, dividend yield allows investors to calculate how much cash flow they will receive for every dollar invested into a business's equity (stock). The formula is:

$$\frac{\text{Annual Dividend per share}}{\text{Market Price per share}}$$

Higher dividend yields imply investors will receive higher amounts of cash flow as dividends for each share of stock they purchase. Conversely, lower dividend yields imply investors will receive a lower amount of dividends for every stock share they purchase.

Caution: Investors should never invest in businesses based on dividend yield only. Investors may perceive higher dividend yields as being more attractive; however, the possibility exists for businesses to cut their dividend payouts. When businesses cut their dividends, investors usually sell the stock, which can cause the price to go lower. Therefore, when considering investing into businesses that pay dividends, investors must also consider the business's payout ratio.

Payout Ratio:

Payout ratio reveals the amount of net earnings paid out as dividends to investors. When we hear the phrase, "Is the dividend safe?" What does this mean? "Safe" dividends are paid out by businesses with low payout ratios. Conversely, businesses with high payout ratios may not be able to continue paying out their high dividends. Payout ratio helps investors determine the level of earnings businesses possess to support their dividend payouts. The formula is:

$$\frac{\text{Annual Dividend per Share}}{\text{Earnings Per Share}}$$

The lower the payout ratio, the more secure or "safe" the dividend is. Conversely, larger dividend payments are more difficult for businesses to sustain over time, and these "unsafe" dividends may be cut in the future.

Payout ratios below 50% are generally safer than businesses with 90% payout ratios. If a business shows a 100% payout ratio, this means the business pays out 100% of its net earnings as dividends to shareholders. If a business shows a payout ratio of 200%, this reveals it is paying twice its amount of net earnings as dividends to shareholders.

If you paid out twice as much as you earn, how long could you sustain that until filing bankruptcy? Businesses with exorbitantly high payout ratios are actually borrowing money to pay dividends to shareholders. Generally, these businesses should be avoided.

There are exceptions. MLPs are Master Limited Partnerships designed to be "pass through organizations" to pay dividends to shareholders. MLPs can also offer tax advantages to investors; however, businesses with high payout ratios tend to offer "unsafe" dividends that are more likely to get cut. Whereas businesses with lower payout ratios are more likely to sustain their "safe" dividend payments to shareholders. Let's do a quick example using the payout ratio formula:

Business A:

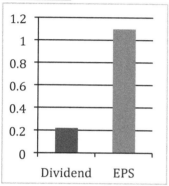

Business B:

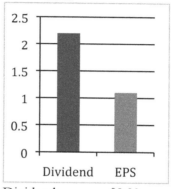

Dividend: $0.22
EPS: $1.10
Payout Ratio = Dividend/EPS
Payout Ratio = $0.22 / $1.10
Payout Ratio: 20.0%

Dividend: $2.20
EPS: $1.10
Payout Ratio = Dividend/EPS
Payout Ratio = $2.20 / $1.10
Payout Ratio: 200%

Question: In which business would you rather invest: Business A showing a **20%** payout ratio, or Business B showing a **200%** payout ratio?
Answer: Business A

Question: Which business is more likely to cut their dividend?
Answer: Business B, because it pays out all its net earnings and borrows twice as much as it earns, just to pay dividends. This leaves no money remaining to reinvest back into the business.

Question: Which business offers a "safer" dividend?
Answer: Business A, because its payout ratio is only 20% of net earnings.

Research & Development (R&D) / Gross Profit (GP):

This ratio reveals the percentage of gross profit allocated toward funding Research and Development (R&D). Warren Buffett seeks businesses with little to no Research and Development (R&D) reinvestment costs. Because businesses with lower Research and Development (R&D) costs, allow a larger percentage of Gross Profit to be available for shareholders. The formula is:

$$\frac{\text{Research and Development}}{\text{Gross Profit}}$$

To demonstrate the usefulness of this R&D / GP Ratio, let's ask the question, why has Warren Buffett avoided technology businesses? Because technology businesses generally have higher Research and Development (R&D) costs, than non-technology businesses.

For example, Warren Buffett never invested Berkshire Hathaway's money into technology business Microsoft (MSFT), despite being personal friends with Microsoft's founder Bill Gates. However, Warren Buffett did choose to invest into California-based chocolate confectioner See's Candies http://www.Sees.com

Question: Why did Warren Buffett invest into a chocolate confectioner business, and not into a technology business?

Answer: Because technology businesses require significantly higher amounts of Research and Development (R&D) capital to be reinvested back into the business. Conversely, chocolate confectionery business See's Candies has little to no Research and Development (R&D) costs.

In other words, Microsoft must continually pour more money out of their Gross Profit dollars into Research and Development (R&D) to continually develop new products.

Whereas, a chocolate confection business, like See's Candies, does not need to continuously pour large amounts of Gross Profit dollars back into Research and Development (R&D). See's Candies can just keep making their same famous candies over and over again, and their customers keep buying them. Can you imagine if Microsoft entirely stopped all of their Research and Development (R&D) reinvestments after "Windows-95?"

Therefore, if businesses are not required to continually reinvest significant percentages of their Gross Profit dollars back into Research and Development (R&D) costs, it just may be a business earning greater profit margins for its shareholders.

When Gross Profit flows back into Research and Development (R&D), it is money shareholders will not receive. Seek businesses with low to no R&D/GP Ratios.

Sales, General, and Administrative (SGA) / Gross Profit (GP):

This SGA/GP ratio describes the percentage of Gross Profit dollars allocated to paying a business's SGA expenses, such as sales commissions, administrative salaries, office supplies, etc. The lower the SGA/GP ratios are the better. Perform sector/industry comparisons to identify businesses showing the lowest SGA/GP ratios within their sector/industry. Generally speaking, businesses showing SGA/GP ratios of 30% or lower do an excellent job controlling SGA costs. The formula is:

$$\frac{\text{Sales, General, and Administrative (SGA)}}{\text{Gross Profit (GP)}}$$

Notice which businesses have the highest SGA /GP ratios, and which have the lowest. The qualitative process of rating a business's management can be nurtured by using quantitative data. For example, businesses showing the lowest SGA/GP ratio within their industry may possess management teams more effective at controlling costs and expenditures, than other businesses within the same sector and industry showing higher SGA/GP ratios.

The SGA/GP ratio is a good general measurement of management's ability to keep SGA-related costs low. Examine the past several years of SGA/GP ratios of a business. Have its SGA/GP ratios been consistently high or low? Or have they been random, showing no signs of a consistent trend? Seek to identify businesses with solid historical trends, possessing the lowest SGA/GP ratios within their sector and industry.

"Nuances of qualitative factors become detectable during quantitative analysis." Scott Thompson

Total Operating Expenses / Gross Profit (GP):

Similar to the SGA/GP ratio, this ratio also serves to quantitatively measure the qualitative aspect of a business's management team's ability to control internal costs. Businesses showing good 5, 7, or 10-year trends of having the lowest Total Operating Expenses / Gross Profit ratios, have outperformed their competitors at controlling internal operating expenses.

"Total Operating Expenses" is found toward the top of the Income Statement. Gross Profit can be found at the top of the Income Statement above Total Operating Expenses. The formula is:

$$\frac{\text{Total Operating Expenses}}{\text{Gross Profit}}$$

Businesses showing trends of lower Total Operating Expenses / GP ratios allow a larger percentage of gross profit dollars to potentially flow down the Income Statement to investors, instead of the money being spent on unnecessary operating expenses. This ratio is one more quantitative measurement of qualitative management effectiveness. Seek businesses showing consistent trends of possessing lower Total Operating Expenses / GP ratios over a 5, 7, or 10-year period.

(Depreciation + Amortization) / Gross Profit (GP) Ratio:

This ratio shows investors which percentage of Gross Profit (GP) is allocated to depreciation and amortization. Remember, depreciation is an allowance made to compensate for a loss in value of an asset due to it wearing out over time as it ages. Amortization refers to the gradual elimination of debt or liability over time as regular payments are made over several consistent time intervals. The formula is:

$$\frac{(\text{Depreciation} + \text{Amortization})}{\text{Gross Profit}}$$

The depreciation and amortization methods a business implements can affect its net profit margins, which can make it appear better or worse than its competitors. Accounting laws and tax codes used by many larger countries (like the USA) organize assets into various asset classes. These asset classes allow either longer or shorter durations to their depreciation and amortization schedules, depending on which asset class the asset gets categorized into.

One depreciation schedule is the "Straight-Line" depreciation process, which depreciates assets evenly over the useful life of the asset. In other words, if an asset costs $100,000 with a useful life of 10 years, then the asset could be depreciated $10,000 each year, over the span of its useful life of 10 years.

However, be aware of the differing accounting methods affecting depreciation, such as the "Double-Declining Balance (DDB)" depreciation process, and the "Sum-Of-the-Years Digits (SOYD)."

As a general rule, if everything else is equal, businesses implementing the "Straight-Line" process tend to show lower expenses, which can appear to increase net income and net profit margins.

Whereas, the "Double-Declining Balance (DDB)" and the "Sum-Of-the-Years Digits (SOYD)" depreciation methods may decrease net income and net profit margins. Notwithstanding this important fact, businesses implementing DDB and SOYD tend to show higher Operating Cash Flows on their Cash Flow Statements, than businesses implementing the more common "Straight-Line" depreciation process. Therefore, a word to the wise: *caveat emptor* while analyzing financial statements and financial ratios!

As a quick example, let's compare the "(Depreciation and Amortization) / Gross Profit (GP)" ratios of two different businesses: Nike (NKE) and General Motors (GM) using their 2012 historical financial statements:

Nike (NKE):

$$\frac{(Depreciation + Amortization)}{Gross\ Profit} = \frac{\$0.405\ billion}{\$10.47\ billion} = 4\%$$

General Motors (GM):

$$\frac{(Depreciation + Amortization)}{Gross\ Profit} = \frac{\$38.76\ billion}{\$10.81\ billion} = 359\%$$

Now that you can calculate this ratio for a single year, try calculating this ratio over a 3-year, 5-year, 7-year, and 10-year history. Using financial ratios for only a single year does not constitute a trend.

The 2012 Income Statements for Nike and General Motors show relatively similar Gross Profits (GP) of $10.41 billion and $10.81 billion, respectively. However, the amount of Depreciation and Amortization shown on their Cash Flow Statements tell a very different story.

As a general rule, lower values for this ratio tend to be better, whereas higher ratios signal accounting anomalies may be present. Businesses showing exorbitantly high values for this ratio may be experiencing periods of financial difficulty, and may be using various accounting methods to affect the numbers.

If we identify a business showing higher values for this ratio (such as General Motors in 2012) we can either walk away and seek investments elsewhere, or we can dig-in and do what Benjamin Graham refers to as "Scuttlebutt." Scuttlebutt is spending the time, and hard work, performing your own research and due diligence process, reading all available annual reports, calling investor relations department, speaking to competitors, visiting their retail stores, sampling the product yourself, etc.

An important point to make in conjunction with this ratio is to retain a healthy skepticism of EBITDA (Earnings Before Interest, Taxes, Depreciation, and Amortization), because the last two letters in EBITDA are "DA," which stand for "depreciation and amortization," which is the numerator in this financial ratio.

Value investors tend to focus more on EBIT (Earnings Before Interest and Taxes) also known as Operating Income, than EBITDA. Be aware EBITDA can be more prone to accounting trickery, whereas, EBIT is more of a raw constant measurement of a business's overall profitability, before accountants have an opportunity to apply their "skills" to the numbers.

Finally, this financial ratio will help investors select better businesses in which to invest. Remember, lower values are better for this ratio; higher values are not. Businesses showing higher values for this ratio may be getting "creative" in their accounting. This financial ratio will help you see through it.

"Every time you see the word EBITDA, you should substitute the word bullshit."
Charlie Munger, Berkshire Hathaway Vice-Chairman to Warren Buffett

Interest Expense / Operating Income:

This ratio shows the percentage of operating income paid out as interest payments to creditors on debt levels incurred by the business. If the business has high debt on its balance sheet, then the business also pays higher amounts of interest payments. Conversely, the lower the debt levels a business has, the lower its interest payments.

To locate Short-Term Debt and Long-Term Debt on the Balance Sheet: Short-Term Debt is listed under Current Assets, and Long-Term Debt is listed under Non-Current Assets on the Balance Sheet. The formula is:

$$\frac{\text{Interest Expense}}{\text{Operating Income}}$$

Conversely, if the business has little or no debt, this is the most desirable scenario because these few "no debt businesses" can then allocate a larger percentage of their operating income (EBIT) to other more beneficial activities, such as: making acquisitions, dividend payments to investors, or initiating share buyback programs, etc., instead of making interest payments on debt.

Capital Expenditure / Operating Income:

Capital Expenditure / Operating Income ratio helps us measure the percentage of Operating Income management allocates toward Capital Expenditures. Capital Expenditure (also commonly referred to as "CapEx") is located toward the bottom of the Cash Flow Statement. Operating Income is located toward the upper-middle of the Income statement.

When calculating this ratio, it is important to remember, Capital Expenditures are shown as a "negative" amount on Cash Flow Statements. Therefore, we must use the "absolute value," or non-negative "above zero" version of Capital Expenditures.

In other words, if Capital Expenditures are shown with parentheses around the number, it is a negative (below zero) amount, and we must remove the "−" minus sign, and use the positive, above-zero version.

When we make a number positive (above zero) despite whether its original form began above or below zero, this is referred to as "absolute value." When we use Capital Expenditures in this ratio, we must always use the "absolute value" (above zero) version of this number.

For example, if Capital Expenditures are shown as (757), this is a negative number. We must convert it from a negative number, to a positive above-zero version of the number, which in this case is 757. The formula is:

$$\frac{\text{Capital Expenditures}}{\text{Operating Income}}$$

Therefore, if Operating Income is 6,000 and Capital Expenditures are (757), then we remove the parentheses from (757), and we use 757, divided by 6,000

$$\frac{757}{6,000} = .126 = 12.6\%$$

Warren Buffett seeks to identify businesses with little to no Capital Expenditures. Why is this? Because businesses with little to no CapEx allows a greater amount of the business's Operating Income to flow directly to Free Cash Flow (FCF), and Free Cash Flow is one of the most important financial metrics we use in identifying rare and wonderful businesses.

Remember, John Burr Williams' Discounted Cash Flow analysis he created in 1938, can use Free Cash Flow (FCF), which helps us identify the Growth Value or Intrinsic Value of the business.

Warren Buffett loves undervalued businesses with abundant Free Cash Flow (FCF). Therefore, seek to identify undervalued businesses with high Operating Income, low Capital Expenditures, and the business will be more likely to offer investors higher levels of Free Cash Flow (FCF).

Remember, just because a business has high Free Cash Flows, is not a sole reason to invest. Perform your own valuation, examine qualitative factors, and determine for yourself if the investment opportunity is: Overvalued, Fairly Valued, or Undervalued. We only invest when the investment is undervalued, offering an adequate Margin of Safety.

Capital Expenditures / Net Income:

Capital expenditures are the equipment businesses must purchase in order to maintain and grow their operations. For example, factory equipment is purchased and categorized as a capital expenditure instead of an operating expense. This way, businesses can depreciate capital expenditure assets annually over the useful life of the equipment. The formula is:

$$\frac{\text{Capital Expenditures}}{\text{Net Income}}$$

Some capital expenditures are necessary, such as the purchase of a number of large excavation trucks by mining corporations. The purchase of the excavation trucks is an example of a capital expenditure. However, the fuel for the truck and the salary of the truck driver are not capital expenditures. Capital expenditures are shown on the Cash Flow Statement as a negative amount, because capital expenditures are an expense.

Honest and capable managers who can optimally allocate capital and finite resources toward their highest and best use run businesses with durable competitive advantages. This benefits shareholders. These managers avoid frivolously allocating finite resources toward buying expensive capital equipment that does not produce optimal results for the business and its shareholders.

Warren Buffett seeks businesses that are not capital intensive, and do not require large amounts of net income to be reinvested regularly back into the business. Businesses with lower capital expenditures tend to be the more profitable businesses, and tend to be run by better management teams, in industries that do not require regular capital reinvestments back into the business.

Be aware, some industries are more capital intensive than others. For example, a railroad requires the capital expenditure purchases of new railroad cars on a regular basis, as old ones wear out. Whereas, businesses like chocolate confectioner See's Candies, is not subject to replace its capital equipment as often, and therefore, does not make regular capital expenditure reinvestments.

Businesses like See's Candies, with lower capital expenditures allow a greater amount of net income dollars to flow through the cash flow statement to becoming free cash flows (FCFs), which benefits shareholders. Therefore, seek businesses showing low CapEx/Net Income ratios.

Long-Term Debt / Net Income:

The LTD/NI ratio is helpful in determining the multiple of times greater a business's long-term debt is, over its Net Income. This ratio is helpful for investors to estimate how many years it would take a business to pay off all of its long-term debt, if it were to hypothetically use 100% of its Net Income to pay off its long-term debt. We explain further in the following example.

Billionaire value investor Warren Buffett seeks businesses with little to no long-term debt. Businesses possessing little to no debt, pay little to no interest payments. This allows a greater amount of net income to flow through their financial statements toward Free Cash Flows (FCFs), which benefits shareholders.

Conversely, businesses possessing higher long-term debt tend to be less desirable, because these businesses must pay higher interest payments. Higher interest payments result in lower net income. Therefore, businesses should seek to minimize debt levels, so lower amounts of interest payments need to be paid to creditors. Lower interest payments serve to invest net income. Higher net income benefits shareholders in many ways such as lowering the PE ratio and increasing the stock price.

The formula for the LTD/NI ratio is:

$$\frac{\text{Long-Term Debt}}{\text{Net Income}}$$

To illustrate an example, let's use the long-term debt and net income amounts from the 2012 year-end financial statements of publicly traded business CenterPoint Energy (CNP)

CenterPoint Energy (CNP) 2012 financial statements show Long-term debt of $8,357,000,000 and Net Income of $417,000,000. So,

$$\text{Long-term debt} \div \text{Net Income} = \text{LTD/NI ratio}$$

$$\$8,357,000,000 \div \$417,000,000 = 20$$

This means, even if CenterPoint Energy (CNP) were to hypothetically use all 100% of its current Net Income to pay down its existing long-term debt, it would take 20 years, because this ratio shows CenterPoint's long-term debt is 20 times greater than its Net Income. Very eye opening, isn't it?

This is why Warren Buffett prefers to invest in healthy businesses carrying little or even no debt. This way, Net Income can flow through the business's financial statements toward Free Cash Flow (FCF), benefitting shareholders, instead of going toward paying off its long-term debt, which is 20 times greater than its 2012 net income.

A positive example of a business with little to no debt and healthy net income is Visa (V). Visa's 2012 financial statements show Long-term debt of $0 and Net Income of $2,144,000,000. So,

$$\text{Long-term debt} \div \text{Net Income} = \text{LTD/NI ratio}$$

$$\$0 \div \$2,144,000,000 = 0$$

Since Visa (V) has $0 long-term debt, there is no debt to pay, and no interest payments to pay. This way, Visa's Net Income can flow through its financial statements toward free cash flows (FCFs), which will benefit shareholders. Note: As of August 2012, Visa (V) is a low-debt, high-profit business in which Warren Buffett's Berkshire Hathaway is invested.

(Long-Term Debt + Capital Expenditures) / Net Income:

This ratio is similar to the previous ratio, however, CapEx spending is also included. Warren Buffett seeks businesses with low-debt, low-CapEx, and high profit.

If we were to add together a business's long-term debt and capital expenditures, then divide this amount by the business's net income. This is the percentage businesses pay out using net income. Lower debt, lower CapEx, and higher Net Income amounts are preferred.

The formula is:

$$\frac{\text{(Long-Term Debt} + \text{Capital Expenditures)}}{\text{Net Income}}$$

This ratio can be very useful because if the business shows a ratio higher than 100, then the business possesses more long-term debt and capital expenditures in the current year than the net income they are annually producing.

Long-Term Debt is located on the Balance Sheet. Capital Expenditures are located on the Cash Flow Statement. Net Income is located on the Income Statement.

Businesses with lower ratios are more desirable than business with higher ratios. Management teams focusing on lowering the numerator and increasing the denominator of this ratio, run businesses that generate more Free Cash Flow (FCF) for shareholders.

Current Ratio:

Current ratio is a measure of a business's ability to pay its current liabilities over the next 12 months using its current assets. The higher the Current Ratio, the stronger the business's ability to meet its 12-month short-term debt obligations. The formula is:

$$\frac{\text{Total Current Assets}}{\text{Total Current Liabilities}}$$

For example, if a business's balance sheet shows total current assets of $500 million, and total current liabilities of $500 million, the business has a current ratio of 1.

Because: $500 million ÷ $500 million = 1

A current ratio of 1 means the business possesses the same amount of total current assets as total current liabilities.

Similarly, if a business's balance sheet shows total current assets of $250 million, and total current liabilities of $500 million, the business has a current ratio of .5.

Because: $250 million ÷ $500 million = .5

A current ratio of .5 means the business possesses half the amount of total current assets as total current liabilities. These types of businesses may have difficulty meeting their short-term liability obligations in the next 12 months.

Finally, if a business's balance sheet shows total current assets of $500 million, and total current liabilities of $250 million, the business has a current ratio of 2.

Because: $500 million ÷ $250 million = 2

A current ratio of 2 is better than a current ratio of 1, because a current ratio of 2 means the business possesses twice the amount of total current assets as total current liabilities. Businesses like these should have no difficulty meeting their short-term liability obligations over the next 12 months. Seek businesses showing higher current ratios.

The Current Ratio is also known as the Working Capital Ratio, because net Working Capital is Total Current Assets minus Total Current Liabilities.

Total Current Assets − Total Current Liabilities = Net Working Capital

If you were to divide total Net Working Capital by the number of total shares outstanding, it would reveal the Net Working Capital per Share. Ben Graham would invest in businesses if the stock price were 2/3rd below Net Working Capital per Share. Ben Graham would call these "Net Net stocks," because their stock prices were selling below Net Working Capital.

"On the subject of the working-capital ratio (Current Ratio), a minimum of $2 of current assets for $1 of current liabilities was formerly regarded as a standard. We are unable to suggest a better figure than the old 2-to-1 criterion to use as a definite quantitative test of a sufficiently comfortable financial position." Benjamin Graham

Quick Ratio (Acid Test):

Quick Ratio (Acid Test) is a measure of the short-term liquidity of a business, since it indicates a business's ability to pay off its current liabilities immediately, using its "quick assets." The higher the ratio, the stronger the business's ability to meet all of its short-term business obligations. The formula is:

$$\frac{(\text{Current Assets} - \text{Inventory})}{\text{Current Liabilities}}$$

A more conservative version of the formula is:

$$\frac{(\text{Current Assets} - \text{Inventory} - \text{Accounts Receivable})}{\text{Current Liabilities}}$$

Inventory Turnover:

Inventory Turnover is a measure of how many times a business turns over (sells and replaces) its inventory over a period of time, usually 1 year. Generally, higher inventory turnover ratios are better than lower inventory turnover ratios.

Value investors can compare inventory turnover ratios of businesses within the same industry to identify businesses with the highest inventory turnover ratios. The formula is:

$$\frac{\text{Sales}}{\text{Inventory}}$$

A simple example illustrating the power of the inventory ratio and its usefulness in identifying businesses with durable competitive advantages and pricing power is; imagine if a business sold cookies. The business could sell 100,000 cookies per year at $1 each, or the business could sell 1 cookie per year at $100,000 each.

It's true both businesses will generate the same annual revenue of $100,000 per year. However, "Business A" that sold 100,000 cookies per year at $1 each would show a very high inventory turnover ratio, with very low gross margins. Conversely, "Business B" would show a very low inventory turnover ratio, with very high gross margins.

Remember, both businesses earn the same annual revenue amount of $100,000 per year, but "Business B" possesses greater pricing power, because it can charge more for its product. Pricing power is the ability to raise your prices and the customers keep on buying.

Managers at "Business A" are very likely trying to find ways to increase their prices and gross profit margins, without affecting their high inventory turnover ratio. Meanwhile, managers at "Business B" are very likely trying to find ways to increase their inventory turnover ratio without cutting prices or decreasing gross profit margins.

Identifying the different strategies of businesses within the same industries can be a fascinating process. It is important value investors understand the businesses in which they invest (Filter #1). Identify businesses with durable competitive advantages (Filter #2), possessing honest capable management teams (Filter #3), selling at an attractive price/value (Filter #4), with sufficient margins of safety.

Therefore, the inventory turnover ratio is an important element value investors use in order to identify businesses with durable competitive advantages.

Return On Assets (ROA):

Return On Assets (ROA) reveals how many dollars of earnings a business can generate relative to each dollar of assets. ROAs will vary across different sectors and industries. Hence, do not compare ROAs of businesses residing in two different sectors and industries. In other words, it is best to compare ROAs only of businesses within the same sector and industry.

ROA is a good measurement showing how profitable a business is. Generally speaking, higher ROA values are better than lower ROA values, since higher ROA values suggest the business is earning higher net income on smaller investments into assets. The formula is:

$$\frac{\text{Net Income}}{\text{Total Assets}}$$

If "Business A" earns Net Income of $100 million, on Total Assets of $500 million, its ROA is 20%, because $100,000,000 ÷ $500,000,000 = 20%.

Whereas, if another business, "Business B," were to earn the same Net Income of $100 million, but had Total Assets of $1 billion, its ROA would be only 10%, because $100,000,000 ÷ $1,000,000,000 = 10%.

Therefore, "Business A" is earning a higher Return On Assets (ROA) than "Business B" despite earning the same amount of Net Income. Because "Business A" earns its Net Income based on a lower amount of Total Assets of only $500 million, instead of $1 billion. This shows managers at "Business A" are doing a better job at allocating their assets. Anyone can earn Net Income by spending a lot of money on a problem; however, very few businesses can earn higher Net Incomes spending very little investing in assets. Seek businesses with the highest Returns On Assets (ROA) within each industry.

Return On Equity (ROE):

Return On Equity (ROE) reveals how much Net Income a business can generate for investors as a percentage of shareholders' equity. Return On Equity (ROE) gauges a business's ability to generate Net Income using the money shareholders have invested. Use ROE to compare businesses within the same sector or industry. The formula is:

$$\frac{\text{Net Income}}{\text{Shareholders' Equity}}$$

Shareholders' equity is also referred to as stockholders' equity. Use the "After Tax" Net Income amount. This is shown on the business's Income Statement.

The average Return on Equity (ROE) for businesses in the S&P 500 is 12. This is a useful fact to know, because you can search for businesses earning Returns On Equity (ROE) higher than "12." Because these businesses are earning above-average Returns On Equity (ROE) relative to the S&P 500. Businesses earning Returns On Equity (ROE) of 15, 18, or greater, and also using little to no debt, may be excellent businesses.

However, be wary of businesses showing high ROEs and also possessing high amounts of debt. ROE may falsely appear higher due to the business using higher amounts of debt. Businesses with high ROEs and also using little to no debt, tend to be better businesses with better managers, making better asset allocation decisions, earning greater than the $1 invested.

Debt-Adjusted Return On Equity (DA-ROE):

The DA-ROE was created by Scott Thompson and Bud Labitan to help investors more accurately compare Returns On Equity (ROE) of businesses possessing differing amounts of debt.

For example, if "Business A" and "Business B" both possess Returns On Equity (ROE) of 15, but "Business A" has a Debt/Equity ratio of "0" (no debt), and "Business B" has a Debt/Equity ratio of .40, all else being equal, "Business A" would be a more attractive business in which to invest, because it has the same ROE, but with 0 debt. The formula is:

$$ROE \times (1 - Debt/Equity) = Debt\text{-}Adjusted\ Return\ On\ Equity$$

Let's apply this formula to "Business A" and "Business B" from the example above:

Business A: ROE $15 \times (1 - 0) = 15 \times 1 = 15$ DA-ROE
Business B: ROE $15 \times (1 - .4) = 15 \times .6 = 9$ DA-ROE

After we factor in the debt and apply the debt to its ROE, the DA-ROE of "Business B" falls from 15 to 9. (Scott Thompson and Bud Labitan 2013)

Instead of ranking businesses by their ROE, we may suggest ranking businesses by their DA-ROE, so businesses possessing the highest ROE and the lowest debt, rise to the top of this ratio. Similarly, businesses possessing the lowest ROE and highest debt will sink toward the bottom of the list.

Therefore, the DA-ROE can become a useful tool to more accurately compare ROEs of businesses possessing widely varying amounts of debt.

Return On Invested Capital (ROIC):

By: James Hua: Opal Advisors
Scott Thompson, MBA: Ameritrust Group

Warren Buffett often uses the word "moat" to describe businesses with durable competitive advantages. One of the best indicators of whether a business "moat" exists is to measure its "Return on Invested Capital (ROIC)." Generally a high ROIC percentage indicates a moat exists that allows the company to earn excess returns (defined below).

ROIC is similar to ROA and ROE in that it's a metric of return but different in that it requires more calculations and assumptions but can also reveal more about the quality of the business and allows investors to view returns on an unleveraged basis. ROA adjusts for neither excess cash nor working capital. The ROE measurement tells us nothing about leverage and the financial engineering that might be used to boost equity returns.

ROIC formula:

$$\frac{\text{Net Operating Profit After Taxes}}{\text{Invested Capital}}$$

Numerator: Net Operating Profit After Taxes (NOPAT) is Net Income with Interest expenses added back. (Do not add taxes back in, as the numerator must be based on an "after tax amount.") This is done so the capital structure of the business does not affect the amount used in the numerator. To calculate NOPAT, use the following formula:

NOPAT = (Operating Earnings) x (1 – Tax Rate)

Operating Earnings, also known as Operating Income, are found on the Income Statement. To determine the tax rate, locate "Provision for income taxes" and "Income before taxes" on the income statement. Divide the "Provision for income taxes" by "Income before taxes" to identify the effective tax rate.

The formula is:

Tax Rate = (Provision for income taxes) ÷ (Income before taxes)

For instance, if (Provision for income taxes) is 86, and (Income before taxes) is 222, then…

Tax Rate = (86) ÷ (222) = .387 = 38.7%

So, if our effective tax rate is .387 and assumed Operating Earnings is 231 million, NOPAT would be calculated as follows:

NOPAT = (Operating Earnings) x (1 – Tax Rate)

NOPAT = (231 million) x (1 – .387)

NOPAT = (231 million) x (.613)

NOPAT = 141.603 million

Denominator: "Invested Capital" is our denominator, is a little trickier:

Invested Capital = Fixed Assets + Current Assets – Current Liabilities - Cash

Fixed Assets can be found on the balance sheet and are usually property, plant, and equipment carried at book value (net of depreciation).

Current Assets and Liabilities can also be found on the balance sheet and are assets and liabilities that are expected to turn to cash or be paid within a year. Last, to keep it simple, we deduct cash (ideally, it's better to deduct excess cash). Making a cash adjustment to the denominator is important as companies sometimes carry large cash balances not required for the business. The cash is unneeded, and in theory can be readily returned to shareholders in the form of dividends or stock buybacks. However, in practice, an investor might even discount the cash on the balance sheet if managers prove to be poor allocators of capital.

After you've calculated ROIC you should have an idea of the quality of business you're dealing with. As a general rule, if a business maintains an ROIC of 15 or higher for a period of time, it likely possesses an economic "moat."

Finally, an investor should make sure the company is creating value for shareholders by generating excess returns as defined by having an ROIC greater than the business's WACC (Weighted-Average Cost of Capital). WACC is the total combined cost of capital for a company's debt, equity, preferred shares, if any, and other sources of capital.

If a business has a WACC of 10 and an ROC of 15, then it is generating 5% excess returns and vice versa. Conversely, if the business's WACC exceeds its ROIC, the business is earning less than its cost of capital and is essentially liquidating itself.

For now, you have a good grasp of ROIC and its importance in helping to determine whether a business possesses an economic moat.

Net Net Working Capital (NNWC):

Warren Buffett's mentor Benjamin Graham was notorious for investing into businesses he identified as being "Net Net stocks." The "Net Net" Ratio can be calculated a few different ways. Remember to divide the final Net Net amount by Total Shares Outstanding to determine Net Net Working Capital per share. The three formulas for Net Net Working Capital (NNWC) are:

Net Working Capital = Current Assets − Current Liabilities

Graham's Net Working Capital = Current Assets − Total Liabilities

Net Net Working Capital = Cash + Short Term Marketable Investments + (Accounts Receivable x 75%) + (Inventory x 50%) − Total Liabilities

Ben Graham did not consider qualitative factors, and instead focused on quantitative financial ratios. It is important to note, although Warren Buffett began his investment career focusing on Net Net stocks, Warren soon outperformed his mentor Ben Graham by incorporating other qualitative factors, as well as quantitative factors, into his investment strategy.

Back when Ben Graham was investing, investors did not know how to identify Net Net Stocks, and as a result, higher quantities of Net Net stocks were available in which to invest. However, there are not as many Net Net Stocks available today in which to invest. They do exist, but when you find them remember to look at these businesses based on what they are likely to do in the future, and not based on what they've done in the past.

"Investors make money looking through the windshield, not the rear-view mirror." Scott Thompson

Next, we'll explore Warren Buffett's screening criteria, and how you can create your own screening criteria next in Chapter 6: Screening Criteria

CHAPTER SIX:

Screening Criteria

6.1 Overview:

There are thousands of publicly traded equities (stocks) in the world. In 1997 there were 8,823 stocks traded on US exchanges (according to the World Federation of Exchanges) NYSE, Euronext U.S., and NASDAQ OMX. In 2012, the number of publicly traded stocks traded on U.S. exchanges dropped about 44% to 4,943. If we total up the number of all publicly traded stocks in the world (according to the World Federation of Exchanges) there were a total of 46,231 in 2012, including the Americas, Asia – Pacific, Europe, Middle East, and Africa.

http://world-exchanges.org/

For many sole investors without huge teams of multiple analysts, 46,231 equities are simply not manageable to analyze within a realistic timeframe. Therefore, analysts must time-efficiently narrow the field of thousands of potential investments in which to analyze and invest, down to a smaller, more manageable amount.

How is this done? Do we start with qualitative first? Do we start with quantitative first? Which is more effective?

If we were to start with the qualitative first, investors would need to read thousands of annual reports. Then all quarterly securities filings, study various sectors, research the industries, evaluate management teams, identify durable competitive advantages of thousands of businesses. This is simply not feasible for most 1-person investors.

Instead, if we were to start with the quantitative first, analysts could create initial quantitative screens through which equities would be screened. This is a more time-efficient solution to reduce the field of available investments. Then the question becomes, "What criteria do I use to identify the great businesses, and screen out average and weak businesses?"

Berkshire Hathaway seeks businesses with little to no debt, high profit margins, high free cash flows, low capital expenditures, high returns on equity, high returns on invested capital, and other factors, which we will discuss now.

6.2 Warren Buffett's Criteria:

What does Warren Buffett look for? Here's a list of criteria Warren Buffett often considers when evaluating business fundamentals and items found on financial statements.

Income Statement:

Revenue: *steadily increasing over several years*

Gross profit margins: *40% or higher*

Operating (EBIT) income margins: *30% or higher*

Net income margins: *20% or higher*

Research and development (R&D) / Gross Profit: *below 10%, or lower than competitors*

Sales, General, Administrative (SGA) / Gross Profit: *below 80%, or lower than competitors*

Total Operating Expenses / Net Income: *below 80%, or lower than competitors*

Interest Expense / Net Income: *lower than competitors*

Price-to-Earnings (P/E) ratio: *16 or lower*

Decreasing # of shares outstanding: *steadily decreasing over several years*

Stock Buybacks to Increase Earnings per Share (EPS)

Balance Sheet

Return On equity (ROE): *15 or higher*

Return On Invested Capital (ROIC): *15 or higher*

Current Ratio: *1 or higher*

Little to no debt

- Short-term debt / Net Income: *lower than competitors*
- Long-term debt / Net Income: *80% or lower than competitors*
- Increasing Retained Earnings: *steadily increasing over several years*

<u>Cash Flow Statement:</u>
Operating Cash Flow / Sales: *15% or higher*
Capital Expenditures (CapEx) / Net Income: *30% or lower*
Free Cash Flow (FCF) / Sales: *10% or higher*

6.3 Create Your Own Screening Criteria:

The number of publicly traded businesses in the world can be daunting. As value investors we must narrow the field of potential investments down to a more manageable amount. Online stock-screening tools can prove helpful in aiding the investor during the process of thoughtfully narrowing the field of potential investments. This is especially true if you're just one analyst, and must narrow a vast field of potential investments.

Now that you've seen the criteria successful billionaire value investor Warren Buffett uses, how will you create your own? Here's some helpful information explaining the reasons why Berkshire Hathaway's billionaire chairman, Warren Buffett, chose these financial ratios to identify above-average businesses with durable competitive advantages:

Revenue:

Revenues, also known as Sales, are the total of money generated from all sales activities. A business showing a long-term consistent history of steadily increasing revenues, means the business is experiencing growth, and expanding its market share.

Conversely, businesses showing declining revenues are experiencing contraction within their industry, and are not expanding their market share.

Warren Buffett prefers to invest in businesses with increasing revenue growth.

Gross Margins:

Gross Margin = (Gross Profit ÷ Revenue)

A business showing 40% or higher gross margins means the business has "pricing power," and may operate in an industry not as price-sensitive. Conversely, businesses with lower gross margins of 20% or lower, may operate in more price-sensitive competitive industries. Gross margins can be revealed using the income statement.

Operating Margins:

Operating Income = (Operating Income ÷ Revenue)

A business showing 30% or higher operating margins means the business has "pricing power" and operates within an industry that is not as price-sensitive as other businesses operating in more competitive industries, which show lower gross margins on their income statements of only 15% or less.

A business with 40% gross margins and 30% operating margins likely has a talented management team that only spends a smaller portion of gross profits on total operating expenses. This shows the management team is successfully controlling total operating expenses.

Net Margins:

Net Margin = (Net Income ÷ Revenue)

A business showing 20% or higher net margins means the business has "pricing power" and operates within an industry not as price-sensitive, and likely has a management team in place successful at controlling the expenses, interest, and taxes of the business. Businesses showing net margins below 10% tend to operate in more price-sensitive competitive industries.

Research and Development (R&D) / Gross Profit:

Businesses with Research and Development (R&D) costs consisting of 10% or less of their gross profit, are businesses that do not require reinvestment of finite gross profit dollars back into the business as R&D costs. Furthermore, businesses with lower Research and Development (R&D) costs within their industry may be better potential investments, than businesses with the highest R&D costs.

Conversely, technology businesses, like Intel (INTC) and other semiconductor businesses, are extremely R&D intensive. These types of businesses require large amounts of gross profit to be reinvested back into their Research and Development (R&D) costs every year, just to maintain the business.

Every dollar the business reinvests back into Research and Development (R&D) is a dollar that doesn't flow through to investors.

If you invest in technology businesses, it may be impossible to find a business with low R&D costs. Therefore, seek businesses with management teams able to better control R&D expenses. These businesses will also show lower R&D costs on their income statements.

Non-technology businesses like Hershey's chocolate are not as R&D intensive. In fact, Hershey's showed $0 R&D costs on their income statement, which allows a greater portion of gross profit dollars to flow through the firm's financial statements toward free cash flows (FCFs), which benefits investors.

Warren Buffett prefers to invest in businesses with low, to no R&D costs.

Sales, General, and Administrative (SGA) / Gross Profit:

Sales, General, and Administrative (SGA) costs are business expenses such as salaries, commissions, advertising costs, travel expenses, warranty expenses, payroll costs, telephone, postage, that businesses incur as shown on their income statement.

Good management teams closely monitor SG&A expenses, and keep them under control. If management can keep SG&A costs among the lowest in their industry, then this allows a greater amount of gross profits to flow through the income statement toward increasing net income.

Good management teams will maintain the lowest SGA/GP ratios within their industry. Businesses showing consistently low SG&A expenses year-after-year, for a long-term consistent history, may possess better management teams. These businesses tend to be better run with lower costs and higher profitability.

Warren Buffett prefers to invest in businesses with lower SGA costs, compared with competitors in the same industry.

Total Operating Expenses / Net Income:

Businesses showing lower Total Operating Expenses tend to have management teams able to successfully control costs, and lead employees to engage in more efficient behaviors conducive to lowering the amount of total operating expenses for the business's income statement.

Warren Buffett prefers to invest in businesses with lower total operating expenses, compared with other businesses in their industry.

Interest Expense / Net Income:

Businesses with lower interest expenses within their respective sectors tend to be healthier businesses with lower debt amounts on their balance sheets. These types of businesses pay little to no interest expenses, and as a result are able to allocate their capital more efficiently toward other important investments instead of paying interest expenses on debts.

Therefore, businesses paying little to no interest payments have little to no debt, and are able to retain a larger portion of net income since little to no money is being allocated toward paying interest expenses on debt. Warren Buffett prefers to invest in businesses with lower interest expenses.

Price-to-Earnings (P/E) Ratio

Warren Buffett's mentor, Benjamin Graham, wrote in his book "Security Analysis" that he invested in businesses showing Price to Earnings (P/E) values of 16 or less. Businesses selling at low Price to Earnings (P/E) ratios tend to be more undervalued, than businesses trading at higher P/E ratios. This is not always the case, but generally speaking, it is wise for value investors to seek investments into businesses trading at lower P/E multiples of 16 or less.

However, if you're a growth investor, investing into high-growth stocks, the P/E ratio of the proposed investment should never be higher than its earnings growth rate. For example, if a high-growth stock has an average earnings growth rate over the past 3 years of 30%, it may not be a good time to invest into this business when the P/E is 50. In other words, anytime the P/E ratio exceeds the growth rate, it is wise to take a deep breath, wait, do nothing, move on, and seek another business that is more undervalued.

Remember the three ways to invest into a business? When the business is overvalued, fairly valued, or undervalued. Seek low P/E stocks, and the best time to invest into them is when they are undervalued, not fairly valued, or overvalued.

Warren Buffett prefers to invest in businesses with low P/E ratios. However, Warren Buffett and Charlie Munger are willing to pay a little more to invest in high-quality businesses. Warren confirms this in his original quote:

"It's better to invest in wonderful businesses at a fair price, than fair businesses at a wonderful price." Warren Buffett and Charlie Munger

Decreasing number of total shares outstanding:

The income statement reveals the amount of total shares outstanding. Look at the number of total shares outstanding for a multi-year period. If the business's income statement shows the number of total shares outstanding decreasing, the business has implemented a share repurchase program. This is proven by a decreasing number of total shares outstanding on the income statement.

Conversely, if the business's income statement shows the number of total shares outstanding to be increasing, the business is trying to raise capital through equity share offerings, which actually increase the number of total shares outstanding. This dilutes the value of the existing shares outstanding, which are owned by existing shareholders.

Businesses with income statements showing a steadily decreasing number of total shares outstanding tend to be run by higher quality, shareholder-oriented management teams. When businesses buy back equity shares of their own stock, the number of total shares outstanding decreases. This is desirable to investors, as it increases the value of existing shares owned by shareholders.

Share repurchase programs increase the value of shares outstanding because net income is divided by the number of total shares outstanding. If we reduce the value of the denominator, which is total shares outstanding, this produces a higher value per share. For example, if a business has $100 million net income, and 12 million total shares outstanding, the business has $8.33 earnings-per-share. ($100,000,000 ÷ 12,000,000 = $8.33). If the business initiates a share repurchase program, buying back 2 million shares, this would leave 10 million total shares outstanding remaining. Then the value per share would rise from $8.33/share to $10/share, because $100,000,000 divided by 10 million total shares outstanding equals $10 earnings-per-share. ($100,000,000 ÷ 10,000,000 = $10).

Billionaire value investor Warren Buffett loves share repurchase programs. Share repurchase programs are a great way for investors to increase the value of their shares without taking any further action. In the early 1990s, Warren Buffett owned 14% of Wells Fargo Bank. Through share repurchase programs of Wells Fargo, Warren Buffett's ownership amount of Wells Fargo Bank has increased from 14% to 17%.

Wells Fargo could have used their free cash flow (FCF) to pay a dividend to shareholders, but this is a taxable event. Instead, Wells Fargo chose to initiate a share repurchase program, buying back millions of total shares outstanding, which accreted the value of existing shares outstanding owned by investors.

This way investors in Wells Fargo stock enjoyed the appreciation of their stock holdings, due to the Wells Fargo share repurchase program, without investors paying any taxes on this event.

Sure, investors will pay taxes on the gains when they eventually sell their stocks, but Warren Buffett does not plan to sell his Wells Fargo stock, allowing his billions invested in Wells Fargo to compound and compound.

Warren Buffett prefers to invest in businesses with decreasing total shares outstanding.

Stock Buybacks to Increase Earnings per Share (EPS):

Businesses that engage in stock repurchase programs are able to actually decrease the number of total shares outstanding. In order to calculate Earnings per Share, we divide net income by the number of total shares outstanding. If there are a lower number of shares outstanding due to a stock buyback, then the Earnings per Share amount will be higher, and this benefits shareholders.

Seek businesses with a steadily decreasing number of total shares outstanding, and steadily increasing Earnings per share. Both of these items are shown on the income statement, and may also be available via online computer-based stock-screening financial websites.

High Returns On Equity (ROE):

ROEs above 15% are most desirable. The average return on equity in the U.S. stock market is 12%. Therefore, businesses with above-average Return On Equity (ROE) of 15% or higher are most desirable.

It's important to note that businesses implementing higher debt levels may show higher levels of Return On Equity. Therefore, be certain to closely analyze the amount of outstanding short-term and long-term debt possessed by the business, on the business's Balance Sheet.

High Returns On Invested Capital (ROIC):

ROICs above 15% are most desirable. Businesses with above-average Return On Invested Capital (ROIC) of 15% or higher are most desirable. ROIC is one of the best tools to identify businesses with "economic moats" against which competitors find it difficult to compete. Businesses possessing economic moats have "pricing power," which allows them to charge a premium price for their products and services. Seek to invest in businesses with high Return On Invested Capital (ROIC).

Current Ratio:

High current ratios, above 2, are most desirable. Current ratios of 2 mean that the business has twice the amount of current assets as current liabilities, in order to meet all of its short-term liability commitments within the next 12 months. Businesses showing current ratios of 1 mean the business has the same amount of current assets to current liabilities. Businesses showing current ratios below 1 may not be able to meet their short-term liability obligations within the next 12 months. The Current Ratio is easily calculated by dividing total current assets by total current liabilities. Seek businesses with higher current ratios of 2 or greater, to identify the strongest businesses.

Little to no debt:

Low interest expense on the income statement and little to no debt on the balance sheet go hand-in-hand. If the business possesses little to no debt on its balance sheet, then the business will not show a high interest expense on the income statement.

Conversely, businesses possessing high amounts of short-term and long-term debt on their balance sheets must pay higher amounts of their finite operating income to pay interest expenses, in order to service their debt.

As value investors, it is wise to avoid businesses possessing high amounts of debt, and instead identify businesses with little to no debt. Businesses with little to no debt are most attractive to value investors, since these are the healthier businesses often run by higher quality management teams, and are more likely to possess a durable competitive advantage.

Warren Buffett prefers to invest in businesses with little to no debt.

"It is easier to stay out of debt, than to get out of debt." Scott Thompson

Retained Earnings Consistently Increasing:

Warren Buffett seeks to invest in businesses showing steadily increasing Retained Earnings on their balance sheets. One of the best examples of this is Warren Buffett's own Berkshire Hathaway. If we look at Berkshire's balance sheet, it shows an impressive long-term history of steadily increasing retained earnings.

Instead of paying out dividends to shareholders, Berkshire Hathaway retains 100% of their earnings. This allows Warren Buffett to efficiently reinvest Berkshire's retained earnings into making strategic acquisitions of high-quality businesses with durable competitive advantages that remunerate superior results for Berkshire's shareholders.

Berkshire Hathaway shareholders avoid the taxable event of receiving dividends, and instead gain the benefits of owning a great long-term business like Berkshire Hathaway, whose balance sheet continues to grow consistently, increasing their book value by about 22% per year for the past several decades. Buffett's Berkshire Hathaway is an incredible business that started with a stock price of about $7 per share. In June 2013, shares of Berkshire were worth over $172,000.00 per share!

Operating Cash Flow / Sales:

Operating Cash Flow is located toward the bottom of the cash flow statement, and represents the cash flow of the business before capital expenditures. Sales, also known as revenues, is located at the top of the income statement.

The formula is:

$$\frac{\text{Operating Cash Flow}}{\text{Revenue}}$$

If this ratio is 15% or higher, it may be a sign of a business with a durable competitive advantage. Higher ratios are better. Seek to identify above-average businesses showing higher Operating Cash Flow / Sales ratios.

Capital Expenditures / Net Income:

Capital expenditures, referred to as CapEx, are capital reinvestments the business must make in order to maintain and grow its operations. Generally, businesses with CapEx/Net Income ratios below 30% tend to be better businesses. Lower ratios are better. 0% is the best, but most businesses have at least some outlay for annual Capital Expenditures.

Capital Expenditures are found on the Cash Flow Statement, and Net Income is found on the Income Statement. Warren Buffett seeks to invest in businesses that are not capital intensive, and possess low CapEx / Net Income ratios.

Free Cash Flow / Sales:

Free Cash Flow (FCF) is one of the most important financial metrics value investors use to identify high-quality businesses with durable competitive advantages. Ideally, value investors seek to find undervalued businesses generating high amounts of Free Cash Flows (FCFs). Searching for businesses with strong consistent free cash flows can be a good place to start in your search to find healthy undervalued businesses in which to invest.

Free Cash Flow (FCF) is the amount of money a business retains after it pays for all its expenses including Capital Expenditures, "CapEx," investments back into the business. Free Cash Flow (FCF) is important because it allows high-quality businesses to invest in opportunities that increase shareholder value such as stock buybacks, debt reduction, making acquisitions, paying dividends, developing new products and services, etc.

The formula is:

Free Cash Flow = Operating Cash Flows – Capital Expenditures

Or, you can calculate Free Cash Flows (FCFs) this way:

Free Cash Flow = (Operating Income x (1 – Tax Rate)) + (Depreciation and Amortization) – (Change in Net Working Capital) – (Capital Expenditures)

Operating Income, also known as EBIT, is found on the income statement. Depreciation and Amortization is found toward the top of the Cash Flow Statement. Remember, Net Working Capital is a balance sheet calculation that is the difference between Total Current Assets and Total Current Liabilities.

Net Working Capital = Total Current Assets – Total Current Liabilities

Capital Expenditures are found toward the bottom of the Cash Flow Statement. Many Cash Flow Statements will show Free Cash Flow (FCF) as a line item toward the bottom of the page.

The Discounted Cash Flow (DCF) analysis that John Burr Williams published in 1938 in his book "The Theory of Investment Value" uses Free Cash Flows (FCFs) to estimate the intrinsic value of businesses. (We'll explain this intrinsic value estimation process further in Chapter 9).

Generally speaking, FCF/Sales ratios of 10% or higher are desirable. Higher ratios are better. Seek businesses with higher Free Cash Flow / Sales ratios.

6.4 Summary:

In summary, continue to experiment with different combinations of financial ratios to create your own set of unique screening criteria. Combine your screening criteria with Buffett and Munger's "Four-Filters" investment process, as discussed in Chapter 3.

Quantitative factors tend to exist with Filter #4, whereas qualitative factors tend to exist within Filters #1, #2, and #3. Remember to consider potential "catalyst" events that may occur in the near future, that could affect business's stock price.

Now you have developed a solid skill set, understanding financial statements, financial ratios, and screening criteria. You should now be able to begin identifying potential high-quality businesses in which to invest.

Remember, billionaire value investors Warren Buffett and Charlie Munger seek to identify high-quality undervalued businesses possessing durable competitive advantages, run by honest and trustworthy managers, available at attractive prices, with adequate margins of safety.

CHAPTER SEVEN:

Net Asset Value (NAV)

7.1 Overview:

At Columbia University, Professor Bruce Greenwald and his colleagues teach a three-stage approach to valuation. (Greenwald, 2001) In order to value the various elements of a business, it is important to be able to calculate:

Net Asset Value (NAV): Balance sheet.

Earnings Power Value (EPV): Income statement.

Growth Value (GV): Cash flow statement.

The balance sheet, income statement, and cash flow statement, are the three primary financial statements. The balance sheet shows the book value (accounting value) of the assets the business owns, as of this particular day.

The income statement shows the firm's revenues, cost of goods sold, gross profit, net income, earnings per share, and other pertinent information regarding the firm's ability, or lack thereof, to generate earnings for shareholders.

The cash flow statement shows the incoming and outgoing flows of cash of a business over an accounting period, usually reported quarterly or annually.

If we were to graph all 3 values (NAV, EPV, GV) side-by-side into a bar chart, Net Asset Value (NAV) should be the lowest bar, Earnings Power Value (EPV) should be middle height, and Growth Value (GV) should be the tallest bar, as shown in the diagram (below).

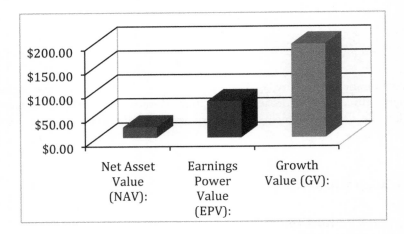

As you can see, calculating NAV, EPV, and GV using this quantitative process, helps us determine which businesses possesses durable competitive advantages, which businesses are average, or are below-average businesses. For best results, the author recommends implementing rigorous qualitative research, in addition to your rigorous quantitative analysis.

Combining both qualitative and quantitative approaches together will give the analyst a more complete picture of the business, and its past, present, and future. After all, investors don't make money on what's already happened in the rearview mirror, they make money on what happens next, looking forward through the windshield.

7.2 How to calculate NAV:

Net Asset Value (NAV) is calculated using the Balance Sheet. Net asset value offers a rough "back of the envelope" valuation of assets on a firm's balance sheet, after making necessary adjustments. To calculate Net Asset Value (NAV) we often make adjustments to items on the firm's balance sheet to determine "reproduction value" or "liquidation value."

136

If a business, like General Motors (GM), possesses specialized inventory items like car seats and dashboards, these types of specialized inventories will likely not bring full value in a liquidation sale of assets. Specialized inventories would most likely sell for 45%-50% of their actual value in a liquidation sale. Therefore, we use "liquidation value" for these types of specialized inventory assets.

If a firm like BHP Billiton (BBL) were to possess inventories of desirable commodities like raw silver and copper, "reproduction value" would most likely be used to value these assets. Raw commodities like these would likely earn higher amounts in a hypothetical asset sale, if the business were to be suddenly forced into an asset sale, or find itself in a distressed financial situation.

Therefore, it is important to make clear distinctions between "liquidation value," used to value more specialized inventories, and "reproduction value," used to value raw material or commodity type inventories.

7.3 Adjustments on the Balance Sheet (Haircut Method):

Balance sheets tend to show book value (accounting value), which we know may not accurately reflect the true value of the assets shown on the balance sheet. We now begin to make notes on the side of the Balance Sheet next to the original values listed. You may also use a spreadsheet, and create a column next to the actual value shown on the Balance Sheet, into which you will make adjustments.

Start by allowing 100% of total cash. For accounts receivables, we use 75%, because if the firm went out of business, not every firm that owes the business money will pay in full. For inventories, we use 50%, because most assets would not garner more than .50 cents on the dollar in a forced liquidation sale. Reproduction values may be higher, however, depending on the type of inventory. Your estimate of the value of the assets may vary. Allow a value of 0% for deferred income taxes.

For plant, property, and equipment, also known as (PP&E), we use the Net PP&E, not the Gross PP&E, because the Accumulated Depreciation amount has already been removed from Net PP&E. This gives us a more conservative valuation. Use 45% of the total amount shown.

Use 0% for goodwill, because goodwill is rather worthless in an asset sale. Goodwill is an accounting term referring to the value of an acquired business's purchase price, higher than the value of its underlying assets. Goodwill occurs on a Balance Sheet when a business is purchased at an amount higher than the fair value of the net assets of the business purchased.

In other words, the difference between the price at which the business was purchased, and the total fair value of the acquired business's net assets is "goodwill" of the purchased business. Goodwill helps the balance sheet stay in balance, because total assets minus total liabilities equals shareholders equity. Another way to state this is, shareholders equity plus total liabilities equals total assets.

For intangible assets, use 0%–5% for liquidation value, since in a forced liquidation sale, intangible assets hold little to no value. In a forced liquidation sale, businesses tend to be sold for the value of their tangible assets.

7.4 Example: NAV:

Book Value, also known as Accounting Value, is very different from Net Asset Value and Liquidation Value. Book value is based on accounting values, and not the true underlying value of the assets. Balance sheets just show book value, not net asset value or liquidation value. Therefore, it is necessary to make adjustments to a firm's balance sheets in order to determine an approximation of the firm's actual underlying asset value, and not the firm's "accounting" book value.

Remember, this "back of envelope" process of making adjustments to a firm's balance sheets only shows us a very rough approximation of the true value of the underlying assets. There are plenty of books, experts, and consultants who are more than happy to delve into the intricacies of detailed asset valuation. You may encounter a situation where enlisting the expertise of a consultant is necessary. However, for our general purposes the "back of the envelope" process will often suffice.

Now we calculate the Net Asset Value (NAV) of "CF Industries Holdings Inc." (CF). The balance sheet of CF Industries Holdings Inc. (CF) shows:

Balance Sheet: CF Industries Holdings Inc. (CF): 2012
USD in millions except per share data

Current Assets:

Cash and cash equivalents	$ 2,275
Short-term investments	$ 0
Total cash	**$ 2,275**
Receivables	$ 213
Inventories	$ 278
Deferred income taxes	$ 10
Prepaid expenses	$ 0
Other current assets	$ 32
Total current assets	**$ 2,808**

Non-current Assets:

Gross property, plant and equipment	$ 6,658
Accumulated Depreciation	($ 2,757)
Net property, plant and equipment	$ 3,900
Equity and other investments	$ 936
Goodwill	$ 2,064
Intangible assets	$ 0
Other long-term assets	$ 459
Total non-current assets	$7,359
TOTAL ASSETS:	**$10,167**

Current Liabilities:

Short-term debt	$17,874
Accounts payable	$ 1,969
Taxes payable	$ 471
Accrued liabilities	$ 6,711
Other current liabilities	$ 796
Total current liabilities	**$27,821**

Non-Current Liabilities:

Long-term debt	$14,736
Deferred taxes liabilities	$ 4,981
Minority interest	$ 378
Other long-term liabilities	$ 5,468
Total non-current liabilities	$25,563
TOTAL LIABILITIES:	**$53,384**

Stockholders' Equity:

Preferred stock	$ 1,760
Common stock	$ 1,760
Additional paid-in capital	$11,379
Retained earnings	$58,045
Treasury stock	($35,009)
Accumulated other comprehensive income	($ 3,385)
Total stockholders' equity	$32,790

TOTAL LIABILITIES & STOCKHOLDERS' EQUITY: $86,174

Balance Sheet Adjustments (Haircut Method):

Now let's apply the following adjustments to the balance sheet to find our Net Asset Value (NAV):

Total cash = Remove 0%, so 100% remains
Receivables = Remove 25%, so 75% remains
Inventories = Remove 50%, so 50% remains
Deferred income taxes = Remove 100%, so 0% remains
Net property, plant, and equipment (PP&E) = Remove 55%, so 45% remains
Goodwill = Remove 100%, so 0% remains
Intangible assets = Remove 100%, so 0% remains

	Original	+/−	Adjusted
Total cash =	$ 2,275	100%	$ 2,275
Receivables =	$ 213	75%	$ 159.75
Inventories =	$ 278	50%	$ 139
Deferred income taxes =	$ 10	0%	$ 0
Net property, plant, and equipment (PP&E) =	$ 3,900	45%	$1,755
Goodwill =	$ 2,064	0%	$ 0
Intangible assets =	$ 0	0%	$ 0

The original amount of total assets (before adjustments) was $10,167 (million). The amount subtracted was: $4,411.25 (million). Next, simply add up all the assets on the balance sheet using the remaining newly "adjusted" amounts, to arrive at: $5,755.75 (million). Congratulations. You've just calculated Net Asset Value (NAV).

Next we determine the Net Asset Value (NAV) per Share, by simply dividing the Net Asset Value (NAV) of $5,755.75 (million) by the number of total shares outstanding of 65 (million). The formula is:

NAV per Share = NAV ÷ (Total Shares Outstanding)
NAV per Share = $5,755,750,000 ÷ 65,000,000
NAV per Share = $88.55

Net Asset Value (NAV) uses the balance sheet, and is the first element of value. In the next two chapters, we will calculate the other two elements of value, which are Earnings Power Value (EPV) using the income statement, and Growth Value (GV) using the cash flow statement.

7.5 Liquidation Value:

To estimate an approximate "back of envelope" Liquidation Value, we begin by applying the same adjustments to specific assets on the balance sheet you just learned in our Net Asset Value (NAV) calculation (above):

Total cash = Remove 0%, so 100% remains
Receivables = Remove 25%, so 75% remains
Inventories = Remove 50%, so 50% remains
Deferred income taxes = Remove 100%, so 0% remains
Net property, plant, and equipment (PP&E) = Remove 55%, so 45% remains
Goodwill = Remove 100%, so 0% remains
Intangible assets = Remove 100%, so 0% remains

For this example, let's use the 2012 balance sheet of a business we'll refer to as "(XYZ)."

Total Assets on XYZ's balance sheet are: $2,722 million. However, after applying adjustments, as shown above, XYZ's Net Asset Value is: $1,294 million. Next, locate XYZ's "Total Liabilities" on their balance sheet, which are $1,173 million. Perform the following simple calculation to estimate an approximate liquidation value:

Liquidation Value = Net Asset Value − Total Liabilities
Liquidation Value = $1,294,750,000 − $1,173,000,000
Liquidation Value = $121,750,000

Next, let's calculate Liquidation Value per Share. This is easily calculated by dividing Liquidation Value by the number of Total Shares Outstanding.

Liquidation Value per Share = Liquidation Value ÷ Total Shares Outstanding

Liquidation Value per Share = $121,750,000 ÷ 88,863,530
Liquidation Value per Share = $1.37

On March 19th, 2013, shares of XYZ were trading at only .68 cents per share, but their liquidation value was $1.37 per share. Therefore, .68 cents per share is 50% below XYZ's estimated liquidation value. We're not recommending you run out and buy shares of "XYZ," but merely illustrating the point that value investors can identify businesses trading below liquidation value. This idea of buying businesses below liquidation value is difficult for many investors to grasp, but the concept is actually very simple.

Businesses trading below their liquidation value are extremely rare, but do occur. Value investors just need to know how to identify them. Be cautious to determine whether a business is a value trap or high-quality bargain, and always perform rigorous due diligence before you invest.

7.6 Summary:

Many investors ignore the balance sheet. We recommend you do not. The balance sheet shows many important items to consider such as the amount of assets or debt held by the business. If a business has little to no debt, it may be an attractive candidate. If a business has exorbitant debt, it may be best to pass and search for a more attractive business that holds less debt.

In many cases, skilled valuation consultants should be hired to determine more precise asset values and liquidation values of businesses. However; this estimated "back of the envelope" valuation process allows value investors to analyze more businesses in less time. This being said, do not hesitate to hire skilled valuation consultants to perform more in-depth, detailed valuations when the need arises.

CHAPTER EIGHT:

Earnings Power Value (EPV)

8.1 Overview:

Earnings Power Value (EPV) is calculated using a business's Income Statement. Ideally, one dollar invested into assets on the balance sheet should generate more than one dollar in earnings on the income statement. Therefore, as a general rule, the better–performing businesses will show Earnings Power Values (EPVs) higher than Net Asset Values (NAVs).

The difference between the Earnings Power Value (EPV) and Net Asset Value (NAV) is the Franchise Value (FV). (Greenwald, 2001) We will show how to calculate Franchise Value (FV) later in this chapter.

First, we must learn how to calculate Earnings Power Value (EPV). The examples of EPV interwoven into this chapter as the concept is being explained will help solidify your understanding of how to calculate EPV.

8.2 Calculating (EPV):

To calculate Earnings Power Value, first determine the "Normalized EBIT Margin percentage." EBIT is an acronym for "Earnings Before Interest and Taxes," also known as Operating Earnings. Operating Earnings is located on the Income Statement.

To calculate Normalized EBIT Margin percentage, first determine the average of the most recent individual 10-year EBIT margins. Then determine the average of the most recent individual 5-year EBIT margins. Then average these two numbers together. This gives you the average long-term average EBIT margin percentage.

8.3 Example (EPV):

If the most recent 10-year Operating Margin % is:
0, 19.6%, 23.7%, 30.8%, 44%, 45.9%, 40.2%, 23.9%, 37.6%, 44.3%

10-year Average = 31.0%
 5-year Average = 38.4%
Then we average these two numbers together to arrive at: 34.7%

Next, multiply the long-term average EBIT margin percentage against the annual revenue amount for the most recent full year shown on the Income Statement. This gives you the "Normalized EBIT earnings, also known as normalized Operating Earnings."

For example,
The most recent full year revenue amount is: $71,739 million.
$71,739 million X 34.7% = $24,893 million
Therefore, Normalized EBIT = $24,893 million

The next step is to determine Normalized NOPAT. NOPAT is an acronym for "Net Operating Profit After Tax." This is calculated by first determining the average tax rate the business has paid over the most recent 10-year period. Then calculate the 5-year average over the most recent 5-year period. Now average these two numbers together.

Tax Rate %:
0, 106.38, 23.06, 24.15, 22.64, 23.17, 28.95, 45.44, 33.53, 23.39 = 33.1%

10-year Average = 33.1%
 5-year Average = 30.9%
Then we average these two numbers together to arrive at: 32%

Then multiply the Normalized EBIT by the 10-year average tax rate, to give you Normalized NOPAT (Net Operating Profit After Tax).

$24,893 million X (1 – 32%) = $16,927 million
Normalized NOPAT   = $16,927 million
(NOPAT means Net Operating Profit After Tax).

Next, we must determine the Excessive Depreciation amount from the Balance Sheet, but only for the most recent full year, not trailing 12 months (ttm). This is done by locating the "Accumulated Depreciation" on the Balance Sheet for the most recent two years, and simply subtracting the most recent year's Accumulated Depreciation amount from the Accumulated Depreciation amount from the prior year.

Remember to first remove the negative signs, to use the "absolute value" of each number. *(See example below)*. This shows us how much depreciation occurred in the most recent year, alone. The Accumulated Depreciation line on the Balance Sheet is exactly what it sounds like – simply a cumulative total of all depreciation that occurred from all prior years up to the present). We only need the amount that occurred in the past year alone. The previous paragraph explains how we isolate this amount.

For example,
If our two most recent Accumulated Depreciation amounts are:

Most recent full year:	*$34,023 million*
2 years ago:	*$29,569 million*
Equals:	*$4,454 million*

(Remember, the Balance Sheet shows these Accumulated Depreciation numbers as negative, so we must first remove the "negative" signs to use the "absolute value" of each number before subtracting).

Therefore, the absolute value of the depreciation for the most recent year alone is: $4,454 million

Now, we must multiply the depreciation amount we just calculated, that occurred in the most recent year, by the average 10-year tax rate we determined earlier. The result is our Excessive Depreciation After Tax.

For example,
$4,454 million X (1 – 32%) = $3,029 million
Therefore, our Excessive Depreciation After Tax = $3,029 million

Then we add the Normalized NOPAT amount and the Excessive Depreciation After Tax amounts together, to give us our Earnings Power Value (EPV). Congratulations, you did it! You can now analyze business's financial statements and create models to help determine if they possess a positive or negative Franchise Value (FV).

For example,
$16,927 million (Normalized Net Operating Profit After Tax)
$ 3,029 million (Excessive Depreciation After Tax)
$19,956 million (Normalized Earnings)

The final step is to apply this EPV formula. (It is time to discuss WACC).

$$\textbf{Normalized Earnings} \div \textbf{WACC} = \textbf{EPV}$$

8.4 Weighted Average Cost of Capital (WACC):

The Weighted Average Cost of Capital (WACC) is different for each business. All capital sources are included in WACC, such as: common stock, preferred stock, bonds, and other long-term debt. (Analysts often use WACC as the discount rate in NPV and DCF analysis). The formula is:

$$WACC = \frac{E}{V} \times Re + \frac{D}{V} \times Rd \times (1 - Tr)$$

Where,

Re = Cost of Equity	V = E+D
Rd = Cost of Debt	E/V = % of equity financing
E = Market Value of Equity	D/V % of debt financing
D = Market value of Debt	Tr = Tax Rate

For more information on WACC, visit http://ThatsWacc.com For simplicity sake, we'll just use 10% to keep this example simple for now.

For example, Normalized Earnings ÷ WACC = EPV, therefore;

Normalized Earnings $19,956 million ÷ 10% WACC = $199,560 million

Therefore, Earnings Power Value (EPV) is: $199,560 million

Congratulations! You now know how to calculate EPV. This will help you identify businesses with strong, average, or weak Franchise Values (FV). Discard average and weak businesses. Focus on the businesses possessing strong Franchise Values (FV).

What is Franchise Value (FV), and how is Franchise Value (FV) calculated? Franchise Value (FV) is the difference between EPV and NAV, and is calculated by subtracting the NAV from EPV. If we express this as an equation, it looks like this:

EPV – NAV = FV

For example, if EPV is $199,560 million, and NAV is $59,367 million, then;

$199,560 million (EPV)
$ 59,367 million (NAV)
$140,193 million Franchise Value (FV)

8.5 NAV, EPV, and GV:

When EPV is higher than NAV, the business has a positive Franchise Value (FV). Conversely, when EPV is lower than NAV, the business has a negative Franchise Value (FV). When EPV is equal to NAV, there is 0 Franchise Value (FV). As a general rule, the best businesses will possess EPVs significantly higher than their NAVs. The following diagram shows some different examples of NAV, EPV, and GV.

Elements of Value:

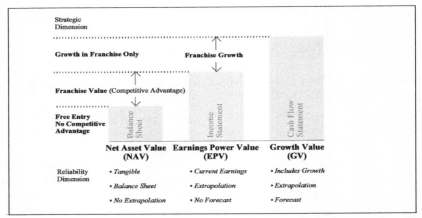

Diagram from Bruce Greenwald's, "Value Investing: From Graham to Buffett and Beyond."

The "Above-Average Business " diagram on the left, shows that every $1 invested into the business's assets on their Balance Sheet, is generating more than $1 of earnings on their Income Statement.

The middle diagram shows that if a business's NAV and EPV are equal, there is no franchise value, and every $1 invested into assets is only generating $1 in earnings.

The "Below-Average Business " diagram on the right shows EPV below NAV, then every $1 invested into assets on the Balance Sheet is generating less than $1 of earnings on the Income Statement.

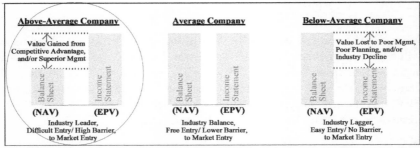

Diagram from Bruce Greenwald's, "Value Investing: From Graham to Buffett and Beyond."
(Greenwald, 2001)

Net Asset Value (NAV) inherently does not require any forecasting, and instead uses available known data from the balance sheet. Net Asset Value (NAV) is an excellent way to measure asset values without making any assumptions, or working with any forecasted or unknown data. With Net Asset Value (NAV), all data is known.

The same is true for Earnings Power Value (EPV), which also does not require any forecasting. With EPV, all data is also known, and can be gathered from the income statement. Earnings Power Value (EPV) does not require any forecasting, estimating, or trying to predict future performance.

Growth Value (GV), however, does require an element of forecasting future performance. Can future performance be based partially on successful past performance? In some cases, yes, but not in all cases. As a general rule, Growth Value (GV) is most accurate for businesses that have demonstrated consistent upward earnings trends over the past several years.

Businesses with consistent earnings histories are more likely to continue into the future than firms with no earnings histories. Forecasting is an art as much as it is a science. NAV and EPV do not require any forecasting and tend to be more reliable. However, when it comes to estimating the future intrinsic values (GV) of businesses,

"I'd rather be approximately right than precisely wrong." Warren Buffett

As we remember from our example of the concert violinist in Chapter 3, the talented concert violinist would be an example of an "Above-Average Business," because her Earnings Power Value (EPV) exceeds the value of her Net Asset Value (NAV). Conversely, "Person B" from this same example would illustrate a "Below-Average Business," because his Earnings Power Value (EPV) is below his Net Asset Value (NAV).

CHAPTER NINE:

Intrinsic Value: Growth Value (GV)

9.1 Overview:

Warren Buffett defines Intrinsic Value as, "… the discounted value of the cash that can be taken out of a business during its remaining life. Anyone calculating intrinsic value necessarily comes up with a highly subjective figure. This figure will change both as estimates of future cash flows are revised and as interest rates move. Despite its fuzziness, however, intrinsic value is all-important and is the only logical way to evaluate the relative attractiveness of investments and businesses."

On the subject of intrinsic value, Warren Buffett also stated, "The calculation of intrinsic value, though, is not so simple. As our definition suggests, intrinsic value is an estimate rather than a precise figure, and it is additionally an estimate that must be changed if interest rates move or forecasts of future cash flows are revised. Two people looking at the same set of facts, moreover – and this would apply even to Charlie and me – will almost inevitably come up with at least slightly different intrinsic value figures. This is one reason we never give you our estimates of intrinsic value. What our annual reports do supply, though, are the facts that we ourselves use to calculate this value."

There are many different strategies used to estimate intrinsic value. Benjamin Graham invented the formula V = EPV x (8.5 + 2g) to estimate intrinsic value. In 1938, John Burr Williams released his book, "The Theory of Investment Value," to measure intrinsic value using the Net Present Value (NPV), or Discounted Cash Flows (DCF) process. In Berkshire Hathaway's 2010 annual report, Warren Buffett released his "two-column method" of measuring intrinsic value. Let's begin with Ben Graham's Formula:

9.2 Ben Graham's Formula:

Ben Graham created the following formula for calculating intrinsic value:

$$V = EPS \times (8.5 + 2g)$$

Where,
V = Intrinsic Value
EPS = Earnings Per Share (ttm, trailing twelve months)
8.5 = Price/Earnings (P/E) ratio for a non-growth business
g = reasonable expected 7–10 year growth rate

For example, let's estimate the intrinsic value for a business with Earnings Per Share (EPS) of $16, that is growing at a 8.25% growth rate per year.

V = EPS x (8.5 + 2g)
V = $16 x (8.5 + (2 x 8.25))
V = $16 x (8.5 + 16.5)
V = $16 x (25)
V = $400/share

If the business has a stock price of $200/share, and intrinsic value of $400/share, this implies a margin of safety (MOS) of 50%.

Let's solidify this concept in your mind with the following example: Estimate the intrinsic value for a business with Earnings Per Share (EPS) of $5, that is growing at a 5.75% growth rate per year.

V = EPS x (8.5 + 2g)
V = $5 x (8.5 + (2 x 5.75))
V = $5 x (8.5 + 11.5)
V = $5 x (20)
V = $100/share

If the business has a stock price of $25/share, and intrinsic value of $100/share, this implies a margin of safety (MOS) of 75%. Similarly, if the stock price were to be $80/share, and intrinsic value of $100/share, the margin of safety (MOS) would be only 20%. Sometimes we identify wonderful businesses using Buffett's Filters #1, #2, and #3, but do not invest until the stock price (Filter #4) falls back below a certain price, where we can establish a wider margin of safety (MOS).

It's rumored that Warren Buffett can quickly estimate intrinsic value in his head. Therefore, Buffett's modified Graham formula may resemble something like this:

$$V = EPS \times (8 + 2g)$$
$$V = \$5 \times (8 + (2 \times 6))$$
$$V = \$5 \times (8 + 12)$$
$$V = \$5 \times (20) = \$100/share$$

After beginning his career using Ben Graham's quantitative value investing strategies, Warren later began to calculate intrinsic value using John Burr Williams' process of Net Present Value (NPV), and Discounted Cash Flow (DCF) analysis, using Free Cash Flows.

9.3 Net Present Value (NPV), Discounted Cash Flow (DCF):

Intrinsic Value is calculated using the Net Present Value (NPV) process invented by John Burr Williams in 1938, in his doctoral thesis, "The Theory of Investment Value." John Burr Williams also refers to this as the Discounted Cash Flow (DCF) valuation process. DCF is based on using a business's Free Cash Flows (FCFs), and discounting them back to the present, according to an appropriate discount rate. (Williams, 1938)

In other words, Net Present Value (NPV) is the present value of all future cash flows, discounted back to the present. This is consistent with Warren Buffett's definition of intrinsic value from his quote at the outset of this chapter. Download a free two-stage DCF model at: ProValueSource.com

The formula is:

$$NPV = 0 = -CF_0 + \frac{CF_1}{(1+r)^1} + \frac{CF_2}{(1+r)^2} + \frac{CF_3}{(1+r)^3} + \ldots + \frac{CF_n}{(1+r)^n}$$

Or

$$NPV = \sum_{t-1}^{T} \frac{C_t}{(1+r)} - C_0$$

Don't be intimidated by this formula. Let's simplify using the following example.

1. First, we estimate the investment's cash flows it generates each year, and its discount rate. (We explain discount rates in greater detail later in this chapter). If a business is contemplating reinvesting $1,500 of its capital back into itself, to purchase new machines that are expected to generate the following new cash flows over the next three years:

$1,200 in Year 1
$1,100 in Year 2
$1,000 in Year 3

2. For this example, let's assume an 8% discount rate.

3. Enter each of the cash flows into each of the first three periods, according to the NPV formula (above). As you enter the first year's free cash flow, it should look like this:

[Free Cash Flow / ((1 + discount rate) ^year)] + ...
[$1,200 / ((1 + .08) ^1)] + ...

Now let's add the remaining two cash flows and years two and three to this formula. It will look like this:

154

[Free Cash Flow / ((1 + discount rate) ^year)] + ...

[$1,200 / ((1 + .08) ^1)] + [$1,100 / ((1 + .08) ^2)] +[$1,000 / ((1 + .08) ^3)]

[$1,200 / ((1.08) ^1)] + [$1,100 / ((1.08) ^2)] +[$1,000 / ((1.08) ^3)]

Excellent. Now let's solve this equation to estimate the intrinsic value of this potential investment. You can do this manually or using spreadsheet software.

Raise 1.08 to the power of the exponent of the first period, which is 1, to get 1.08. Divide the free cash flow in the numerator by the denominator in the first period, which is 1.08. So,

$1,200 / 1.08 = $1,111

Calculate the result of periods two and three, remembering to raise 1.08 to the exponent of 2 in period two, and raise 1.08 to the exponent of 3 in period three. You should arrive at: $943 in period two, and $794 for period three. Let's put it all together now:

DCF = $1,111 + 943 + $794
DCF = $2,848

The business is expected to earn $2,848 in new free cash flows by purchasing the new machines. If the capital reinvestment required to purchase the new machines were $1,500, then,

$2,848 – $1,500 = $1,348
Therefore, this investment would generate a profit of $1,348.

However, what if the cost to purchase these new machines were $4,000 instead of $1,500?

$2,848 – $4,000 = (–$1,152)
Therefore, this investment would lose (–$1,152).

As Buffett says, "Price is what you pay. Value is what you get." This illustrates the point that a bargain is not a bargain at any price! In other words, at some price, a bargain is no longer a bargain.

Instead of assuming these numbers represent machines, now let's assume they represent the total free cash flows (in millions) of a publicly traded business on the stock market.

$1,200 (million) in Year 1
$1,100 (million) in Year 2
$1,000 (million) in Year 3

Using the same formula and math (above), we estimate an intrinsic value of $2,848 (million), or $2,848,000,000. This is the present value of the business's expected free cash flows discount back to the present.

If you were Warren Buffett, how much would you rather pay for a business worth $2,848 (million)?

A. $1,500 (million)
B. $4,000 (million)

The obvious answer is A.

If you paid $1,500 (million) for a business worth $2,848 (million), your margin of safety would be: [($2,848 − $1,500) / $2,848] = 47.3%. However, if you paid $4,000 (million) for a business worth $2,848 (million), your margin of safety would be: [($2,848 − $4,000) / $2,848] = (−40.4%). This is a negative margin of safety, so a purchase price of $4,000 is not a bargain.

DCF Example #1:

If you were to deposit $100 into a bank at 3% interest, $100 is your beginning amount, and $3 is the amount of interest you will receive at the end of "Year 1."

Therefore, at the end of Year 1, you will have at total of $103. Because your starting amount was $100, and you received 3% interest at the end of Year 1. So what happens if you leave the $103 in the bank at 3% interest? How much would the $103 be worth at the end of Year 2? Year 3? Year 4? Year 5? Etc.

Starting Amount $100

Year 1: $100 x .03 = $3.00
$100 + $3 = $103
$103 is new starting amount for next year.

Year 2: $103 x .03 = $3.09
$103 + $3.09 = $106.09
$106.09 is new starting amount for next year.

Year 3: $106.09 x .03 = $3.18
$106.09 + $3.18 = $109.27
$109.27 is new starting amount for next year.

Year 4: $109.27 x .03 = $3.28
$109.27 + $3.28 = $112.55
$112.55 is new starting amount for next year.

Year 5: $112.55 x .03 = $3.38
$112.55 + $3.38 = $115.93
$115.93 is new starting amount for next year.

Year 6: $115.93 x .03 = $3.48
$115.93 + $3.48 = $119.41
$119.41 is new starting amount for next year.

Year 7: $119.41 x .03 = $3.58
$119.41 + $3.58 = $122.99
$122.99 is new starting amount for next year.

Year 8: $122.99 x .03 = $3.69
$122.99 + $3.69 = $126.68
$126.68 is new starting amount for next year.

Year 9: $126.68 x .03 = $3.80
$126.68 + $3.80 = $130.48
$130.68 is new starting amount for next year.

Year 10: $130.48 x .03 = $3.91
$130.48 + $3.91 = $134.39
$134.39 is new starting amount for next year.

Now let's assume hypothetically, there were to be no growth during years 11–15. So, your ending amount of $134.39 at the end of Year 10 stayed the same for years 11-15.

Year 11: $134.39 x 0% growth = $134.39
Year 12: $134.39 x 0% growth = $134.39
Year 13: $134.39 x 0% growth = $134.39
Year 14: $134.39 x 0% growth = $134.39
Year 15: $134.39 x 0% growth = $134.39

This example simply illustrates what a two-stage Discounted Cash Flow (DCF) model looks like in its simplest form. You started with $100. Then you applied a 3% growth rate for years 1–10, and you applied a 0% growth rate for years 11–15.

If we were to create a simple two-stage DCF model using Excel, it would resemble this.

Starting Amount	$100.00		
Year 1	$103.00	3%	$3.00
Year 2	$106.09	3%	$3.09
Year 3	$109.27	3%	$3.18
Year 4	$112.55	3%	$3.28
Year 5	$115.93	3%	$3.38
Year 6	$119.41	3%	$3.48
Year 7	$122.99	3%	$3.58
Year 8	$126.68	3%	$3.69
Year 9	$130.48	3%	$3.80
Year 10	$134.39	3%	$3.91
Year 11	$134.39	0%	$0.00
Year 12	$134.39	0%	$0.00
Year 13	$134.39	0%	$0.00
Year 14	$134.39	0%	$0.00
Year 15	$134.39	0%	$0.00

If you have not already created a DCF "two-stage" model spreadsheet using Excel or other spreadsheet software to calculate Net Present Value (NPV), please create one now. Or, download a free two-stage DCF model at: www.ProValueSource.com

Set up your spreadsheet to calculate NPV for 15 annual periods. Apply a growth rate to years 1–10, and a lower growth rate to years 11–15.

You just learned how to set-up a DCF two-stage model through our example of receiving 3% interest on $100 deposited into a bank account. After you set-up your model in Excel, what happens if the interest rate for years 1–10 were 4%? Higher growth rates increase earnings for investors. Conversely, lower growth rates decrease earnings for investors.

Caution: models do not always accurately predict the future. The outputs of models are only as good as the inputs you put into them. Do your own research. More accurate data yields more accurate results.

DCF Example #2:

Next, instead of using the previous example of $100 deposited into a bank account as our starting amount, let's use a starting amount based on the Free Cash Flows (FCFs) shown on the Cash Flow Statement of a business. Then, let's average these Free Cash Flows together for the most recent 3-year or 5-year periods.

For instance, if the most recent Free Cash Flows for a business over the past 5 years were:

2008: $560 million
2009: $619 million
2010: $655 million
2011: $731 million
2012: $786 million

The 5-year average is: $670.2 million
The 3-year average is: $724.0 million
If we average these two together, we get: $697.1 million

	Starting Amount	$697,100,000		
Year 1	$738,926,000	6%	$41,826,000
Year 2	$783,261,560	6%	$44,335,560
Year 3	$830,257,254	6%	$46,995,694
Year 4	$880,072,689	6%	$49,815,435
Year 5	$932,877,050	6%	$52,804,361
Year 6	$988,849,673	6%	$55,972,623
Year 7	$1,048,180,654	6%	$59,330,980
Year 8	$1,111,071,493	6%	$62,890,839
Year 9	$1,177,735,782	6%	$66,664,290
Year 10	$1,248,399,929	6%	$70,664,147
Year 11	$1,248,399,929	0%	$0.00
Year 12	$1,248,399,929	0%	$0.00
Year 13	$1,248,399,929	0%	$0.00
Year 14	$1,248,399,929	0%	$0.00
Year 15	$1,248,399,929	0%	$0.00

In this example, our starting Free Cash Flow amount of $697.1 million is similar to the starting amount of $100 from our first example. We just simply selected an appropriate starting amount. Then, we applied an appropriate growth rate for years 1–10, and 11–15.

In this example, we selected a 6% growth rate for years 1–10, and 0% growth rate (which may be overly conservative) for years 11–15.

Now we know our starting amount is $697.1 million. We also know our Free Cash Flow amounts for years 1–10 and 11–15 are as shown in the chart above. Now let's simply input these 15 numbers into our DCF two-stage model. Then, we'll apply a discount rate, and estimate intrinsic value.

You can build your own customized DCF two-stage model in Excel. Download a free two-stage DCF model at: www.ProValueSource.com

Or, simply use Excel's Net Present Value (NPV) function to calculate the NPV of these 15 FCF amounts (above) over a 15-year period. For this example, let's assume:

Market Price: $20/share
Total shares outstanding (diluted): 240,000,000
Discount rate: 6% *(We will explain discount rates later in this chapter).*

Based on this info, we estimate the intrinsic value to be $9,907,438,795. Next, we divide our intrinsic value of $9,907,438,795 by the number of total shares outstanding 240,000,000. This equals an intrinsic value Per Share of $41.28.

Market Price	$20.00	Intrinsic Value		$9,907,438,795
Shares Outstanding	240,000,000	**Intrinsic Value/Share**		**$41.28**
Growth Rate: Years 1-10	6.0%	**Margin of Safety**		**51.6%**
Growth Rate: Years 11-15	0.0%	*Price-to-Value*		*0.484*
Discount Rate	6.00%	Bargain		$21.28

15-Year: 2-Stage DCF Model

Starting FCF Amount	$697,100,000			
Year 1	$738,926,000	end of year	6.0%	growth
Year 2	$783,261,560	end of year	6.0%	growth
Year 3	$830,257,254	end of year	6.0%	growth
Year 4	$880,072,689	end of year	6.0%	growth
Year 5	$932,877,050	end of year	6.0%	growth
Year 6	$988,849,673	end of year	6.0%	growth
Year 7	$1,048,180,654	end of year	6.0%	growth
Year 8	$1,111,071,493	end of year	6.0%	growth
Year 9	$1,177,735,782	end of year	6.0%	growth
Year 10	$1,248,399,929	end of year	6.0%	growth
Year 11	$1,248,399,929	end of year	0.0%	growth
Year 12	$1,248,399,929	end of year	0.0%	growth
Year 13	$1,248,399,929	end of year	0.0%	growth
Year 14	$1,248,399,929	end of year	0.0%	growth
Year 15	$1,248,399,929	end of year	0.0%	growth

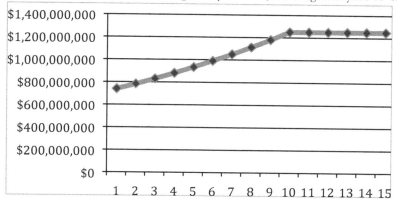

If the current stock price is $20/share, and our intrinsic value per share is $41.28/share, this implies a margin of safety of 51.6%.

(Intrinsic Value per Share – Stock Price) ÷ (Intrinsic Value per Share) = Margin of Safety

($41.28 – $20) / $41.28 = Margin of Safety
$21.28 / $41.28 = Margin of Safety
51.55% = Margin of Safety

Price-to-Value = ($20 / $41.28)
Price-to-Value = .484

The Price-to-Value ratio can also be calculated this alternative way:

Price-to-Value = (1 – Margin of Safety)
Price-to-Value = (1 – .5155)
Price-to-Value = .484

The key to correctly using this DCF two-stage model (above) is to use an appropriate starting Free Cash Flow amount, appropriate discount rate, and appropriate growth rates for years 1–10 and years 11–15.

Discounted Cash Flow (DCF) analysis can help us determine the intrinsic value of a potential investment. Therefore, we make a variation on John

Burr William's NPV formula, to create the following two-stage Discounted Cash Flow (DCF) formula:

Two-stage DCF model, for years 1–10:

$$DCF = \frac{FCF_0 \times (1 + g)}{(1 + r)^1} + \frac{FCF_1 \times (1 + g)}{(1 + r)^2} + \frac{FCF_2 \times (1 + g)}{(1 + r)^3} + \dots \frac{FCF_9 \times (1 + g)}{(1 + r)^{10}}$$

Where,

DCF: Intrinsic Value, or Present value of future cash flows discounted back to the present.
FCF_0 **: Starting Free Cash Flow Amount**
g: Free Cash Flow growth rate
r: Discount Rate

> *Note: In the numerator:*
> $FCF_0 \times (1 + g)$, becomes FCF_1
> $FCF_1 \times (1 + g)$, becomes FCF_2
> $FCF_2 \times (1 + g)$, becomes FCF_3
> Etc.

Two-stage DCF model, for years 11–15:

$$DCF = \frac{FCF_{10} \times (1 + g)}{(1 + r)^{11}} + \frac{FCF_{11} \times (1 + g)}{(1 + r)^{12}} + \frac{FCF_{12} \times (1 + g)}{(1 + r)^{13}} + \dots \frac{FCF_{14} \times (1 + g)}{(1 + r)^{15}}$$

Where,

DCF: Intrinsic Value, or Present value of future cash flows discounted back to the present.
FCF_0 **: Starting Free Cash Flow Amount**
g: Free Cash Flow growth rate
r: Discount Rate

> *Note: In the numerator:*
> $FCF_{10} \times (1 + g)$, becomes FCF_{11}
> $FCF_{11} \times (1 + g)$, becomes FCF_{12}
> $FCF_{12} \times (1 + g)$, becomes FCF_{13}
> Etc.

Download a free two-stage DCF model at: www.ProValueSource.com
Next, we introduce the concept of Minimum Safety Threshold (MST).

9.4 Minimum Safety Threshold (MST)

By establishing a Minimum Safety Threshold (MST) investors can predefine their minimum required margin of safety. For instance, if an investor requires a minimum margin of safety of 50%, how do we determine what the Minimum Safety Threshold (MST) is for each potential investment? The formula is:

MST = [(NPV Per Share – Market Price Per Share) / NPV Per Share]

Using the current example, let's assume there are 100 (million) total shares outstanding. We simply divide NPV of $2,848 (million) by 100 (million) = $28.48 = Intrinsic Value Per Share. Next, we simply divide the market capitalization of $1,500 (million) by 100 (million) shares = $15 = Market Price Per Share.

So, now we know:
MST = [(NPV Per Share – Market Price Per Share) / NPV Per Share]
[($28.48– $15) / $28.48]
($13.48 / $28.48) = 47.33% Margin of Safety

Now, let's calculate our Minimum Safety Threshold (MST). If we were to require a Minimum Safety Threshold (MST) of 50% (or 0.5), and we know the NPV Per share is $28.48, what would be the Minimum Market Price Per Share we would accept?

MST = [(NPV Per Share – Minimum Market Price Per Share) / NPV Per Share]

50% or 0.5 = [($28.48 – Minimum Market Price Per Share) / $28.48]
0.5 x $28.48 = ($28.48 – Minimum Market Price Per Share)
$14.24 = ($28.48 – Minimum Market Price Per Share)
$14.24 + Minimum Market Price Per Share = $28.48
Minimum Market Price Per Share = $28.48 – $14.24
Minimum Market Price Per Share = $14.24/share

Similarly, if you were to require a Minimum Safety Threshold (MST) of 33% (instead of 50%), we simply calculate:

MST = [(NPV Per Share − Minimum Market Price Per Share) / NPV Per Share]

33% or 0.33 = [($28.48 − Minimum Market Price Per Share) / $28.48]
0.33 x $28.48 = ($28.48 − Minimum Market Price Per Share)
$9.40 = ($28.48 − Minimum Market Price Per Share)
$9.40 + Minimum Market Price Per Share = $28.48
Minimum Market Price Per Share = $28.48 − $9.40
Minimum Market Price Per Share = $19.08/share

Later in this chapter we will show a Minimum Growth Threshold (MGT), where the investor can find the minimum required growth rate an investment needs in order to meet the required minimum margin of safety.

Next, we will show you how to select appropriate growth rates to input into your DCF Analysis. You will learn to apply appropriate growth rates to Free Cash Flows (FCFs) using a 2-stage DCF model to measure Intrinsic Value like Warren Buffett and other successful value investors.

In a 2-stage DCF model, the first stage applies to years 1–10, and the second stage applies to years 11–15. The second stage of the 2-stage DCF model (years 11–15) is also referred to as the "terminal growth rate."

Download a free two-stage DCF model at: ProValueSource.com

9.5 Selecting Growth Rates:

There are many ways to select appropriate growth rates to use in your DCF model at which Free Cash Flows will likely increase for Years 1–10. However, we tend to be very conservative in our growth rates chosen for Years 11–15 (terminal value) and often choose 0%, 1%, or 2%, etc.

Conservative growth rates cause the investor to estimate lower intrinsic valuations. This in turn allows a smaller number of businesses through the investor's valuation screen to meet his criteria. On the other hand, selecting too conservatively low growth rates may cause the investor to miss good investment opportunities because the valuation estimate was too low. Use your best judgment. Your skills will improve over time, as Warren's have.

One process helpful to choosing appropriate growth rates is to:

1. Identify the firm's 10-year average Free Cash Flow (FCF) growth rate.

2. Identify the firm's 10-year average Net Income growth rate.

3. Averaging these two numbers together may be a starting point to discovering an appropriate growth rate.

4. Or, to be conservative, you could divide this average number by 2 again, to keep your growth estimate extremely conservative.

5. For years 11–15, select a conservative growth rate between 0%– 5%, based on what the business will likely achieve in years 11–15.

9.6 Compound Annual Growth Rate (CAGR):

The Compound Annual Growth Rate (CAGR) process of selecting an appropriate growth rate is based on extrapolating long-term growth rates the business already achieved in the past. This process has its limitations. Businesses may no longer achieve growth rates achieved in the past.

For instance, if the business was a buggy-whip manufacturer around the time automobiles first began being sold. Sales of buggy-whips surely dropped precipitously as fewer and fewer customers purchased buggy-whips for their horses, and instead purchased new automobiles. In this case, applying past growth rates to the future would cause the mathematical model to not be consistent with reality. This demonstrates the need for investors to exercise caution when applying CAGR to the future.

If a business had Free Cash Flow of $50 million 10 years ago, and Free Cash Flow of $250 million for the current year, then we can calculate its CAGR like this:

CAGR = {[(ending value / starting value) ^(1/periods)] – 1} X 100

CAGR = {[(250 / 50) ^(1/10)] – 1} X 100
= [(5) ^(0.1) - 1] X 100
= [1.1746 - 1] X 100
= 0.1746 X 100 = 17.46%

This means the CAGR is 17.46% per year, over a 10-year period. In other words, the business with $50 million has grown its free cash flows by 17.46% per year, over a 10 year period, from $50 million 10 years ago to $250 million in the current year.

Another way to verify the CAGR from a spreadsheet is:
FV = 250, PV = 50, periods = 10, PMT = 0
CAGR is the RATE formula in Excel: =RATE (10, 0 ,-50, 250) = 17.46%

The CAGR can be a good place to begin when selecting a growth rate to apply to future periods of your model. However, make certain you understand the major limitations of CAGR, such as it is based on the past, and not the future.

"Investors make money looking out the windshield, not the rear view mirror." Scott Thompson

9.7 Selecting Discount Rates:

Business schools teach MBA students to select discount rates equal to Weighted Average Cost of Capital (WACC). However, throughout the 1980's Warren Buffett selected discount rates that correlated closely to the US long-term government treasury yield, which at the time was around 8.5%. Since the 1980's, treasury yields have fallen significantly, and are now below 4%. Even back in the 1980's when U.S. Treasury yields first dropped below 8%, Buffett would still select a conservatively higher discount rate closer to 9%, giving him an added margin of protection.

The weighted average cost of capital (WACC) may be noticeably higher than long-term U.S. Treasury bond yields. Furthermore, over the past 150 years, the average annualized return of the stock market is about 9%. Therefore, using a conservative discount rate of 9% would be closer to the discount rates Buffett selected during the 1980's. Using a discount rate of 10% would be even more conservative.

If you are in doubt about which discount rate to select, a discount rate between 7%–10% may be a good general place to start. However, we recommend selecting more appropriate discount rates based on the particular business you are evaluating.

9.8 Case Study: DCF/FCF Analysis

XYZ Business shows the following Free Cash Flows (FCFs) on their Cash Flow Statement. We will perform a Discounted Cash Flow (DCF) analysis.

(in millions)

2009	2010	2011	TTM
$90	$120	$160	$210

We add all (4) FCF amounts together to arrive at: $580,000,000.

We divide by 4 to determine the average FCF amount: $145 million. We could also use the 5-year average, (instead of a 3-year average plus ttm). Use your own discretion as to what the best starting free cash flow (FCF) amount is for your DCF analysis.

For this exercise, there are 20,000,000 total shares outstanding (diluted). Let's select a growth rate of 8% for years 1–10, and growth rate of 2% for years 11–15.

Let's begin with our starting free cash flow amount of $145,000,000. Next we apply our 8% growth rate for years 1–10, then our 2% growth rate for years 11–15. After you've completed these 15 calculations, your 15 annual periods will look like this:

Starting: $145,000,000

Growth Rate (years 1—10): 8%
Year 1: $156,600,000
Year 2: $169,128,000
Year 3: $182,658,240
Year 4: $197,270,899
Year 5: $213,052,571
Year 6: $230,096,777
Year 7: $248,504,519
Year 8: $268,384,880
Year 9: $289,855,671
Year 10: $313,044,125

Growth Rate (years 11–15): 2%
Year 11: $319,305,007
Year 12: $325,691,107
Year 13: $332,691,107
Year 14: $332,204,929
Year 15: $345,626,009

Discount Rate: 9%

20,000,000 total shares outstanding (diluted)

			Intrinsic		
Market Price	$42.00		Value	$1,922,992,796	
Shares			**Intrinsic**		
Outstanding	20,000,000		**Value/Share**	**$96.15**	
Growth Rate: Years 1-10	8.00%		**Margin of Safety**	**56.3%**	
Growth Rate: Years 11-15	2.00%		*Price-to-Value*	*0.437*	
Discount Rate	9.00%		Bargain	$54.15	

15-Year: 2-Stage DCF Model

Starting FCF Amount	$145,000,000			
Year 1	$156,600,000	end of year	8.0%	growth
Year 2	$169,128,000	end of year	8.0%	growth
Year 3	$182,658,240	end of year	8.0%	growth
Year 4	$197,270,899	end of year	8.0%	growth
Year 5	$213,052,571	end of year	8.0%	growth
Year 6	$230,096,777	end of year	8.0%	growth
Year 7	$248,504,519	end of year	8.0%	growth
Year 8	$268,384,880	end of year	8.0%	growth
Year 9	$289,855,671	end of year	8.0%	growth
Year 10	$313,044,125	end of year	8.0%	growth
Year 11	$319,305,007	end of year	2.0%	growth
Year 12	$325,691,107	end of year	2.0%	growth
Year 13	$332,204,929	end of year	2.0%	growth
Year 14	$338,849,028	end of year	2.0%	growth
Year 15	$345,626,009	end of year	2.0%	growth

Download a free "two-stage DCF model" at: www.ProValueSource.com

Free Cash Flow (FCF) Growth: 8% growth years 1–10, and 2% growth years 11–15

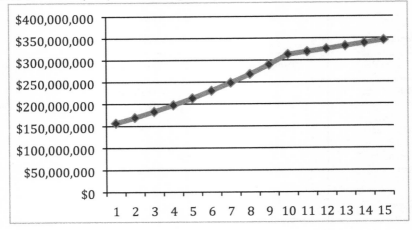

We estimate an Intrinsic Value of: $1,922,992,796

We simply divide Intrinsic Value by the number of total shares outstanding: 20,000,000

$$\$1,922,992,796 \div 20,000,000 = \$96.15$$

Intrinsic Value Per Share: $96.15 / share
Market Price: $42 / share
Margin of Safety: 56.3%
Price-to-Value: 0.437
Bargain: $54.15

If the business passes Buffett and Munger's Four Filters (discussed in Chapter 3), it may be a business on which to spend more time and due diligence. The best investors decline over 99% of potential investments. Don't be swayed by Mr. Market. Remember, Ben Graham taught us, Mr. Market is there to serve you, not to instruct you.

Instead of a market price of $42/share, let's imagine this same business with an overvalued market price of $90 / share. Is it still a bargain? Here's the same "2-stage DCF model" showing the same fundamentals, except for the market price was changed to $90/share.

			Intrinsic	
Market Price	$90.00		Value	$1,922,992,796
Shares			**Intrinsic**	
Outstanding	20,000,000		**Value/Share**	**$96.15**
Growth Rate:			**Margin of**	
Years 1-10	8.00%		**Safety**	**6.4%**
Growth Rate:				
Years 11-15	2.00%		*Price-to-Value*	*0.936*
Discount				
Rate	9.00%		Bargain	$6.15

15-Year: 2-Stage DCF Model

Starting FCF Amount	$145,000,000			
Year 1	$156,600,000	end of year	8.0%	growth
Year 2	$169,128,000	end of year	8.0%	growth
Year 3	$182,658,240	end of year	8.0%	growth
Year 4	$197,270,899	end of year	8.0%	growth
Year 5	$213,052,571	end of year	8.0%	growth
Year 6	$230,096,777	end of year	8.0%	growth
Year 7	$248,504,519	end of year	8.0%	growth
Year 8	$268,384,880	end of year	8.0%	growth
Year 9	$289,855,671	end of year	8.0%	growth
Year 10	$313,044,125	end of year	8.0%	growth
Year 11	$319,305,007	end of year	2.0%	growth
Year 12	$325,691,107	end of year	2.0%	growth
Year 13	$332,204,929	end of year	2.0%	growth
Year 14	$338,849,028	end of year	2.0%	growth
Year 15	$345,626,009	end of year	2.0%	growth

We still estimate an Intrinsic Value of: $1,922,992,796

We still divide Intrinsic Value by the number of total shares outstanding: 20,000,000

$$\$1,922,992,796 \div 20,000,000 = \$96.15$$

Intrinsic Value Per Share is still: $96.15/share
However, the Market Price is now: $90/share *(instead of $42/share)*
Therefore, the following ratios change to...
Margin of Safety: 6.4%
Price-to-Value: 0.936
Bargain: $6.15

In this example, $90/share is not as attractive as $42/share. Remember there are three ways to invest... when the business is either:

• Overvalued

• Fairly valued

• Undervalued

Obviously, it's best to invest in wonderful businesses when they are undervalued. What do we do when wonderful businesses pass the first three of Buffett and Munger's Four Filters, but are selling for higher market prices and lower margins of safety? In these overvalued cases, we wait, make a note, or set an alert to inform us if/when the business ever trades in a lower price range offering a wider margin of safety (and lower market price).

9.9 Minimum Growth Threshold (MGT):

Minimum Growth Threshold (MGT) is a newer concept introduced to the field of value investing. It's a variation or expansion on John Burr Williams' Discounted Cash Flow (DCF) model. The concept of MGT functions similarly to the concept of Minimum Safety Threshold (MST) introduced earlier in this chapter, where the investor chooses his minimum margin of safety, and we solve for the missing intrinsic value or intrinsic value per share.

MGT allows the investor to calculate which minimum growth rate for each cash flow in each time period is necessary to arrive at the minimum margin of safety.

For example, in a DCF analysis, inputs to the DCF model that investors provide are cash flows for each time period, discount rate, and growth rate. If the investor requires a 50% Margin of Safety (MOS), the MGT is the minimum growth rate the business must sustain in order to achieve the minimum required "margin of safety," which in this case is 50%. *Also refer to the Minimum Safety Threshold (MST) example earlier in this chapter.*

To illustrate this concept we'll use a 2-stage DCF model with one growth rate for years 1–10, and another growth rate for years 11–15. For this example, enter the following cash flows into your DCF model. Download a free two-stage DCF model at: ProValueSource.com

EXAMPLE #1: MGT

With a total starting free cash flow amount of $46,000,000, and 28,581,110 total shares outstanding, the starting Free Cash Flow amount is $1.77 (per share). Stock price: $8.75 per share. For this example, use a conservative discount rate of 9%. Then, apply a growth rate of 10% for years 1–10 and a terminal growth rate of 2% for years 11–15. We estimate the following annual cash flows (per share) as follows:

	Cash Flows 10% growth rate	MGT 4.78% Minimum Growth Threshold
Year 1:	$1.77	$1.69
Year 2:	$1.95	$1.77
Year 3:	$2.14	$1.85
Year 4:	$2.36	$1.94
Year 5:	$2.59	$2.03
Year 6:	$2.85	$2.13
Year 7:	$3.14	$2.23
Year 8:	$3.45	$2.34
Year 9:	$3.80	$2.45
Year 10:	$4.17	$2.57
Year 11:	$4.26	$2.62
Year 12:	$4.34	$2.67
Year 13:	$4.43	$2.72
Year 14:	$4.52	$2.78
Year 15:	$4.61	$2.83

Next, this is where MGT gets interesting. At which minimum growth rate would this investment meet our minimum margin of safety (MOS) of 50%? Answer: 4.78%. If we were to require a minimum margin of safety (MOS) of 50%, this investment meets our minimum margin of safety requirement, because this investment's margin of safety is 63.52%, which is above our minimum required 50% margin of safety (MOS). See diagram below.

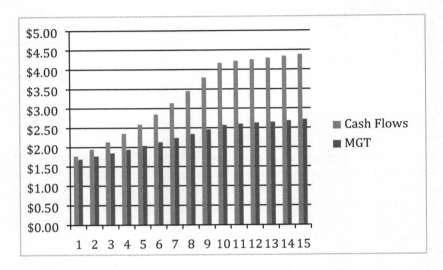

As the diagram shows, the Free Cash Flow growth rate of 10% (for years 1–10) exceeds the Minimum Growth Threshold (MGT) Free Cash Flow growth rate of 4.78% (for years 1–10). In other words, 10% is higher than 4.78%, which exceeds the minimum required margin of safety (MOS), which in this case is 50%.

The 10% growth rate is higher than the MGT of 4.78%, so this investment exceeds our minimum required margin of safety (MOS). Note: Be certain to weigh all qualitative and quantitative factors before investing.

EXAMPLE #2: MGT

This is an example of an investment that does NOT meet the minimum (MGT) test, and is below the minimum required margin of safety (MOS).

With a total starting free cash flow amount of $149,000,000, and 81,000,000 total shares outstanding, the starting Free Cash Flow amount is $1.84 (per share). Market price is $13.75 per share. For this example, use a conservative discount rate of 9%.

Then, apply a growth rate of 5% for years 1–10 and a terminal growth rate of 2% for years 11–15. We estimate the following annual cash flows (per share) as follows:

	Cash Flows	**MGT**
	5% growth rate	_9.91% Minimum Growth Threshold_
Year 1:	$1.93	$2.02
Year 2:	$2.03	$2.22
Year 3:	$2.13	$2.44
Year 4:	$2.24	$2.68
Year 5:	$2.35	$2.95
Year 6:	$2.47	$3.24
Year 7:	$2.59	$3.56
Year 8:	$2.72	$3.92
Year 9:	$2.85	$4.31
Year 10:	$3.00	$4.73
Year 11:	$3.06	$4.83
Year 12:	$3.12	$4.92
Year 13:	$3.18	$5.02
Year 14:	$3.24	$5.12
Year 15:	$3.31	$5.22

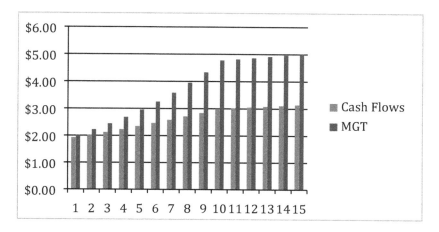

As the diagram shows, the Cash Flows do NOT exceed the Minimum Growth Threshold (MGT) and does NOT achieve the minimum required margin of safety (MOS), which in this example is 50%. Cash Flows growing from years 1–10 at a growth rate of 5%, while the Minimum Growth Threshold (MGT) for years 1–10 is 9.91%. The 5% growth rate is not higher than the MGT of 9.91%, so this investment does not exceed our minimum required margin of safety (MOS), and may not be suitable for investment.

For these examples, if the growth rate were to be exactly matching the MGT, then the margin of safety would be exactly met. The Minimum Growth Threshold (MGT) can be very useful in determining the minimum required growth rate necessary for a potential investment to achieve its minimum required margin of safety, (in this example is 50%).

One practical application of MGT is to quantitatively measure the percentage difference between FCF growth rate and the MGT. For instance, if the MGT for a potential investment were to be only 2%, and its growth rate were to be 12%, investors could rank businesses according to the percentage spread between the MGT and the growth rate. This could help investors rank businesses with highest margins of safety (MOS) in order from best to worst.

The MGT will vary for each potential investment depending on factors such as current stock price, free cash flows, number of time periods in the DCF model, discount rate, and growth rates for years 1–10, and terminal growth rates for years 11–15.

As a general rule, investments with high growth rates, and low MGTs have wide margins of safety, and may perform better than investments with lower margins of safety. There are always exceptions, however, these businesses tend to be the most undervalued, and "spring-loaded." As always, beware of value traps. Don't rely on quantitative analysis alone. Be sure to consider other important qualitative and quantitative factors.

It's important to note many blue chip large cap stocks (stocks with large market capitalizations) rarely trade for 50% margins of safety. It is usually the small-cap and mid-cap businesses that are more likely to temporarily trade at 50% margins of safety (MOS).

"It's better to buy a wonderful business at a fair price, than a fair business at a wonderful price." Charlie Munger and Warren Buffett, Berkshire Hathaway

Therefore, when investing in large cap businesses, as Warren Buffett and Charlie Munger did, they invested when the margins of safety for these large cap businesses were around 25%–33%. Large cap stocks tend to be more stable, and experience less volatility than small cap and mid cap stocks. Therefore, it is up to each investor to establish their own minimum margin of safety (MOS). MGT is a great way to measure the minimum Free Cash Flow (FCF) growth rate required to attain the minimum required margin of safety (MOS) using a Discounted Cash Flow (DCF) Analysis valuation process.

John Burr Williams wrote about Discounted Cash Flow (DCF) analysis back in 1938 in his book, "The Theory of Investment Value." Fortunately, while standing on the shoulders of value investing forefathers, like John Burr Williams, Ben Graham, etc., I humbly submit the concept of Minimum Growth Threshold (MGT) to the value investing community.

It's my hope MGT will continue to evolve and expand in its practical use and range of application. It allows investors to measure the minimum required Free Cash Flow growth rate in order to attain the minimum margin of safety (MOS). In turn, this can help investors earn higher returns, with wider margins of safety, and less risk, based on the intrinsic valuation of the underlying asset.

In 2013, we are the third generation of value investors. Benjamin Graham's generation was the first. Warren Buffett's generation was the second, and my generation is the third generation of value investors.

Value investors like Warren Buffett, Charlie Munger, Phil Fisher, Seth Klarman, and others, expanded on Ben Graham's original value investing strategies, and contributed immensely to the field of value investing.

The wide range of applications of the Minimum Growth Threshold (MGT) continues to be developed. I invite value investors to explore and develop this concept of Minimum Growth Threshold (MGT) and further expand its wide range of applications.

9.10 Warren Buffett's Two-Column Method:

In Berkshire Hathaway's 2010 Annual Report on page 6, Warren Buffett updated his magical, "Two-Column Valuation Method," also called the "Two-Column Method." (Buffett later republished his updated Two-Column Method on page 99 of the 2011 Annual Report, and on page 104 of his 2012 Annual Report). Here's what Warren Buffett wrote:

BERKSHIRE HATHAWAY INC. INTRINSIC VALUE – TODAY AND TOMORROW *

Though Berkshire's intrinsic value cannot be precisely calculated, two of its three key pillars can be measured. Charlie and I rely heavily on these measurements when we make our own estimates of Berkshire's value.

COLUMN #1: The first component of value is our investments – stocks, bonds and cash equivalents. At yearend these totaled $158 billion at market value.

Insurance float – money we temporarily hold in our insurance operations that does not belong to us – funds $66 billion of our investments. This float is "free" as long as insurance underwriting breaks even, meaning that the premiums we receive equal the losses and expenses we incur. Of course, underwriting results are volatile, swinging erratically between profits and losses. Over our entire history, though, we've been significantly profitable, and I also expect us to average breakeven results or better in the future. If we do that, all of our investments – those funded both by float and by retained earnings – can be viewed as an element of value for Berkshire shareholders.

COLUMN #2: Berkshire's second component of value is earnings. This comes from sources other than investments and insurance underwriting. These earnings are delivered by our 68 non-insurance businesses, itemized on page 106. In Berkshire's early years, we focused on the investment side. During the past two decades, however, we've increasingly emphasized the development of earnings from non-insurance businesses, a practice that will continue.

The following tables illustrate this shift. In the first table, we present per-share investments at decade intervals beginning in 1970, three years after we entered the insurance business. We exclude those investments applicable to minority interests. *(Table: COLUMN #1)*

Yearend	Per Share Investments	Period	Compounded Annual Increase in Per-Share Investments
1970	$66		
1980	$754	1970-1980	27.5%
1990	$7,798	1980-1990	26.3%
2000	$50,229	1990-2000	20.5%
2010	$94,730	2000-2010	6.6%

Though our compounded annual increase in per-share investments was a healthy 19.9% over the 40-year period, our rate of increase has slowed sharply as we have focused on using funds to buy operating businesses.

The payoff from this shift is shown in the following table, which illustrates how pre-tax earnings of our non-insurance businesses have increased, on a per-share basis and after applicable minority interests have been excluded. *(Table: COLUMN #2)*

Year	Per-Share Pre-Tax Earnings	Period	Compounded Annual Increase in Per-Share Pre-Tax Earnings
1970	$2.87		
1980	$19.01	1970–1980	20.8%
1990	$102.58	1980–1990	18.4%
2000	$918.66	1990–2000	24.5%
2010	$5,926.04	2000–2010	20.5%

For the forty years, our compounded annual gain in pre-tax, non-insurance earnings per share is 21.0%. During the same period, Berkshire's stock price increased at a rate of 22.1% annually. Over time, you can expect our stock price to move in rough tandem with Berkshire's investments and earnings. Market price and intrinsic value often follow very different paths – sometimes for extended periods – but eventually they meet.

There is a third, more subjective, element to an intrinsic value calculation that can be either positive or negative; the efficacy with which retained earnings will be deployed in the future. We, as well as many other businesses, are likely to retain earnings over the next decade that will equal, or even exceed, the capital we presently employ. Some businesses will turn these retained dollars into fifty-cent pieces, others into two-dollar bills.

This, "what-will-they-do-with-the-money" factor must always be evaluated along with the "what-do-we-have-now" calculation in order for us, or anybody, to arrive at a sensible estimate of a business's intrinsic value. That is because an outside investor stands by helplessly as management reinvests its share of the business's earnings. If a CEO can be expected to do his job well, the reinvestment prospects add to the business's current value. If the CEO's talents or motives are suspect, today's value must be discounted. The difference in outcome can be huge. A dollar of then-value in the hands of Sears Roebuck's or Montgomery Ward's CEOs in the late 1960s had a far different destiny than did a dollar entrusted to Sam Walton.

Reproduced from Berkshire Hathaway Inc. 2010 Annual Report.

"Intrinsic value is an estimate rather than a precise figure, and it is additionally an estimate that must be changed if interest rates move or forecasts of future cash flows are revised. Two people looking at the same set of facts, moreover — and this would apply even to Charlie and me — will almost inevitably come up with at least slightly different intrinsic value figures." Warren Buffett

---

How does Warren Buffett's "Two-Column Method" work?

First, determine the "Per-Share Investments" amount for the most recent year. In Buffett's Annual Report, let's use $94,730. Next, determine the "Per-Share Pre-Tax Earnings" for the most recent year. In Buffett's Annual Report, let's use $5,926.04. Next, determine which multiple to apply to the "Per-Share Pre-Tax Earnings." Choose a multiple to apply this to what other similar businesses show, within the same industry.

Pre-Tax Earnings can also be referred to as Operating Earnings, which are found on the Income Statement. Pre-Tax Earnings are also referred to as EBIT, or Earnings Before Interest and Taxes.

If stock prices of businesses are currently trading at a multiple of Pre-Tax Earnings of 10, then for this example let's use 10 as our multiple we'll apply to Pre-Tax Earnings.

Therefore, if Pre-Tax Earnings are $5,926.04, and we multiple this amount by our multiple of 10, then this equals $59,260.40.

$$\$5,926.04 \times 10 = \$59,260.40$$

Next, we add the business's Per-Share Investments to this amount. Therefore,

$$\$94,730 + \$59,260.40 = \$153,990.40$$

Similarly, if we were to apply a different multiple to Berkshire Hathaway's 2010 Pre-Tax Earnings of $5,926.04, we would arrive at a different estimated intrinsic value. For instance, if we were to use a multiple of 12 (instead of 10), then…

$$\$5,926.04 \times 12 = \$71,112.48$$

Next, if we were to add Berkshire's 2010 Per-Share Investments of $94,730 to $71,112.48, Berkshire Hathaway's estimated intrinsic value at the end of 2010 would be $165,842.48.

$$\$94,730 + \$71,112.48 = \$165,842.48$$

Therefore, using Warren Buffett's "Two-Column Method," the intrinsic value of Berkshire Hathaway at the end of 2010 could be estimated to be somewhere between $153,990.40 and $165,842.48. Comparatively,

Berkshire Hathaway's stock price on December 31, 2010 closed at $120,450, well below its underlying intrinsic value.

"Market price and intrinsic value often follow very different paths — sometimes for extended periods — but eventually they meet." Warren Buffett

"Wall Street is more concerned with correlation than valuation." Scott Thompson

"It's better to be approximately right, than precisely wrong." Warren Buffett

Obviously, the key to mastering Buffett's "Two-Column Method" is correctly calculating Per-Share Investments, selecting an appropriate multiple to apply to Pre-Tax Earnings, and accurately combining these two amounts together to arrive at an estimated intrinsic value.

On one occasion when I met Warren Buffett, I mentioned that John Burr Williams' valuation method of using Discounted Cash Flows (DCF) of Free Cash Flows (FCF) to calculate intrinsic value worked well for some business valuations, but not for others. We also discussed Graham's Net Net Working Capital (NNWC) method, and Buffett's newer "Two-Column Method."

I find Warren to be very genuine and down-to-earth. He has not changed despite his success. During our interaction, we were joking, laughing, and just enjoying the conversation. We discussed many topics, including his past valuation methods and current "Two-Column Method." I find him to be brilliant, and yet having a warm, welcoming personality with a great sense of humor.

Warren and Charlie have developed a simple yet powerful "Four Filters investment process." Buffett's "Two-Column Valuation Method" relates to Filter #4 (price/value) of their powerful "Four Filters investment process." You should know and understand all four investment filters, and not just "Filter #4," relating to quantitative valuation. See Chapter 3 for more information.

Buffett's decision to publish his "Two Column Method" publicly for the first time in his 2010 annual report has gone relatively unnoticed. Value investors can benefit enormously by studying Buffett's "Two Column Method." I'm glad to be one of the few authors to explain it.

CHAPTER TEN:

What Is Risk?

10.1 Defining Risk:

Most people think of risk as the probability of something happening or not happening. How do you measure risk? Over 90% of Wall Street financial firms use Modern Portfolio Theory (MPT) to measure "risk" as "volatility." Is risk the same as volatility? Or is true risk the risk of losing your money? Value investors believe risk is not the same as volatility, and instead believe that risk is actually the risk of possibly losing your money.

Billionaire value investors Warren Buffett and Charlie Munger agree they'd rather earn a 30% gain even if the stock price experienced volatility, than a 3% return from a security that experienced less volatility. If value investors hold their investments for longer time periods, they pay less attention to inevitable short-term volatility and fluctuating market prices.

Most Wall Street firms measure risk as "price volatility." This is the reason so many Wall Street firms often downgrade a stock. In other words, Modern Portfolio Theory (MPT) practitioners measure price volatility as "risk," making stocks that have fallen significantly in price, too "risky" to recommend to clients.

Conversely, billionaire value investor Warren Buffett would likely invest in a stock after its price falls and is downgraded. Value investors prefer lower prices and more attractive valuations. Wall Street firms operate based on Modern Portfolio Theory (MPT), so value investors are often branded as "contrarians," since they appear to be going "against" the market.

"To invest successfully, you need not understand beta, efficient markets, modern portfolio theory, option pricing or emerging markets. You may, in fact, be better off knowing nothing of these. That, of course, is not the prevailing view at most business schools, whose finance curriculum tends to be dominated by such subjects. In our view, though, investment students need only two well-taught courses – How to Value a Business, and How to Think About Market Prices." Warren Buffett

10.2 Value Investing vs. MPT, CAPM, EMH:

Stock Price	Value Investing	Modern Portfolio Theory (MPT)
$100	High Risk	Low Risk
$50	Lower Risk	Higher Risk
$1	Lowest Risk	Highest Risk

Modern Portfolio Theory (MPT) views "risk" as volatility. MPT does not put as much consideration into the business's fundamentals or economic developments. Conversely, value investors view "risk" as the threat of losing money. Volatility can be the friend of the value investor, if we wait to buy when market prices are low. In MPT, Ben Graham's principles of "margin-of-safety" and "price-to-value" are completely ignored, as if a business selling at $50/share is somehow "riskier" than the same business selling at $100/share!

"As long as Wall Street continues to implement Modern Portfolio Theory (MPT) and focus on short-term results, attractive price-to-value dislocations will occur from which value investors can profit." Scott Thompson

Each investor's tolerance for volatility is different. Determine if you would rather earn a volatile 30% or a smooth 3%. Select investments appropriate for your level of volatility tolerance. More importantly, focus on underlying value, not on price.

"Modern Portfolio Theory (MPT), Capital Asset Pricing Model (CAPM), and Efficient Market Hypothesis (EMH) are beautiful equations that don't necessarily equate to the real world." Scott Thompson

10.3 Volatility Is Not Risk:

In this example, the intrinsic value is $100. How does Value Investing differ from Modern Portfolio Theory (MPT), Capital Asset Pricing Model (CAPM), and Efficient Market Hypothesis (EMH)? If the intrinsic value of a stock price is $100, value investors view the $100 stock price as being "fairly valued." Any deviation from this $100 stock price is viewed as volatility by MPT, CAPM, and EMH. Therefore, when a stock price experiences downward volatility, such as a $100 stock going to $50/share, then MPT, CAPM, and EMH view this volatility as increased risk.

"Wall Street is more concerned with correlation than valuation." Scott Thompson

However, value investors view this same volatility differently. Value investors do not view volatility as risk. Instead, value investors view this same volatility as opportunity. For instance, if a fairly valued stock with an intrinsic value of $100 and a market price of $100, suddenly decreased to $50/share, value investors may view this as a buying opportunity to own a $100/share business at only $50/share. (See diagram below).

For this diagram: Assume intrinsic value is $100/share

Stock Price	Value Investing	Modern Portfolio Theory (MPT)
$100	High Risk	Low Risk
$50	Lower Risk	Higher Risk
$1	Lowest Risk	Highest Risk

Similarly, let's say you were shopping for a home to buy. The intrinsic value of the home is $100,000. Suddenly the Seller needs cash fast, and decides to sell it for $50,000. As a value investor, you immediately know the new distressed $50,000 price is half of what the home's intrinsic value is worth ($100,000).

However, the equations of MPT, CAPM, and EMH, all suggest that the new $50,000 price for the home worth $100,000 is higher risk, due to the volatility of $50,000 being farther away from the original $100,000 price.

Value investors would consider buying a $100,000 home for $100,000 as "high risk" because the home would be "fairly valued." However, MPT views buying a $100,000 home for $100,000 as "low risk" due to the low volatility of $100,000 being close (exactly) to $100,000. Value investors would much rather buy the $100,000 home for $50,000, as this would create a 50% margin of safety in this investment. However, MPT investors would perceive buying a $100,000 home for $50,000 as too risky, due to the wide amount of volatility.

Therefore, if you could buy the $100,000 home for only $50,000, would you be a value investor and buy it? Or, would you miss this great investment opportunity because you subscribe to MPT, CAPM, and EMH? The choice is yours. (See diagram below).

For this diagram: Assume intrinsic value is $100k

Home Price	Value Investing	Modern Portfolio Theory (MPT)
$100k	High Risk	Low Risk
$50k	Lower Risk	Higher Risk
$1k	Lowest Risk	Highest Risk

"Basing investment decisions on volatility or anything other than valuation is foolish."
Scott Thompson

"Some erroneously believe that stocks are somehow magically exempt from the laws of valuation." *Scott Thompson*

"Wise value investors know stocks, homes, cars, etc. are sold based on valuation, and can profit from dislocations between price and value caused by Sellers who do not know how to properly value the asset they are selling." *Scott Thompson*

During the times I speak publicly about investing, I often begin by holding up a $10 gift card from a local restaurant, and ask the audience who will give me $20 for this $10 gift card? Then I say, "apparently no one wants to overpay when they know the value of the asset. Then why will you overpay in the stock market?!" This fun example quickly enlightens the audience to consider the concepts of value investing.

The lesson is simply to determine the value of the asset <u>before</u> you invest. Investors should obtain a wide margin of safety (MOS), so the asset is purchased for less than its underlying intrinsic value. A margin of safety is necessary because even if the investor ends up being wrong, there is still enough margin of safety so the investor could sell the asset without losing money. Margin of safety is essential to value investing.

Value investing requires discipline and a calm and rational temperament many investors simply do not possess. In financial markets, sometimes no activity is better then hyper activity, and many investors who follow MPT, CAPM, and EMH are simply unable to control their emotions, and unable to refrain from activity in financial markets for long periods of time.

Wall Street tends to be focused on short-term gains. If portfolio managers do not make gains for clients every quarter, then they risk being fired. Warren Buffett's value investing strategies require patience, and his investments often do not make profits over the short-term. However, over the long-term, there is no doubt Warren Buffett and his value investing strategies have outperformed financial markets, which have made him the wealthiest investor in the history of the world.

Now you have developed a better understanding of the differences between value investing and MPT, CAPM, and EMH.

10.4 Doing Smart Things vs. Not Doing Dumb Things:

Many who call themselves investors are actually not investors, but gamblers and speculators. They hope to make quick, short-term profits. However, the results of these gamblers and speculators usually end with large loses, and losing money over the long-term.

Let's compare value investing to a sport like football. Many football games are won or lost because in one brief moment, very smart, talented athletes with years of experience do dumb things, like throw interceptions or fumble the ball resulting in losing the game. If athletes do this several times, their repeated mistakes can cost a smart, talented, athlete his career!

Investing other peoples' money works very much the same way. In one brief moment, very smart investors with years of experience, might invest in dumb things (like investing in overvalued tech stocks at the height of the "dot.com" boom of the late 1990's). Or they may have invested in real estate at the peak of the real estate market just before the crash of 2007.

"It's not just the smart things you do, but the dumb things you don't do that help make you a successful investor." Scott Thompson

Example:

While performing investment research, I discovered a successful U.S.-based business with millions of dollars of cash on their balance sheet. The business was very successful and had enjoyed much success for many years. A smaller European manufacturer approached executives at this company, and pitched them an opportunity to acquire the exclusive global distribution rights to a new technology-based product still in the development phase.

While the executives at the firm were considering distributing this new product, they discovered another business was also pitched distribution rights for this same product. A bidding war ensued with competitive bids from each of these two firms increasing higher and higher. Each firm raised their bids until ultimately the first firm was chosen as the highest bidder.

"The loser in a bidding war is the winner." Scott Thompson

Remember, the product was still in the development phase, and was not even ready for distribution. But executives at the firm congratulated themselves on winning the bid, and wrote the check anyway. They took delivery of thousands of units, and stored them in their warehouse.

Unfortunately, the product never worked properly. Many customers who initially bought the product, returned it after experiencing an excess of technical problems. The U.S.-based firm tried to return the units back to the European manufacturer, but despite promises from the manufacturer to upgrade firmware in the future for free, the European manufacturer went out of business, leaving the U.S. firm stuck with all that inventory of pre-purchased products that did not work.

The product ended up costing the firm millions of dollars in losses. It would've been best if the firm never won the bidding war in the first place. Furthermore, the product was outside of the firm's core business. The executives realized they would've been better off sticking to reinvesting into their core business, instead of trying to expand into another industry they knew nothing about.

Remember our discussions from Chapter 7 about "Net Asset Value (NAV)," and Chapter 8 about "Earnings Power Value (EPV)." The primary objective of management's capital allocation decisions should be for every $1 invested into Net Asset Value (NAV) to generate greater than $1 in Earnings Power Value (EPV).

Unfortunately, in this example, $1 invested into NAV, generated much less than $1 in EPV. The executives learned from their mistake, and have not repeated it.

The point is, as investors we may be fortunate to enjoy years of success. However, we must remain vigilant, avoiding value traps, investments appearing attractive on the surface, but whose underlying economics result in losing money.

Your skills as a value investor are becoming sharper. You are becoming better at recognizing the differences between bad, good, and great investments!

LTCM: Long Term Capital Management

Long-Term Capital Management (LTCM) was one of the largest hedge funds in the world, consisting of the brightest minds of Wall Street and academia. LTCM's upper-management were Nobel Prize winning economists. They programed incredibly complex algorithms into the fastest super computers to crunch enormous amounts of financial data in very short periods of time.

Billions of dollars poured in to LTCM. For years LTCM performed very well. LTCM's fatal mistake was borrowing exorbitant amounts of money on margin. LTCM leveraged themselves up over 100 times the amount of their actual tangible assets. Therefore, even a 1% move downward in the price of an asset would potentially wipe them out.

During the Russian financial crisis of 1998, LTCM sustained terminal losses from which they could not recover. LTCM was forced to liquidate billions in assets. Just like the mythological flight of Icarus, LTCM flew higher and higher toward the sun, until it came crashing downward in an instant! Wall Street was shocked. How could all the Nobel-prize-winning experts manage a fund that went broke? Billions... gone!

Conversely, there is one guy in Omaha implementing value investing strategies. His outcome is... he remains the wealthiest multibillionaire investor in the history of the world. Meanwhile, LTCM's investors sustained astonishing losses, and were forced to liquidate their assets for just pennies on the dollar.

The lesson here is: No matter how many years you are successful with your investments, if you have just one devastating year, anything times 0 is 0. That is exactly what happened to LTCM. This demonstrates the efficacy of "how not doing dumb things" can be more important than doing smart things.

"It's hard to go broke when you don't owe any money." Scott Thompson

"Capital is finite. Invest it wisely." Scott Thompson

"Rule #1 of investing is: Never lose money. Rule #2 is never forget Rule #1." Warren Buffett

CHAPTER ELEVEN:

Temperament

"Many talk about 'Buy low and sell high,' but few actually possess the rational temperament to achieve it." Scott Thompson

11.1 Overview:

Even if you master the quantitative and qualitative principles of value investing, you must learn to control your emotions. Before you can become a successful value investor it is important to discipline yourself with the right mental temperament. Value investing requires patience and a calm temperament. These are qualities many investors claim to possess, but their actions tell a very different story.

Value investors are not "traders." Value investors do not sit in front of computers making trade after trade all day, focused primarily on short-term gains. These are activities day traders engage in, not value investors. Value investors tend to take a longer-term approach to markets primarily focused on longer-term gains. Day traders are very different from value investors.

Many traders do not possess a calm temperament. Instead they often sit in front of their computers watching the financial markets, grinding their teeth, hyper from drinking coffee, energy drinks, and sugar-rich diets. They often watch their favorite financial news shows, making frequent trades in and out of stocks all day long. Frequent trading activity is not the way to get rich. In fact, frequent trading often has the opposite effect on one's portfolio.

Many treat the stock market like a casino, trading in and out of stocks, without first taking the time to carefully evaluate each investment, or the underlying fundamentals of the business. Most value investors make only a small number of investments per year and hold them for long periods, often years. Whereas, day traders often own businesses for just a few hours or days, then trade out of them, only to repeat the frantic process.

Billionaire value investors Warren Buffett and Charlie Munger exemplify rare, calm and patient temperaments that allow them to focus on carefully assessing the merits of a potential value investment, or lack thereof.

Define what your investment criteria is and isn't before you begin your investment search; analyzing businesses, financial statements, data, SEC filings, annual and quarterly reports, and other important information.

"Don't swing at every pitch. Instead wait for the right pitch." Ted Williams

"Know what you're looking for, before you find it." Scott Thompson

Successful value investing requires a patient, calm temperament, an inner confidence, and sense of certainty that an asset's market price will eventually rise to its intrinsic value. Maintaining this inner confidence and fortitude can be challenging during periods of extreme adverse market conditions. However, during adverse market conditions is often the time to put your capital to work.

"Be greedy when others are fearful, and fearful when others are greedy." Benjamin Graham

Value investors must guard against the foolishness of others who may try to assert influence over the value investor to "join the pack" and drift away from the successful core value investing principles that made billionaire investor Warren Buffett the wealthiest investor in the world.

Only a small percentage of Wall Street firms implement successful value investing strategies. The majority of Wall Street firms select investments based on choosing stocks they believe will perform well over the short term, and ignore businesses that are mispriced (undervalued).

Since the majority of Wall Street firms are short-term focused, their short-term activity helps create price dislocations in the markets from which good investors can profit. Since the majority of Wall Street firms are short-term based, asset managers implementing value-investing strategies producing longer-term results, instead of short-term results, are often shown the door before their investments produce long-term results.

Therefore, being a value investor requires the ability to think independently, and not be influenced by the tremendous pressures to follow the herd. As we know, those who follow the herd just end up scraping their shoes. Value investors do not follow the herd. Value investors are independent thinkers who understand how to value businesses and identify temporary price to value dislocations in financial markets.

Value investors are often frugal in their spending habits. Warren Buffett is a great example of how one who has achieved so much financial success is not a frivolous spender. Instead, Warren has chosen to continually reinvest his capital, which, through the law of compounding, has snowballed into a multibillion-dollar fortune.

Ask yourself these questions: Are you a saver? Are you a spender? Do you have a high consumption lifestyle? Do you have a low consumption lifestyle? Do you spend your money as fast as you get it, or even before you get it? Or, are you more like Warren Buffett who keeps his living expenses low, despite his high income, so he can reinvest his capital and earn above-average market returns?

Are you an investor? Do you select your investments based on a careful, intelligent process? Or, are you a gambler? Do you engage in high-risk financial behavior with very high mathematical probability you will lose money? Or, do you carefully select your investments based on a calm, rational, research process, with very high mathematical probability you will earn money? As you can see, temperament plays a major role in whether value investors are financially successful, or not.

"Calculate the certainty of success, before you invest your money." Scott Thompson

Warren Buffett says many investors have been ruined by the two L's… liquor and leverage. When it comes to money, sometimes <u>not</u> doing a stupid thing keeps more money in your pocket than doing a smart thing. A well-known example is the hedge fund Long-Term Capital Management (LTCM). LTCM employed experienced financial professionals, and Nobel Prize winning economists. For a few years, LTCM earned impressive returns for its investors. However, LTCM was highly leveraged, and when the markets turned against them they were financially ruined, forced to liquidate for just pennies on the dollar.

"Know what you're getting into, before you get into it." Scott Thompson

Berkshire Hathaway does not believe in being highly leveraged, and instead maintains very healthy cash balances of several billions of dollars. When the markets experience major downturns, these are often the times when Berkshire Hathaway puts its billions of cash reserves to work, buying shares of high-quality businesses at temporarily distressed prices. This is what value investors do. Buy low, sell high – not the other way around.

"Price is what you pay. Value is what you get." Warren Buffett

11.2 Financial History:

It's important for value investors to read financial history. The psychological reasons motivating human behavior are just as important as a sound analysis and valuation. Most investors do not know about the North Pacific Corner, Holland's Tulip Bulb Craze, and other major events, which caused the stock market to crash. We recommend investors read financial history. Wall Street tends to be shortsighted and quickly forgets its own history. This creates opportunities for intelligent investors to profit.

"Those who cannot remember the past are condemned to repeat it." George Santayana.

"History doesn't repeat itself, but it rhymes." Mark Twain

On the subject of financial history, here's a letter written by Warren Buffett's father Howard Buffett on July 31st 1962, requesting a copy of a book on financial history for his young son, Warren Buffett:

HOWARD BUFFETT
KIEWIT PLAZA
OMAHA 31, NEBRASKA

July 31, 1962

Mr. Murray N. Rothbard
215 West 88th Street
New York 24, N. Y.

Dear Murray:

This is a somewhat belated note of thanks for your kindness in sending me the two volumes of your work, "Man, Economy and State." I have been reading it part time, intending to write you when I had finished my perusal of it. In saying this, I don't mean that I started on page one and am trying to read every word--that would be something less than accurate.

However, I have been enjoying my reading of the second half of Volume II which gets into an area of economy with which I have had at least some experience. And I am in full agreement with Bill Peterson's comments in the WALL STREET JOURNAL this morning, July 31st. As you might guess, it's his review that has triggered this letter to you.

One thing I want to ask is if you have any suggestions on how I might aid in getting circulation or acceptance of your volumes. I assume that they are designed for textbook use in colleges. If that is correct, I will be glad to recommend them to one or two colleges with which I have some slight acquaintance. Please let me know what is being done in the promotion field, and maybe I can make myself helpful.

Somewhere I read that you had written a book on "The Panic of 1819." If this is correct, I would like to know where I can buy a copy of it. I have a son who is a particularly avid reader of books about panics and similar phenomena. I would like to present him with the book referred to.

Perhaps you saw the folder I have enclosed when it appeared in HUMAN EVENTS. Anyway, I think you will like the front page I added to the article itself.

Sincerely yours,

Howard

Howard Buffett

HB:bf Enc

11.3 Which Investments Do You Decline?

Do you say "Yes" to every investment pitched to you? Or, have you pre-defined your investment selection criteria? What specifically, in advance, have you decided that you will say "No" to? For instance, Warren Buffett says "No" to businesses with high debt on their balance sheets.

Do you adhere to a sound investment philosophy, and only invest in those investment opportunities you fully understand? Or, do you foolishly swing at every pitch? Remember Ted Williams, the #1 hitter in the history of baseball. Did Ted Williams swing at every pitch? No. Ted Williams knew in advance, exactly the type of pitch he was waiting for and he'd only swing at those specific pitches.

The diagram (below) shows Ted Williams' strike zone dissection into 77 component zones.

My first rule of hitting was to get a good ball to hit. I learned down to percentage points where those good balls were. The box shows my particular preferences, from what I considered my "happy zone" - where I could hit .400 or better - to the low outside corner - where the most I could hope to bat was .230. Only when the situation demands it should a hitter go for the low-percentage pitch.

Since some players are better high-ball hitters than low-ball hitters, or better outside than in, each batter should work out his own set of percentages. But more important, each should learn the strike zone, because once pitchers find a batter is going to swing at bad pitches he will get nothing else. The strike zone is approximately seven balls wide (allowing for pitches on the corners). When a batter starts swinging at pitches just two inches out of that zone (shaded area), he has increased the pitcher's target from approximately 4.2 square feet to about 5.8 square feet - an increase of 37 percent. Allow a pitcher that much of an advantage and you will be a .250 hitter.

Investment selection is similar to hitting a baseball. You need to start with a good ball to hit. Fortunately, unlike baseball hitters, value investors are not forced to decide whether to swing or not in a split-second! Instead, value investors have the luxury of spending more time to analyze the "pitch." In baseball there are "called strikes" whether the batter swings or not. However, in value investing, there are no called strikes. Value investors can wait until their right pitch arrives. When it does, this is when they step up and swing for the fences.

Many investors on Wall Street cannot resist the temptation to swing at bad pitches. Many don't even know the difference between a good pitch and a bad pitch, because they cannot properly value a business. Others swing at bad pitches, and whisper stocks, knowing they are bad pitches, but cannot resist the temptation to swing.

Investors do not make money on activity. Investors make money on investing in the right securities. However, Wall Street's investment banks do make money off activity, whether clients make money or not. Therefore, for value investors, activity is not the goal. Instead, carefully selecting the right securities is the goal.

"Don't confuse activity with accomplishment." Scott Thompson

Don't swing at every pitch. Instead, wait for the right pitch. Know what you're looking for in advance, before you step up to the plate, and like Ted Williams, your batting average will greatly improve.

11.4 Independent Thinking:

Do you think independently? Or, are you persuaded by the persistent recommendation of others? Warren Buffett lived in New York for a few years early in his career. However, after Buffett's mentor Benjamin Graham retired from the Graham Newman Partnership, Warren moved back to his hometown of Omaha, Nebraska, so he would not be surrounded by the constant "whisper stock" environment and the distractions of New York.

Warren knew he would not be as distracted by as many "whisper stock" suggestions in Omaha, as he would if he were to remain in New York.

Moving back to Omaha turned out to be a great decision for Warren, as he soon formed his "Buffett Partnership." In the first 13 years following founding his "Buffett Partnership" Warren achieved an average of 23.17% annual returns for investors. In fact, $100 invested into the Buffett Partnership during the first year would be worth $1,502 at the end of the 13th year. Compare Buffett's stellar performance with that of investing the same $100 into the Dow Jones industrial index. The same $100 would've grown to only $152. Warren Buffett exemplifies the advantages of independent thinking. Don't succumb to external pressure. Think independently.

Remember, only single-digit percentages of investors actually adhere to strict value investment philosophies. Therefore, there are an abundance of Wall Street professionals who persistently volunteer their latest stock pick, but you must remain strong and adhere to your successful value investing philosophy. Remember, they are focused on short-term results (if any), whereas you're focused on longer-term stellar results.

11.5 Opportunity Cost:

Another important aspect of investing is the "opportunity cost." To say yes to one thing often requires saying no to another. Value investors have finite amounts of capital to invest, not infinite amounts. Therefore, value investors must examine hundreds or even thousands of potential investments, and choose the best one.

For example, if you invest your limited money to earn only a 5% return, you may have missed a better investment opportunity that may pay a 10% return. Therefore, before value investors commit their hard-earned capital, they must evaluate the full spectrum of available investment opportunities, rank them in order, and invest only into the best investments first. Value investors must make optimal investing decisions, and not randomly invest finite capital without considering "opportunity cost." This way, you can achieve optimal results, instead of only mediocre results, or worse.

Before value investors invest in high return investments, value investors should mentally commit their capital to be invested for the long-term. This way, investors will not liquidate their investment positions at inopportune times when market prices may be trading below intrinsic value, towards the lower end of its 52-week price volatility range.

Charlie Munger says that all intelligent people make investment decisions based on their own individual opportunity costs. For example, if Warren Buffett were to be pitched a potential investment opportunity in an emerging market, Warren would not deem it a better investment than adding to his existing position in Wells Fargo (WFC). Buffett understands Wells Fargo's business, its sustainable competitive advantages, its management team, and his position in its stock. This is an example of opportunity cost, because it's like Warren saying, "Don't pitch me anything else, unless its better than buying more shares of Wells Fargo."

It doesn't matter to Warren where the opportunity is. He has no preconceived ideas about whether Berkshire's money ought to be in this or that. Warren is simply scanning the world trying to get his opportunity cost as high as possible, so his individual decisions will be better. Because Warren's new investment decisions must be better than his existing opportunity cost.

11.6 Berkshire's Culture:

Berkshire Hathaway possesses a culture of exceptional integrity respected by the business world, but it's much more than that. Warren Buffett worked his entire life to build the high-integrity brand, culture, and reputation of Berkshire Hathaway. Berkshire's high-trust culture empowers managers to remain more autonomous and decentralized in their decision-making process. As a result, Berkshire attracts clients, and it closes deals that otherwise would not have closed.

Berkshire Hathaway is run by capable and trustworthy managers who produce superior results. However, not many people understand Berkshire's unique culture. Berkshire's culture is based on four pillars of honesty, integrity, professionalism, and trustworthiness.

Warren Buffett has created an exemplary business culture where experienced managers do the right thing, even when no one is looking. Berkshire's managers are advised to prioritize reputation over money. Warren confirmed this when he testified during the Solomon Brothers trial. "Lose money and I will be understanding. But lose one shred of reputation and I will be ruthless."

Preserving Berkshire's unique culture is so vital to Warren, he established a succession plan where his son Howard Buffett would become non-executive Chairman of the Board to preserve Berkshire's culture.

To better understand Berkshire Hathaway's culture, we can draw an analogy from Ben Graham's concept of "intrinsic value vs. market price." Think of Berkshire's reputation as its intrinsic value, while Berkshire's monetary success is its outward appearance, similar to market price. In other words, Berkshire's culture is its "inner scoreboard," and Berkshire's profitability is its "outer scoreboard."

Warren makes certain Berkshire's balance sheet remains rock solid maintaining at least a $10 billion minimum balance on Berkshire's balance sheet at all times. Warren insists on remaining absolutely certain Berkshire's checks will clear, especially to disabled beneficiaries who rely on receiving insurance checks from Berkshire.

Furthermore, Warren never speculates on risky investments or acquisitions that would jeopardize Berkshire's unwavering ability to pay its contractual obligations. In other words, Warren Buffett makes sure Berkshire Hathaway remains the standard to which others aspire.

Warren's integrity is so high he says, "If I shake your hand, we have a deal." This is commendable and reminiscent of the days when deals were done with only a handshake. If more people were like Buffett who keeps his word no matter what, the business world would be a better place. Let us make no mistake that the world we live in is less than perfect. Therefore, it is even more imperative Berkshire's culture is preserved to remain the shining example of integrity.

We must remember that *our* reputations are also more important than money. As investors, we should only engage in behaviors consistent with building reputations of integrity. Due to its reputation, Berkshire is more successful than other businesses. This enables Berkshire to do deals that others cannot. For instance, when a highly profitable family business is considering a sale of their business to Berkshire, the family must think of the future legacy of the business. This is important because they value their relationships with employees and loyal customers.

Berkshire managers must be able to look these business owners in the eye, and determine if they love the money or the business. It's okay to love the money some, but they must love the business. After Warren buys a business, he relies on its current management team to remain in place to run and grow the business.

I grew up in an American middle-class family with mid-western values similar to that of Warren and his family. My father also taught me that value of a dollar by reminding us to turn off lights when not in use. Phrases like, *"Close the door, I'm not paying to heat the outside!"* were commonly heard while I was growing up. With our similar backgrounds, I understand why Warren has not spent his money, and gave 99% of it away to charity. (See Chapter 16) Berkshire Hathaway's culture is rare and very special. Warren has done an excellent job building it, and I believe Warren's children will do an excellent job preserving it.

11.7 Inner Scorecard vs. Outer Scorecard:

Ask yourself the following two questions to determine if you're Inner Scorecard focused, or Outer Scorecard focused. Would you rather be the world's best chef and no one knew it? Or would you rather be the world's worst chef, but everyone thinks you're the best?

Those who are more focused on learning their craft and doing the work everyday to improve themselves are Inner Scorecard Focused. Those who are more focused on publicity and what others think of them, instead of actually learning their craft and doing the work everyday to improve themselves are Outer Scorecard Focused.

Few would admit to themselves they are Outer Scorecard focused. Take a close look at your behavior and determine if you need to make changes to your life. Warren Buffett loves reading financial statements, annual reports, and valuing businesses. He does not do it for the publicity. The money *followed* Warren Buffett, but it never *led*. Warren says he, "tap dances to work every morning" because he loves his job so much. It is not because of the money, but for the love of his business.

"We enjoy the process far more than the proceeds, though I have learned to live with those also." Warren Buffett

We tend to judge others by their behavior and ourselves by our intentions. However, if we were to judge ourselves by our actual actions and not by our intentions, this is the start of taking responsibility, becoming a better value investor, and choosing the path of being Inner Scorecard-focused, instead of Outer Scorecard-focused.

Being a successful value investor like Warren Buffett requires hours of diligent research, analysis, valuations, and reading annual reports, etc., every day, day after day, month after month, year after year. Like the story of The Little Red Hen, many would love the big reward, but very few are willing to actually do the work!

Establish good habits early. Becoming a successful value investor is like going to the gym. You can't just *think* about lifting weights and get healthy. You actually need to do the work! Someone once said, "Success is 10% inspiration and 90% perspiration."

"The chains of habit are too light to be felt, until they are too heavy to be broken."
Warren Buffett

11.8 Selective Contrarian:

Warren Buffett calls himself a "Selective Contrarian Value Investor." This means he looks for those wonderfully profitable businesses that are selling at a significant discount to their intrinsic value, with an adequate margin of safety. Remember, just because a stock price falls precipitously does not mean you should automatically buy it. Price is part of it, but it is not all about market price alone. It is about fundamentals and the intrinsic valuation of the underlying business.

The term "selective" is important in the phrase "selective contrarian," because it's not just about investing in opposite ways from other investors. Instead, it's about investing in what earns money.

"You are neither right nor wrong because the crowd disagrees with you. You are right because your data and reasoning are right." Warren Buffett and Charlie Munger

Analysts on Wall Street downgrade publicly traded businesses for many reasons. If a business within a particular sector faces regulatory, legal, or other major issues, the share prices of other businesses within this same sector may also fall, even if there is nothing wrong with the business. This can create potentially attractive price to value dislocations. It is the job of the value investor to identify which businesses within a particular sector are most likely to recover and succeed.

What causes price to value dislocations in financial markets? Traders and speculators focused on short-term results. Over time securities become mispriced, and this is when value investors can buy shares of high-quality businesses at attractive prices.

As long as universities continue to teach Modern Portfolio Theory (MPT), Capital Asset Pricing Model (CAPM), Efficient Market Hypothesis (EMH), they will continue to turn out new young Wall Street professionals focused on short-term results. This in turn, will perpetuate the existence of Price-to-Value dislocations in financial markets, from which value investors will profit.

11.9 Donating, Gambling, Speculating, vs. Investing:

It's important to draw clear distinctions between donation, gambling, speculation, and investing. Many who believe they are investing are actually donating!

• Donating refers to giving money away and expecting no financial benefit in return. Philanthropists give money away to help others in need. However, in the financial world, some investors believe they're investing when actually they are about to make an unintentional donation. This occurs when investors invest in overvalued businesses. The stock price often drops. Investors panic-sell, and realize too late they have just made an unintentional donation. This is not investing.

• Gambling is engaging in high-risk behavior with hope of winning money based on luck. Again, the end result is often an unintentional donation. Casinos are known for gambling. Buffett and Munger do not gamble. Gambling is not investing.

• Speculation is engaging in risky financial transactions, attempting to earn a short-term profit. Speculators often risk what they have for something they don't need. There is usually little to no financial analysis in unintelligent speculation. Most retail "investors" in the stock market are at this stage, and do not perform a thorough analysis of the businesses in which they invest.

• Intelligent Speculation is a gray area between unintelligent speculation and investing. These investors perform a moderate amount of analysis, but still don't know all the facts before committing capital.

• Investing is performing a thorough analysis on the underlying business and achieving clear tangible results. Buffett and Munger's "Four Filters" Investment Process is an example of a sound investing strategy. Ben Graham defined the process of investing as requiring:
- Diligent analysis
- Margin of safety
- Adequate return

If an investment process does not possess these three requirements, Ben Graham would deem it speculative. Few investors actually invest. Fewer investors actually achieve consistent compounded returns, year after year. Which of these best describes you? Which of these would you like to evolve to?

11.10 Law of Compounding:

The "Law of Compounding" is the ability of smaller amounts to grow exponentially into becoming exorbitantly large quantities. A Chinese parable helps us understand the power of the law of compounding. A king once offered to compensate a servant in his kingdom after the servant performed a good deed for the king. The king was so pleased with the servant that the king offered to grant him whatever he'd like for compensation. The servant, whose math skills exceeded those of the king, asked the king for the following compensation:

"Oh great King, please grant me just 1 grain of rice on the first checkerboard square. On the next square, double the amount of rice of the previous square. Continue to double the amount of rice onto the next square, until the end of the checkerboard. Then my compensation will be the total amount of rice at the end of the checkerboard." The king laughed because the servant did not ask for gold, jewels, or other lavish compensation. The king thought the servant's request was a pittance, and immediately granted the servant's request. The King did not realize there are not enough grains of rice in the world. Unlike the King, the clever servant understood the power of the law of compounding.

Here's how the servant turned just 1 grain of rice into 9,223,372,036,854,780,000. A checkerboard has 64 squares. One grain of rice on first square "doubled" on each square throughout all 64 squares, until the end of the checkerboard yields the following results:

1)	1
2)	2
3)	4
4)	8
5)	16
6)	32
7)	64
8)	128
9)	256
10)	512
11)	1,024
12)	2,048
13)	4,096
14)	8,192
15)	16,384
16)	32,768
17)	65,536
18)	131,072
19)	262,144
20)	524,288
21)	1,048,576
22)	2,097,152
23)	4,194,304
24)	8,388,608
25)	16,777,216
26)	33,554,432
27)	67,108,864

28)	134,217,728
29)	268,435,456
30)	536,870,912
31)	1,073,741,824
32)	2,147,483,648
33)	4,294,967,296
34)	8,589,934,592
35)	17,179,869,184
36)	34,359,738,368
37)	68,719,476,736
38)	137,438,953,472
39)	274,877,906,944
40)	549,755,813,888
41)	1,099,511,627,776
42)	2,199,023,255,552
43)	4,398,046,511,104
44)	8,796,093,022,208
45)	17,592,186,044,416
46)	35,184,372,088,832
47)	70,368,744,177,664
48)	140,737,488,355,328
49)	281,474,976,710,656
50)	562,949,953,421,312
51)	1,125,899,906,842,620
52)	2,251,799,813,685,250
53)	4,503,599,627,370,500
54)	9,007,199,254,740,990
55)	18,014,398,509,482,000
56)	36,028,797,018,964,000
57)	72,057,594,037,927,900
58)	144,115,188,075,856,000
59)	288,230,376,151,712,000
60)	576,460,752,303,423,000
61)	1,152,921,504,606,850,000
62)	2,305,843,009,213,690,000
63)	4,611,686,018,427,390,000
64)	9,223,372,036,854,780,000

A similar example is, if you were to invest $1,000 into a business that experiences ten 2-for-1 stock-splits over the next 10 years, it would grow into over $1,000,000. Many receptionists working at Microsoft during the 1990's retired early from their MSFT employee stock options worth over $1,000,000.

Here's how it works: Starting with an initial investment of just $1,000, and the stock of a business doubling every year for 10 years would yield the following results: *(starting amount: $1,000)*

Year 1	$2,000
Year 2	$4,000
Year 3	$8,000
Year 4	$16,000
Year 5	$32,000
Year 6	$64,000
Year 7	$128,000
Year 8	$256,000
Year 9	$512,000
Year10	$1,024,000

Billionaire value investor, Warren Buffett, grew his net worth through the Law of Compounding. Warren Buffett started delivering newspapers as a boy, saved the little bit of money he earned, and invested it wisely through Value Investing. To better understand the Law of Compounding, if you put just $1 on a checkerboard square, and doubled it on every square until the end of the checkerboard, there would be $9.2 quintillion at the end of the checkerboard. This is more money than there is in the world.

Even if you start with just <u>1 penny</u> on the first square, there would be $92,233,720,368,547,800   (or $92.2 quadrillion) at the end of the checkerboard!

"I buy dollars for 50 cents." Warren Buffett

"Compound interest is wonderful if you're receiving it, and potentially devastating if you're paying it." Scott Thompson

11.11 Shareholder Oriented:

The phrase "shareholder oriented" refers to businesses run by honest and capable managers who prioritize shareholder interests before their own. Both quantitative and qualitative strategies can be used to identify these "Shareholder-oriented" businesses.

For example, generally speaking, businesses that exhibit the following qualities tend to be "Shareholder-oriented" businesses:

- Steadily decreasing total shares outstanding in which business engages in stock buybacks / share repurchase programs

- Executive pay growing in accordance with the success of the business

- Among the highest gross margins in its sector/industry

- Among the highest operating margins in its sector/industry

- Among the highest net income (net profit) margins in its sector/industry

- Among the highest inventory turnover in its sector/industry

- Steadily rising revenues

- Steadily rising operating income

- Steadily rising net income

- Among the lowest SGA costs in its sector/industry

- Steadily rising retained earnings

Businesses engaging in share buyback programs can be a sign of a shareholder-oriented business. How can you determine if a particular business engages in share buyback programs? Start with the income statement. Toward the bottom of the income statement you will see a line labeled "Shares Outstanding" or "Weighted Average Shares Outstanding." There you will see two subcategories, one labeled "Basic" and the other labeled "Diluted." Using the "Diluted" shares outstanding, the number of shares outstanding should be decreasing over time.

If the number of shares outstanding is increasing, instead of decreasing, the business is raising capital by issuing more shares of its stock, which dilutes the value of the shares of stock owned by shareholders.

Let's assume for a moment that the net income of a business remains relatively stable over time. If we divide net income by total shares outstanding, the result is earnings-per-share (EPS). If there are a higher amount of shares outstanding, then net income divided by shares outstanding will result in lower earnings per share (EPS). Conversely, if there are a lower amount of shares outstanding, then net income divided by shares outstanding will result in higher earnings-per-share (EPS).

For example, a net income of $25,000,000 divided by 10,000,000 total shares outstanding, results in earnings per share (EPS) of $2.50 per share.

Conversely, if this same business with net income of $25,000,000 is divided by only 5,000,000 total shares outstanding, it now results in earnings per share (EPS) of $5 per share.

Therefore, if this business is engaged in a share buyback program and bought back 5,000,000 of its own shares, then it would have only 5,000,000 total shares outstanding, instead of 10,000,000 total shares outstanding.

Then as you can see, when net income is divided by the number of total shares outstanding, "shareholder-oriented" businesses possess a lower number of total shares outstanding. This results in higher earnings per share (EPS). Higher amounts of EPS are desirable for shareholders, and higher EPS, in turn, results in higher stock prices.

Shareholder-oriented businesses should show a steady trend of decreasing total shares outstanding over their financial history over the past 5, 7, or 10 years (or longer).

11.12 Whisper Stocks:

"I find my investments. My investments don't find me." Scott Thompson

Whisper stocks are stocks that others "whisper" to you as uninformed, speculative recommendations for you to purchase. Whisper stocks are stocks that others believe may supposedly rocket upward making investors a lot of fast, easy money. However, these risky "whisper stocks" usually turn out to perform badly.

Caveat Emptor: *Latin: buyer beware,* "Whisper stocks" are sometimes intentionally started as rumors, especially on the internet, to falsely inflate the stock price. Then, others on the inside can find unsuspecting buyers to dump their worthless shares to. It is best to avoid whisper stocks, and perform your own thoughtful, informed analysis. If you currently lack the time or desire to perform your own research, consider enlisting the help of a financial professional who's skilled in valuations.

11.13 Ignoring Market Noise:

Warren Buffett left the bustle of busy New York City, and moved back to the comparatively serene life of Omaha, Nebraska. Once back in Omaha, Warren knew he could better hear his inner voice (signal) more clearly, without being distracted by the market (noise). This way Warren could better choose which businesses to invest in, while avoiding being bombarded daily with "whisper stock" recommendations from others.

In music, there is a specification referred to as the "signal-to-noise ratio," which measures how strong a unit of signal is for every equal unit of noise. "Signal" represents the true content on which you want to focus. "Noise" represents distractions attempting to pull your focus away from the true "signal" (or content) on which you desire to focus.

Know who you are. Know your investment criteria and which businesses you're looking for, in advance. Know which sectors, industries, and types of businesses you seek to invest in, before you begin your search. Don't become distracted by your environment, or change your environment.

Like Buffett, reduce the noise. Avoid distractions. Most of all, listen within to your inner true "signal" and alleviate all the "noise."

11.14 Patience:

One of the most important qualities of successful value investor Warren Buffett is patience. An investment of a mere $7 into Buffett's Berkshire Hathaway, would be worth $220,000 USD as of 2015. Some investors who invested with Warren from the beginning, back in the 1950's and 1960's, have kept their money with Warren. Their patience continues to pay off, as shares of Berkshire Hathaway continue to climb higher.

Most speculators do not possess the patience and temperament to buy and hold shares of a wonderful business for years, even decades. These impatient speculators trade in and out of stocks quite frequently, and do not possess the calm rational long-term mindset that Warren possesses.

While speculators make thousands or millions, Warren's patience has earned him billions. Many speculators think of themselves as investors, but sooner or later they cannot control their urge to sell and buy into the next high-flying overvalued stock.

Warren is patient, and says his favorite holding time is "forever." To this day, Warren has never sold even a single share of his Berkshire Hathaway stock, worth several tens of billions. He just continues to let it compound.

Are you able to control your urge to sell today, next month, next year, over the long-term? If you can, you may possess a patient value investing mindset like Warren Buffett.

11.15 Intrinsic Value Temperament

Healthy, profitable businesses experiencing temporarily adverse situations from which they will recover, can be likened to good people going through temporarily adverse periods during their lives. Eventually, the distressed period passes. Sometimes people in our lives, like great businesses, need someone to see value in them when they are going through a temporarily difficult time.

Value investors are like "friends" who see value within distressed high quality businesses, and invest during these temporary periods of adversity. To do this in the world of finance requires a unique temperament most investors do not possess. This represents a principle of Buffett's value investing temperament. Identify value others do not see.

As successful value investors, we discover high quality businesses going through periods of temporary adversity, but we must ask ourselves whether these businesses will recover, or if they will not. Not all distressed businesses will recover. Know the difference. Avoid value traps.

As Chapter 3 explains, when value investors find a potential investment, they should perform Buffett and Munger's "Four Filters" Investment Process. Is it (Filter #1) a business you understand? Does it possess (Filter #2) a durable competitive advantage? Does it possess (Filter #3) capable and trustworthy management? Is it available at (Filter #4) an attractive price to value ratio, with a sufficient margin of safety? And, is there a "catalyst" event coming soon that may trigger its market price upward toward its underlying intrinsic value?

Remember when you went through a difficult time, or helped a friend through their difficult time? The distressed period was temporary. High-quality businesses may experience temporary periods of distress. However, not all distressed businesses are high quality businesses. As stated previously, know the difference. Avoid value traps.

While most speculators myopically focus on the short-term, you stay focused on long-term results. Find opportunities where others do not. Historically, after the public learns of the newest Berkshire investment or acquisition, many puzzled speculators ask, "Why did Berkshire invest in that?" Stay focused on the fundamentals, on what you know, and like all-star hitter Ted Williams, your success rate will vastly improve.

What's your investing temperament? Can you control your emotions and not speculate? What's the longest period you have owned a stock? Do you trade frequently, or buy and hold high-undervalued quality businesses for the long-term? After reading this book, it will become easier for you to identify higher-quality undervalued investment opportunities others do not see. This is the heart of value investing and the ideal calm, rational, patient, investing temperament.

CHAPTER TWELVE:

When To Buy? When To Sell?

12.1 Overview:

The obvious goal of value investing is to buy low and sell high, but few people ever actually achieve this. Never buy after a big run-up, and never sell after a precipitous decline. Inexperienced investors often do the opposite. Never "panic-sell" after a big market sell off, and never "panic-buy" after a big market increase. Control your emotions. Successful investing is done intelligently and calmly, and not during times of extreme emotional duress. Successful investing is done with a confident, calm, rational mind, after performing valuations, verifying if businesses meet a rigorous set of criteria, and performing due diligence.

12.2 When to Buy:

Here are four answers from four value investors answering the question of: "When to buy?"

"Our goal is to acquire part or all of businesses we believe we understand, that have good sustainable underlying economics, run by managers we like and trust." Warren Buffett

"When fundamentals of high-quality businesses are strong, and market price is significantly below intrinsic value, offering a wide margin of safety." Scott Thompson

"I look for a high 'Quality Bargain' that fulfills all four decision filters of Buffett and Munger. Everything else is a pass." Dr. Bud Labitan

"It's far better to buy a wonderful business at a fair price, than a fair business at a wonderful price. We look for first-class businesses accompanied by first-class managements." Charlie Munger

12.3 When to Sell:

Here are four answers from four successful value investors answering the question of: "When to sell?"

"For a wonderful business producing FCF, the answer is never." Warren Buffett

"When market price rises to its intrinsic value." Scott Thompson

"If you find out that they are cooking the books, sell immediately." Dr. Bud Labitan

"When you find something better." Charlie Munger

In 1999 and 2000 during the dot.com boom, speculators were in a trading frenzy that had nothing to do with valuations. An announcement was made that the laws of valuation no longer apply and a "new economy" is now in place.

Wise value investor Warren Buffett avoided tech stocks, and instead stayed within his "circle of competence" (Filter #1) of what he understands… fundamentals and value investing.

During the tech-stock boom of 2000, the NASDAQ increased over 100 points every day, day after day, for extended periods! Speculators went crazy trying to participate in this trading frenzy! Even rational people eventually jumped into the frenzied market.

However, just a few months later, the market crashed and most lost significant sums of money. Many investors also leveraged their bets on "margin" (borrowed money), which magnified their losses. As value investors, it is wise to avoid using margin. Even Warren Buffett does not invest using margin.

"The market can remain irrational longer than you can remain solvent." John Keynes

"You can't go broke if you don't owe any money." Scott Thompson

"Avoid the two L's: Liquor and Leverage!" Warren Buffett

Remember it takes a confident, independently thinking investor to ignore market booms, like the tech-stock boom of 1999. The time to buy is not when market prices are lofty, but instead when market prices are distressed. Identify healthy businesses whose fundamentals are sound, showing dislocations between (market) price and (intrinsic) value that offer a sufficiently wide "margin of safety."

So you've performed your intrinsic valuations and due diligence. You've identified a wonderful business that meets your rigorous criteria and you're ready to invest. Do you invest all your capital into the business all at once? No. Consider investing 5% of your total assets into 20 different businesses. This way you will own a basket of 20 different businesses with 5% invested in each. This is a more responsible process of portfolio construction instead of betting your entire net worth on a single investment.

12.4 Determine: Entry Point and Exit Point:

Warren Buffett uses only fundamental analysis, and does not use technical analysis. Warren values the business, carefully examines the earnings, profit margins, and debt levels, but does not use charts to determine his entry point. Buffett is a true value investor and uses fundamentals only.

Other value investors who are greatly influenced by Warren Buffett also use fundamental analysis, but sometimes may use technical analysis to determine a more optimal entry point. We will explain these strategies in this chapter, but know that although many modern value investors incorporate technical analysis into their value investing, Warren Buffett does not.

12.5 Dollar-Cost Averaging (DCA):

Dollar-cost averaging process is an alternative to investing all your capital into an investment all at once. Instead, investors "dollar-cost average" or invest regular amounts of capital into an investment on a recurring basis despite the market price. In other words, these investors choose to invest on a certain day of each month, every month, for an extended period.

This way the market prices are averaged together normalizing the cost-bases at which the investor invested.

For instance, many employees choose to invest a portion of their salaries each month into a 401k or other retirement account. A predetermined percentage of their income is automatically invested each month, month after month. This is dollar-cost averaging.

12.6 Market Cycles:

Financial markets often traverse through four major market cycles. These four major financial market cycles are:

EPRT:
- Expansion
- Peak
- Recession
- Trough

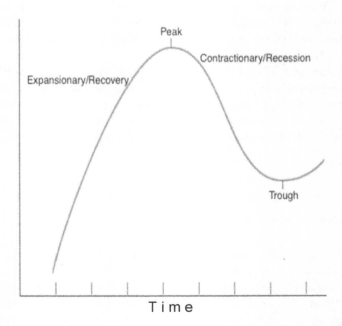

The EPRT process repeats itself. Now that you're aware of the four major market cycles, two prominent questions to be raised are: When to buy? When to sell?

Obviously, investors can look at the graph and surmise that the best time to buy is in the trough, and the best time to sell is at the peak. This is easier said than done. Even skilled value investor Warren Buffett admits he cannot determine when the market is bottoming in the trough, or at the peak.

In 2009, Warren invested $5 billion into Goldman Sachs (GS) at $115 per share. Shortly afterward, shares of Goldman Sachs plummeted to only $57 per share, 50% lower than Buffett's original $115 per share acquisition price. This illustrates two important concepts:

- Stock prices are subject to extreme volatility price swings. Many investors say they can handle market volatility, until it actually happens. Adhere to your value investing strategies, even during periods of extreme market volatility cycles.

- Even billionaire Warren Buffett did not see a 50% price drop coming just weeks after he made his investment into Goldman Sachs (GS). Maintain your strong conviction for the undervalued investments you choose, especially during extreme price volatility.

12.7 Fundamental Analysis:

Warren Buffett only uses fundamental analysis within the Four Filters investment process to make his investment decisions. Warren Buffett does not use technical analysis.

Fundamental Analysis focuses on the fundamentals of the underlying business, such as earnings, profit margins, and free cash flows. Fundamental analysis also includes reading annual reports, performing valuations, analyzing financial statements, management team, competitors, patents, credit risk, etc.

12.8 Technical Analysis: *(Selecting entry point)*

Technical analysis is a process to analyze securities based mostly on prices, volume, and charting. As value investors, we almost exclusively implement fundamental analysis. However, if you've already performed your fundamental analysis, valuations, due diligence, the business meets your criteria, and you're ready to invest, sometimes technical analysis can be helpful to select a more optimal entry point.

Visit a financial website offering financial stock charts such as: Yahoo.com, Morningstar.com, Valueline.com, etc. Type in a ticker symbol such as Coca Cola's ticker symbol "KO". The stock chart appears. Click on the "1 Year" chart view. In the "technical indicators" section of the chart, activate the following technical indicators:

- **50-day Moving Average**: The 50-day moving average shows a normalized line representing the average stock price averaged over the previous 50-day period.

- **200-day Moving Average**: Similarly, the 200-day moving average shows a normalized line representing the average stock price averaged over the previous 200-day period.

- **Bollinger Bands**: Bollinger Bands show a high and low range, above and below the past and present stock price that measure volatility using standard deviation, over a simple moving average period that is defined by the user. For instance, a common simple moving average period used in Bollinger Bands is "20" day moving averages, and common standard deviation values is a value of "2" standard deviations.

- **Volume**: Displays the number of shares traded during a specified period.

- **Other technical indicators**: Other technical indicators can also be useful in helping to determine an optimal entry point into undervalued stocks such as: Slow Stochastic Oscillator, Relative Strength Index (RSI), Moving Average Convergence/Divergence (MACD), etc. We will not list them all here, as there are numerous technical indicators.

12.9 Death Cross:

When the 50-day moving average crosses <u>below</u> the 200-day moving average, this is called a "death cross." Some believe the "death cross" to be a leading indicator preceding negative, downward movement in the stock price. Many believe a buying opportunity may follow as the market price heads lower toward a bottom.

Death Cross: *50-day crosses <u>below</u> 200-day moving average*

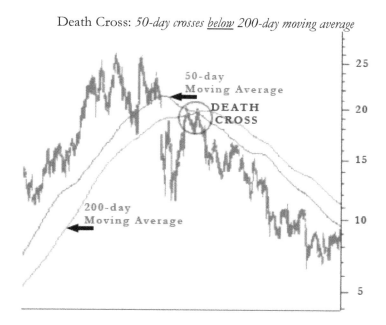

If your intrinsic valuation looks attractive, and all other criteria is met, when market price is below the 50-day moving average, and the 50-day moving average is below the 200-day moving average, and the market price is at the bottom of the Bollinger Band range, it may indicate a more optimal time to buy.

12.10 Golden Cross:

When the 50-day moving average crosses <u>above</u> the 200-day moving average, this is called a "golden cross." Some believe the "golden cross" to be a leading indicator preceding positive, upward movement in the stock price. Many believe a selling opportunity may soon follow as the market price heads higher toward a top.

Golden Cross: *50-day crosses above 200-day moving average*

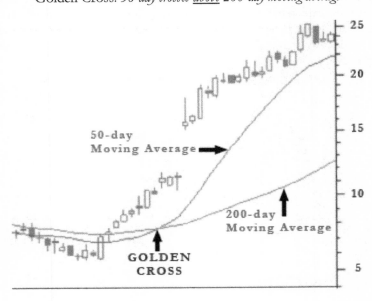

If your intrinsic valuation looks attractive, and all other criteria is met, when market price is above the 50-day moving average, and the 50-day moving average is above the 200-day moving average, and the market price is at the top of the Bollinger Band range, it may indicate a more optimal time to sell.

This book focuses on fundamental analysis, not technical analysis. Therefore, these aforementioned technical indicators are all we will mention about them.

Next, we move on to Chapter 13: Case Studies.

CHAPTER THIRTEEN:

CASE STUDIES

Warren Buffett stated the best way to learn value investing is "case studies." Therefore, we present the following three case studies to help solidify the concept of intrinsic valuation value investing using real world examples:

CASE STUDY #1: The 1988 Historic Valuation of Coca-Cola (KO): The Year Warren Buffett invested $1 billion into Coca-Cola Company.

By: Dr. Bud Labitan, MBA and Scott Thompson, MBA

CASE STUDY #2: FactSet Research Systems (FDS):

By: Bakul Lalla and Scott Thompson, MBA

CASE STUDY #3: Colgate-Palmolive Company (CL):

By: Dr. Maulik Suthar, MD, and Scott Thompson, MBA

13.1 CASE STUDY #1:

1988 Historical Valuation of Coca-Cola:
Ticker Symbol: (KO)
Dr. Bud Labitan, MBA and Scott Thompson, MBA
(Labitan/Thompson, 2013)

For years, we have wondered how Warren Buffett valued Coca-Cola (NYSE: KO) stock at such a deep bargain in 1988. In this book, we estimate the intrinsic value of each Coca-Cola share when Warren Buffett purchased 7% of the company that year. This book describes a simple 2-stage discounted cash flow model that delivers a close approximation of the stock's intrinsic value at that point in time.

In 1987, Coca-Cola was refocusing on its core business and sold its Columbia Pictures subsidiary. The "New Coke" fiasco of 1985 was past. The company was repurchasing common stock. So, how did the business look in the eyes of Buffett and Munger?

As some of you know, "The Four Filters Invention of Warren Buffett and Charlie Munger" book explored their investment decision making process. We believe that Buffett and Munger made a major contribution to the field of Behavioral Finance by applying these four sequential filter steps:

Filter #1: Look for a business you understand, within your "circle of competence."

Filter #2: Look for a Durable Competitive Advantage.

Filter #3: Insist on Able and Trustworthy Managers.

Filter #4: Insist on Ben Graham's Margin of Safety where your purchase price is significantly below intrinsic value.

Coca-Cola passed these filters. Consider the significance of each filter like this. Filter #1: Understanding means finding an understandable business with good economics. Filter #2: Look for a Durable Competitive Advantage. This means having repeat customers. Filter #3: Insist on Able

224

and Trustworthy Managers because management must have both qualities. Why? The able, but untrustworthy manager can lead to disaster.

Filter #4: Insist on a Margin of Safety where your purchase price is significantly below the intrinsic value. This is Ben Graham's quest to buy a business at a significant bargain so that the risk of capital loss is minimized, and the probability of capital appreciation is maximized. Therefore, let us look at Coca-Cola's intrinsic value per share in 1988. Coca-Cola is a business with a differentiated and continuing competitive advantage. Its economic moat is deep and wide. It has a combination of a special brand advantage, a large-scale "cost of production" advantage, and a global network distribution advantage. We could say that it has three moats around its economic castle. In addition, its managers work to build this moat bigger every day.

A customer generally asks for a Coke by name. Customers do not buy a 'cola'. Charlie Munger said, "The social proof phenomenon, which comes right out of psychology, gives huge advantages to scale – with global distribution, making it available almost everywhere in the world."

In 1988, Warren Buffett and Charlie Munger began buying stock in the Coca-Cola Company for the Berkshire Hathaway portfolio. They purchased about 7% of the company for $1.02 billion. This turned out to be one of Berkshire's most lucrative investments. Berkshire Hathaway now owns 8.9%, or 400 million shares of Coca-Cola.

Buffett and Munger knew that commodity companies sell products or services that can be reproduced. In 1982, Buffett said this about commodity companies: "Businesses in industries with both substantial over-capacity and a 'commodity' product, undifferentiated in any customer-important way by factors such as performance, appearance, service support etc., are prime candidates for profit troubles." There are also companies that market commodity products so well that they distinguish their commodity product from that of their competitors. These put their own special brand upon their product. They can achieve this by the marketing mix of price, product, placement, and promotions. In addition, continuous improvement, in terms of higher quality production and service, is always a plus.

In 1993, Warren Buffett said this about companies with competitive advantages, "Is it really so difficult to conclude that Coca-Cola and

Gillette possess far less business risk over the long term than, say, any computer company or retailer? Worldwide, Coke sells about 44% of all soft drinks, and Gillette has more than a 60% share (in value) of the blade market. Leaving aside chewing gum, in which Wrigley is dominant, I know of no other significant businesses in which the leading company has long enjoyed such global power."

Coca-Cola has a strong brand identity in the global market and it has pricing power. It is one of most respected brands in the world. Coca-Cola utilizes a great amount of positive advertising to maintain the Coke brand. The amount of advertising is also a barrier to entry; it makes it impossible for brands with low capital to gain a comparable amount of brand awareness. This creates an expensive barrier to entry.

Coca-Cola's 5Yr Gross Margin (5-Year Avg.) is approximately 62%. Its Net Profit Margin (5-Year Avg.) is approximately 22%, while the industry's Net Profit Margin (5-Year Avg.) is 18.0%. Coca-Cola also has better earnings power efficiency in terms of Free Cash Flow per unit of sale.

In 2012, Coca-Cola had a 5-Year Average Return on Equity (ROE) of 29.9. Its worldwide distribution system is also major competitive advantage.

Are these advantages sustainable for the next 10 years? Yes. However, Coca-Cola has recently dropped out of the top-ten brand value list for the first time. This may be underpinned by a consumer trend towards healthier, non-carbonated drinks. Coca-Cola recognized "obesity and health concerns" as potential risks for the company in the 2010 annual report. However, there is little doubt that Coca-Cola's loyal brand following will sustain its competitive advantage. Coca-Cola recognizes the need to sustain marketing and increase innovation.

In its 2010 annual report, they acknowledged the need to continue to selectively expand into other profitable segments of the nonalcoholic beverages segment.

From the 2012 annual report: "Obesity and other health concerns may reduce demand for some of our products. Consumers, public health officials and government officials are highly concerned about the public health consequences associated with obesity, particularly among young people. In addition, some researchers, health advocates and dietary guidelines are encouraging consumers to reduce consumption of sugar-sweetened beverages, including those sweetened with HFCS (High-Fructose Corn Syrup) or other nutritive sweeteners.

Increasing public concern about these issues; possible new taxes on sugar-sweetened beverages; additional governmental regulations concerning the marketing, labeling, packaging or sale of our beverages; and negative publicity resulting from actual or threatened legal actions against us or other companies in our industry relating to the marketing, labeling or sale of sugar-sweetened beverages may reduce demand for our beverages, which could adversely affect our profitability."

A historically wonderful business, Coca-Cola's able and trustworthy managers are motivated to invest in its supply chain network to "leverage the size and scale of the Coca-Cola system to gain a competitive advantage." With this moat building in mind, we believe that Coca-Cola will be successful in maintaining its economic franchise and current barriers to entry.

On October 18, 2012, Coca-Cola announced that it planned to purchase up to 500 million shares of the company's common stock. Such actions add value to the "intrinsic value" of each remaining share outstanding.

Consider why the Coca-Cola Company is such a good business from an investor's point of view. Both Coke and Pepsi make products we enjoy. As an investor, we prefer the Coca-Cola Company. One reason is the amount of Free Cash Flow generated for every sale. Another reason is the amount of Free Cash Flow generated after expenses.

Charlie Munger once stated: "Warren often talks about these discounted cash flows, but I've never seen him do one." Warren Buffett responded: "It's sort of automatic... It ought to just kind of scream at you that you've got this huge margin of safety." Buffett went on to state, "We define intrinsic value as the discounted value of the cash that can be taken out of a business during its remaining life."

Anyone calculating intrinsic value necessarily comes up with a highly subjective figure. This figure will change both as estimates of future cash flows are revised and as interest rates move. Despite its fuzziness, however, intrinsic value is all-important and is the only logical way to evaluate the relative attractiveness of investments and businesses.

This exercise is our quantitative estimation of Coca-Cola's Intrinsic Value Per Share in 1988. First, we describe our 2-stage "discounted cash flow" valuation model. This estimating model is strict. It assumes a good business will only "live" for 20 years. Within this model, we apply compounding growth to the first 10 years. Then, we assume a lower growth rate for years 11 until the end of year 20. This restriction of lesser growth in years 11 through 20 means this restriction imposes a degree of conservatism on top of the estimator's optimism during the model's early growth years. Then, after we sum up all the individual end of year cash, we should apply a discount rate and bring that sum back to present value. At this point, we divide by the number of shares outstanding.

Warren Buffett said, "Intrinsic value is the discounted value of the cash that can be taken out of a business during its remaining life. Anyone calculating intrinsic value necessarily comes up with a highly subjective figure. This figure will change both as estimates of future cash flows are revised and as interest rates move. Despite its fuzziness, however, intrinsic value is all-important and is the only logical way to evaluate the relative attractiveness of investments and businesses."

Again, we emphasize that our model is an "estimation method" that imposes conservatism by limiting growth in the final ten years. It is just a model for 1988. At that time, KO stock traded between $35 and $45.25. From 1987 to 1988, the net income grew 14% and the net income per common share grew 17.3%. The number of shares outstanding in 1988 was 364,612,000 shares. We used a discount rate of 6.0% because that is the approximate 20-year average from 1988 to 2008. (see diagram)

Average: 10-Year US Treasury Rates from 1988–2008

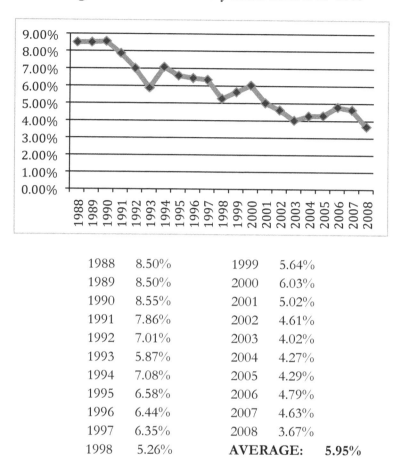

1988	8.50%	1999	5.64%
1989	8.50%	2000	6.03%
1990	8.55%	2001	5.02%
1991	7.86%	2002	4.61%
1992	7.01%	2003	4.02%
1993	5.87%	2004	4.27%
1994	7.08%	2005	4.29%
1995	6.58%	2006	4.79%
1996	6.44%	2007	4.63%
1997	6.35%	2008	3.67%
1998	5.26%	**AVERAGE:**	**5.95%**

Coca-Cola's 1988 Annual Report does not show Free Cash Flow. We can calculate FCF using available information from its 1988 financial statements like this:

The formula for calculating Free Cash Flow (FCF) is:

Free Cash Flow = Operating Cash Flow – Capital Expenditures

Or, this formula can be used to calculate Free Cash Flows:

Free Cash Flow = (EBIT x (1–Tax Rate)) + (Depreciation & Amortization) – (Changes in Working Capital) – Capital Expenditure

Remember that Operating Income is referred to as EBIT or (Earnings Before Interest and Taxes, shown on the Income Statement.

Working Capital = (Current Assets) – (Current Liabilities)

EBIT (also known as Operating Income) = \$1,598,300,000
EBIT = Earnings Before Interest and Taxes

Tax Rate in 1988 = .34 or 34%

Depreciation & Amortization = \$169,768,000

Changes in Working Capital = \$227,993,000

1988's Working Capital = 1988 Total Current Assets – 1988 Total Current Liabilities
\$376,535,000 = \$3,245,432,000 – \$2,868,897,000

1987 Working Capital = 1987 Total Current Assets – 1987 Total Current Liabilities

\$148,542,000 = \$4,231,921,000 – \$4,083,379,000

Capital Expenditures = \$387,000,000

Now, let's plug these numbers into our Free Cash Flow formula:

(EBIT x (1–Tax Rate)) + (Depreciation & Amortization) – (Changes in Working Capital) – Capital Expenditure = Free Cash Flow

($1,598,300,000 x (1–.34)) + $169,768,000 – $227,993,000 – $387,000,000 = FCF
($1,598,300,000 x (.66)) + $169,768,000 – $227,993,000 – $387,000,000 = FCF
$1,054,878,000 + $169,768,000 – $227,993,000 – $387,000,000 = FCF
$1,054,878,000 + $169,768,000 – $227,993,000 – $387,000,000 = $609,653,000

We used an assumed FCF annual growth of 15% for the first 10 years, and we assume 12% growth from years 11 to the end of year 20. Keep in mind, this is how our estimating model was designed. In the real world, you should adjust your model to better fit a superior or inferior business's longevity.

In fact, for a great company like Coca-Cola, you could lengthen the second stage of your model out to another 5-20 years. For the purpose of conservatism, we chose to stay with our 20-year, 2-stage model with the compounding growth set at 15% and 12% respectively. These are reasonable expectations for that period, based on Warren Buffett's 1990 letter, where he wrote: "We hope to have look-through earnings grow about 15% annually."

In our model, the resulting estimated intrinsic value per share (after discounting the sum back to the present) is approximately $78.67. If Warren Buffett bought at or around the Market Price of $40, he obtained a margin of safety of around 49%.

At this point, it is important to remember that Intrinsic Value is not a precise number. It is an estimated range. It is better to be approximately right, than precisely wrong. As you can see below, both valuation models have estimated valuations that are fairly close to one another. The DCF/FCF model inspired by John Burr Williams estimates Coca-Cola's intrinsic value at around $79. Alternatively, Benjamin Graham's classic formula estimates the value of Coca-Cola to be approximately $87.48.

We believe that it is better to go with the more conservative estimation, and examine the business qualities within the Four Filters Process. The Four Filters are a search for: "Understandable first-class businesses, with enduring competitive advantages, accompanied by first-class managements, available at a bargain price." This is discussed in the next chapter.

Here is the Ben Graham formula: **V = EPS = (8.5 + 2g)**

Where:
V = Intrinsic Value
EPS = Earnings Per Share for ttm (trailing twelve months)
8.5 = Price/Earnings (P/E) ratio for a no-growth business
G = reasonable expected 7–10 year growth rate
For our 1988 Coca-Cola valuation:

V = $2.43 x (8.5 + (2x14))
V = $2.43 x (8.5 + 28)
V = $2.43 x 36.5
V = $88.70

Alternatively, if we imagine Buffett performing this calculation in his head, his modified Graham formula might resemble something like this:

V = EPS = (8 + 2g)
V = $2.43 x (8 + (2x14))
V = $2.43 x (8 + 28)
V = $2.43 x 36
V = $87.48

A word of caution, intrinsic value estimations comprise Filter #4 of Buffett and Munger's Four Filters investment process. Be sure to consider all four filters during your investment research and analysis.

No matter which estimation method you adopt, bear in mind Warren Buffett bought an understandable business with sustainable competitive advantages, able and trustworthy managers, and a significant bargain, relative to its intrinsic value. These four filter factors describe the wonderfulness or magic of a business.

A Guide to Coca-Cola's 1988 Financial Ratios

When calculating financial ratios, it's best to use longer-term 10-year, 7-year, 5-year, or 3-year historical data. In this particular Case Study, longer-term financial data was not available at the time of this writing, so the following financial ratios have been calculated based on available data shown in Coca-Cola's 1988 annual report.

Price/Earnings (P/E) = 14.04
1988 average market price = $40/share.
1988 Net Income = $1,038,277,000 (available to common shareholders)
1988 Total Shares Outstanding = 364,612,000
1988 Earnings Per Share (EPS) = $2.85
Price ÷ EPS = P/E ratio
$40 ÷ $2.85 = 14.04

Therefore, Coca-Cola's 1988 Price/Earnings ratio = 14.04. Although, some investors may not consider a P/E ratio of 14.04 an extreme bargain, Coca-Cola's financial statements reveal a consistent long-term history of increased earnings growth, year-after-year. Buffett correctly predicted that Coca-Cola's long-term history of increasing earnings growth would continue into the future.

Coca-Cola remains one of Warren Buffett's most profitable investments. In fact, Warren Buffett's Berkshire Hathaway now owns 400 million Coca-Cola (KO) shares. Warren's initial investment of $1 billion into Coca-Cola in 1988 was worth $14.5 billion in 2013.

Price/Book (P/B) = 4.79
1988 average market price = $40/share.
1988 Common Shareholders Equity = $3,045,300,000
1988 Total Shares Outstanding = 364,612,000
1988 Book Value per Share = $8.35

Price ÷ Book Value = P/B ratio
$40 ÷ $8.35 = 4.79

Therefore, Coca-Cola's 1988 Price/Book ratio = 4.79 times book value. This is not necessarily cheap, however, Charlie Munger influenced Warren Buffett by saying: "Let's go for the wonderful business!" Wonderful businesses rarely sell at a significant discount.

Price/Sales (P/S) = 1.75

1988 average market price = $40/share.

1988 annual Sales revenue = $8,337,800,000

1988 Total shares outstanding: 364,612,000

($8,337,800,000 ÷ 364,612,000 = $22.87/share) and Coca-Cola's 1988 annual sales revenue per share was $22.87/share.

Coca-Cola's 1988 Price/Sales ratio = 1.75 from ($40 ÷ $22.87 = 1.75)

Free Cash Flow/Sales (FCF/S) = 7.31%

1988 Free Cash Flow (FCF) = $609,653,000

1988 annual Sales revenue = $8,337,800,000

$609,653,000 ÷ $8,337,800,000 = 7.31%.

In other words, for every dollar of revenue Coca-Cola generated in 1988, 7.31% of that dollar became Free Cash Flow, benefiting shareholders.

Research & Development/Gross Profit (R&D/GP) = 0%

Coca-Cola's 1988 Annual Report and financial statements show no R&D expenses. Buffett likes business with little or no R&D costs. This allows a greater portion of Gross Profit dollars to flow through financial statements to become free cash flow, benefiting shareholders.

Sales, General, & Administrative/Gross Profit (SGA/GP) = 65.54%

1988 SGA = $3,038,058,000

1988 Gross Profit = $4,636,358,000

$3,038,058,000 ÷ $4,636,358,000 = 65.54%

234

In 1988, Coca-Cola paid 65.54% of every Gross Profit dollar it earned toward SGA expenses, which include sales, commissions, salaries, administrative and advertising costs. Coca-Cola spends a lot of advertising dollars to create one of the most widely recognized brands in the world. SGA is the line on the income statement where advertising costs are shown. Although, 65.54% may seem excessive, Coca-Cola has built one of the strongest durable "wide-moat" brands in the world.

Depreciation & Amortization/Gross Profit (DA/GP) = 3.66%
1988 Depreciation & Amortization = $169,768,000
1988 Gross Profit = $4,636,358,000
$169,768,000 ÷ $4,636,358,000 = 3.66%

Lower values for this ratio tend to be better. Higher ratios can signal accounting anomalies. Businesses showing exorbitantly high values for this ratio may be experiencing periods of financial difficulty, and may be using various accounting methods to affect the numbers. Coca-Cola's 1988 financial statements show a low value for this ratio, quantitatively identifying a qualitative aspect of Coca-Cola's exemplary management team.

Interest/Operating Income (I/EBIT) = 14.42%
1988 Interest Expense = $230,513,000
1988 Operating Income = $1,598,301,000
$230,513,000 ÷ $1,598,301,000 = 14.42%

In 1988, Coca-Cola spent 14.42% of every Operating Income (EBIT) dollar earned toward paying Interest Expense. Interest is paid on short-term and long-term debt the business carries on its balance sheet. Coca-Cola carries little debt, and maintains a low weighted average cost of capital. Warren likes to invest in businesses with little to no debt.

Capital Expenditures/Operating Income (CapEx/EBIT) = 24.21%
1988 Capital Expenditures = $387,000,000
1988 Operating Income = $1,598,301,000
$387,000,000 ÷ $1,598,301,000 = 24.21%

In 1988, Coca-Cola spent 24.21% of every Operating Income (EBIT) dollar earned toward paying Capital Expenditures. Capital Expenditures are dollars reinvested into buying machinery and equipment the business needs in order to maintain and grow the business. Some businesses are more capital intensive than others. Lower values for this ratio are better.

Long-term Debt/Net Income (LTD/NI) = .7

1988 Long-term debt = $761,000,000
1988 Net Income = $1,038,000,000
$761,000,000 ÷ $1,038,000,000 = .7

If Coca-Cola were to decide to pay off all of its Long-term debt, hypothetically, using all of its Net Income, it would take only .7 years, or 8.8 months. This is less than 1 year, and a very strong financial position to be in. Buffett likes businesses with little to no debt.

Current Ratio = 1.31

Total Current Assets ÷ Total Current Liabilities = Current Ratio
$3,245,432,000 ÷ $2,868,897,000 = 1.31
Coca-Cola's 1988 Current Ratio = 1.31

Coca-Cola possesses a Current Ratio above 1, which puts them in a strong financial position to pay for all upcoming financial obligations due within the next 12 months.

Inventory Turnover = 10.71

1988 annual Sales revenue = $8,337,800,000
1988 Inventory = $778,816,000
$8,337,800,000 ÷ $778,816,000 = 10.71

Higher values for this ratio are better, because it means the business is "turning over its inventory" and selling higher quantities of its products & services. Buffett seeks to invest in businesses that have either a high turnover ratio, or high profit margins.

Now let's look at Coca-Cola's Gross profit margins, Operating profit margins, and Net profit margins.

Gross Profit Margin = 55.6%
1988 Gross Profit = $4,636,358,000
1988 annual Sales revenue = $8,337,800,000
$4,636,358,000 ÷ $8,337,800,000 = 55.6%

55.6% Gross Profit Margins are excellent, as 55.6% of each dollar of revenue earned becomes Gross Profit for Coca-Cola. High Gross Margins are a sign of "Pricing Power" and a business with a durable competitive advantage. (In 2012, Coca-Cola shows Gross Profit Margins of 60.3%). High values for this ratio are better. Warren Buffett seeks businesses with high gross profit margins.

Conversely, if a business shows low gross profit margins, this is typically a sign the business exists within a highly competitive, price-sensitive environment.

Operating Profit Margin = 19.2%
1988 Operating Income (EBIT) = $1,598,000,000
1988 annual Sales revenue = $8,337,800,000
$1,598,000,000 ÷ $8,337,800,000 = 19.2%

This means 19.2% of each dollar of revenue earned becomes Operating Profit. High Operating Profit Margins are a sign of a business with high gross margins, a durable competitive advantage, and a management team that maintains tight control of their operating expenses. In 2012, Coca-Cola showed Operating Profit Margins of 22.4%. High values for this ratio are better. Warren Buffett seeks businesses with high operating margins.

Conversely, if a business were to show low operating margins, this would typically be a sign of a business within a highly competitive, price-sensitive environment, with a management team that doesn't control operating expenses as effectively.

Net Profit Margin = 12.5%
1988 Net Income = $1,038,000,000
1988 annual Sales revenue = $8,337,800,000
$1,038,000,000 ÷ $8,337,800,000 = 12.5%

This means 12.5% of each dollar of revenue earned translates into Net Profit for Coca-Cola. High Net Margins are a sign of "Pricing Power" and a business with a management team able to control costs. In 2012, Coca-Cola showed Net Profit Margins of 18.8%. High values for this ratio are better. Warren Buffett seeks businesses with high net profit margins. Conversely, if a business shows a low net profit margin, this can be a sign of a business within a highly competitive, price-sensitive environment.

Return On Assets (ROA) = 13.9%
1988 Net Income = $1,038,000,000
1988 Total Assets = $7,451,000,000
$1,038,000,000 ÷ $7,451,000,000 = 13.9%

Higher values are better. Seek businesses with higher ROA.

Return On Equity (ROE) = 34.1%
1988 Net Income = $1,038,000,000
1988 Shareholders' Equity = $3,045,300,000
$1,038,000,000 ÷ $3,045,300,000 = 34.1%

According to Warren, Return on Equity (ROE) is one of the most important financial ratios he considers in his investment decisions. Higher values are better. Warren seeks businesses showing high Return on Equity (ROE). Buffett and Munger consider "return on shareholders' equity" to be an important yardstick of economic performance.

In 1988, Warren Buffett wrote: "Here's a benchmark: In its 1988 Investor's Guide issue, Fortune reported that among the 500 largest industrial companies and 500 largest service companies, only six had averaged a return on equity of over 30% during the previous decade. The best performer among the 1000 was Commerce Clearing House at 40.2%."

Summary:

Originally invented as a medicine by John Pemberton, Coca-Cola was bought by Asa Candler. Candler helped incorporate Coca-Cola as a Company on March 24, 1888. Candler marketed the product into a popular brand on top of an amazing and efficient business. Coca-Cola is truly an amazing business. It sells products that are simple and understandable. Coke's respected brand is over 125 years old. It is run by able and trustworthy managers.

In 1988, Warren Buffett purchased shares in KO when he found them selling near a 50% bargain. This gave Buffett and Berkshire Hathaway a wide margin of safety in a wonderful and growing business. It has rewarded him with dividends, capital appreciation, and a remarkable Yield On Cost. See the YOC discussion by my friend Bud Labitan in the reference section of this book. It will surprise you. For now, simply consider that Berkshire Hathaway's cost of $1.299 billion divided by 400 million shares gives Buffett and Berkshire a $3.25 per share cost per share of Coca-Cola, KO.

13.2 CASE STUDY #2:

FactSet Research Systems, Inc:
Ticker Symbol: (FDS)
Bakul Lalla and Scott Thompson

Filter #1: Business you understand, Circle of Competence

Remember the gold rush days when pioneers and prospectors risked everything to find gold? In those days, the search for gold created a tremendous demand for mining tools for such activity. Regardless of whether the gold diggers found gold, the mining tool makers were the beneficiaries. One can think of the mining tool maker business as a "toll bridge"-type of business. In today's age, information is the gold, and FactSet (FDS) is the tool maker supplying the demand for information tools.

The subscription based business model can be thought of as a "toll bridge"-type of business and is simple to understand. FDS sources financial data from providers of disparate computer systems or databases and receives the financial data in various formats, then aggregates that data using FDS developed "information tools" into information consumed by its customers. Once the aggregated data and the information tools are sold to customers, they become imbedded in the business process allowing customers to make financial analysis and decisions as a value-add, compelling them to retain these tools on an on-going basis. Sound like a simple toll bridge that can be sustained over the long haul? Yes, indeed!

Filter #2: Durable Competitive Advantage

FDS's durable competitive advantage lies in the fact that the company can balance the needs of various stakeholders including employees, shareholders, and customers. For employees, FDS has provided a work environment conducive to attract and retain talented employees. Over the last four years, the company has been identified by Fortune and Forbes magazines as one of the best places to work in the U.S. and U.K. For its shareholders, the company has generated returns well above the cost of capital. For its customers, the company has demonstrated an intense focus on customer satisfaction, regardless if these customers are in the buy side or sell side of the equity research area.

Let's assume the equity premium above the risk free rate for FDS is 5%–6% and the current, 1.86% ten-year treasury yield trends toward three to four percent. FDS's cost of capital can be estimated to be between 8%–10%. Taking the upper threshold, let's assume FDS's cost of capital is 10% as a benchmark. FDS has created shareholder value by generating returns well above this 10% cost of capital benchmark as will be shown in later sections.

FDS has reported customer retention rates in annual reports and SEC filings over many years. Figure 1 shows customer retention rates for the last ten years:

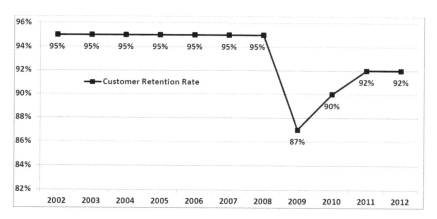

Figure 1: Customer Retention Rates

The trend of the customer retention rate is impressive over the 10-year period. During the Great Recession, the customer retention rate dipped below 90%. For fiscal 2011 and 2012, the customer retention rate recovered to the 92% level. It remains to be seen if the 92% level reached

241

is the "new normal" in the new environment after the financial crises. Also, we have to see if the company can reach the 95% level, as in years past. Regardless, I construe a 90% level or higher as a durable competitive advantage, which is evident in the company's financials described in the Financial Statement and Financial Ratios sections.

Competitors:

Thomson Reuters (ticker: TRI) is a close competitor to FDS. TRI has $13.3 billion of revenue. Comparatively, FDS has $834 million of revenue on a trailing twelve month (TTM) basis. The net profit margin and return on equity of a big competitor like TRI is much lower than FDS. Other competitors are Bloomberg, L.P., Standard & Poor's Capital IQ business unit, Dow Jones & Company, and Wilshire Associates. FDS's competitive advantage allows the company to command premium prices for their products allowing management to maintain higher margins.

Filter #3: Management

The fact that FDS sustains high customer retention rates indicates that the company's management understands its customer base better than its competitors. Since the company has been identified in lists of "best companies to work for," this could be a reflection of happy employees translating good morale into higher customer satisfaction allowing management to maintain high customer retention rates. In addition, FDS management has delivered return on equity (ROE) and cash return on invested capital (CROIC) that are very attractive and well above the assumed cost of capital benchmark of 10%. Taking all this into consideration, management is able to balance the needs of all the stakeholders, i.e. customers, employees, and shareholders. It is a virtuous circle of meeting the needs of all stakeholders.

Looking at the proxy statement filed on October 30th 2012, directors and executive officers own 8.9% of the company's common stock. Performance based executive compensation is tied to metrics such as an increase in annual subscription value (ASV), earnings per share growth greater than ASV growth, improving competitive position, and optimizing capital allocation, among others. Management's interests are unquestionably aligned with shareholders to generate long-term shareholder value, even though I prefer directors and executive officers to have more skin in the game to the tune of 15% or more ownership of the company's stock.

Filter #4: Price to Value

Price to value of FDS was quite attractive during the Great Recession just as many other high cash flow generators had pricing that was reaching attractive levels. I am not sure if such price to value opportunity may arise in the future. Currently, the estimated intrinsic value is $103.90 while the price at close of market on April 5th 2013 stood at $90.08 per share. So, an 86.7% price-to-value is not too attractive for accumulation of shares for an existing shareholder or for taking a new position.

Catalyst Events

Value investors take advantage of significant price movements in either direction, depending on catalyst events that may unfold over time. There are three catalyst events that could potentially make the price move.

First, the capitalization of the company indicates FDS has no long-term debt; thus, the company is incurring the cost of capital associated with equity owners only. In this unusually low interest rate environment, the company could lower its cost of capital by taking on debt to the tune of 25% of capitalization. With the current market capitalization of $4.0 billion, a maximum issuance of $1.0 billion would mean interest cost of $50 million per annum, assuming cost of long-term debt is 5%. For a company that generates $209.6 million of free cash flow, the interest cost is only 23.85% of this free cash, which means that interest coverage is more than acceptable to allow the debt to be classified as investment grade. Suppose such a debt issuance transaction of $1.0 billion is consummated with 44.455 million shares outstanding, FDS could affect an accelerated stock repurchase program to retire 25% of outstanding stock in an accretive and opportunistic manner.

Second, an unwillingness of the company to take on debt might attract an institutional investor to take on a 10% or greater equity position. The institutional investor would negotiate with the company to take a board seat, either in a shareholder friendly manner or via a proxy battle. Then the institutional investor would address the reduction of cost of capital by proposing issuance of debt and subsequent stock repurchase. This strategy may or may not work, depending on whether the institutional shareholder is acting in the best interest of all shareholders or whether the institutional investor uses hostile tactics.

Third, a private equity entity makes an outright bid for the company to take it private with an offer price that is above the current market price, i.e. a premium price is offered by a private equity buyer. In this case, a quick profit is realized at the opportunity cost of potential long-term growth of free cash and growth of dividend payouts for existing shareholders.

Discounted Cash Flow (DCF) Valuation

Discounted cash flow (DCF) models involve the time value of money, and the financial formulas are non-linear. What this means is that slight changes in input assumptions cause large fluctuations in the estimated output intrinsic value. It does take a little effort to understand the limits and use of the DCF model, just as in the use of any other model. It does not mean that the model should be rendered unusable.

DCF Assumptions

FCF growth rate is assumed to decrease gradually using a half-life decay formula starting from a 15% high threshold, and ending toward 10% in the forecasted period as shown in Figure 2.

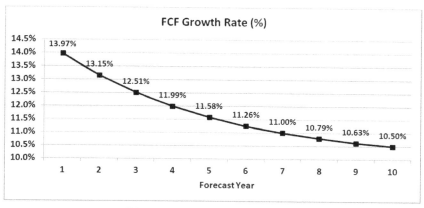

Figure 2: FCF Growth Rate

The remaining DCF assumptions are: residual or perpetuity growth rate of 3% beyond the forecast period, discount rate of 12%, diluted shares outstanding of 44.455M, cash and equivalents (C&E) of $151.314M, and long term debt of $0, as shown in Figure 3.

Company Name	FactSet Research, Inc.
Ticker	FDS
Starting TTM FCF i.e. Year 1	15.00%
Ending TTM FCF i.e. Year 10	10.00%
Residual (aka perpetuity) value growth rate (g)	3.00%
FCF Decay (half-life)	10
Discount rate (k)	12.00%
Price Per Share (at close of 4/5/2013)	$90.08
Free Cash Flow (TTM)	$209.6
Shares Outstanding	44.455
Cash & Equivalents (C&E)	$151.3
Long-Term Debt	$0.0

Figure 3: DCF Assumptions

Intrinsic Value

Estimated intrinsic value of the company is $4,618.9 million or intrinsic value per share of $103.90, given 44.455 million diluted shares outstanding. These intrinsic values are shown in Figure 4.

	Year									
	1	2	3	4	5	6	7	8	9	10
Prior year FCF	$209.6	$238.9	$270.3	$304.1	$340.6	$380.0	$422.8	$469.3	$519.9	$575.2
Growth rate (add)	13.97%	13.15%	12.51%	11.99%	11.58%	11.26%	11.00%	10.79%	10.63%	10.50%
FCF	$238.9	$270.3	$304.1	$340.6	$380.0	$422.8	$469.3	$519.9	$575.2	$635.6
Discount Factor (multiply)	0.8929	0.7972	0.7118	0.6355	0.5674	0.5066	0.4523	0.4039	0.3606	0.3220
Discounted value per annum	$213.3	$215.5	$216.4	$216.4	$215.6	$214.2	$212.3	$210.0	$207.4	$204.6
Cum. Discounted Value	$213.3	$428.7	$645.2	$861.6	$1,077.2	$1,291.4	$1,503.7	$1,713.7	$1,921.1	$2,125.7

Sum of present value of FCFs	$2,125.7	46%
Residual Value		
FCF in year 10	$635.6	
Growth rate (g) (add)	3.00%	
FCF in year 11	$654.6	
Capitalization rate (k-g)	9.00%	
Value at end of year 10	$7,273.6	
Discount factor at end of year 10 (multiply)	0.3220	
Present Value of Residual (Perpetuity) Value	$2,341.9	51%
Present Value of FCFs (in millions)	$4,467.6	
Add: Non-Operating Assets	$151.3	3%
Less: Long-Term Debt	$0.0	0%
Intrinsic Value of Company (in millions)	$4,618.9	100%
Intrinsic Value per Share	$103.90	
Shares Outstanding Latest Yr (millions)	44.455	
Price Per Share (at close of 4/5/2013)	$90.08	
Total Market Value (in millions)	$4,005	
Margin of Safety	13.30%	

Figure 4: Estimated Intrinsic Value Based on Assumptions

Additional insight brought forth by this DCF model is that the estimated $4,618.9 million intrinsic value is comprised of (1) $2,125.7 million in the forecasted 10-year period, (2) $2,341.9 million as the perpetuity value or going concern value, (3) $151.3 million as cash and equivalents. In short, the 10-year forecast period constituted 46% of intrinsic value, going concern value constitutes 51% of intrinsic value, and the remaining 3% of intrinsic value is due to cash.

Summary of Valuation

Intrinsic Valuation: We start with Free Cash Flows (FCFs) of $ 209.6M on a trailing twelve month (TTM) basis.

Intrinsic Value: $ 103.90 per share.

Market Price: $ 90.08 per share (at close of 4/5/2013).

Price-to-Value: 86.7 %

Margin of Safety: 13.3 %

Note: For a 35% margin of safety requirement, price per share is $67.54 derived from a what-if analysis.

Financial Statements

When I look at financial statements, I examine the balance sheet, cash flow, and income statement, in that order. Rather than being fixated on earnings first, understanding the balance sheet in terms of capitalization structure and how cash flow rolls up into balance sheet accounts is a good starting point. Next, I look at the cash flow statement in terms of generation and use of cash, since it allows me to examine the capital allocation strategy of the company. Finally, I look at the income statement. Following is a discussion of some observations in these statements, followed by a few ratios that caught my eye.

Balance Sheet

The company enjoys a pristine balance sheet. Debt and equity capital are primary sources of funds. FDS has no long-term debt and generates sufficient cash to fund its operations and growth. Since the company is in the information business, there is no capital tied up in the inventory line item of working capital. High cash flow generators usually have an increasing accumulation of cash on the balance sheet after capital expense is allocated for growth, and dividend payouts are taken into consideration. Cash and equivalents (C&E) range from 19% to 34% of total assets in the last 10 years. Beginning fiscal 2006, the company started making acquisitions, evidenced by the goodwill account on the balance sheet, and the goodwill to total assets ratio increased from 9.42% in 2006 to 35.4% in 2012. I would prefer goodwill to total assets ratio to be under 20%, so organic growth is the driver of future growth rather than an increase in acquisitions.

Cash Flow Statement

The cash flow statement indicates the free cash flow, i.e. cash generated from operations, less capital expenses, has increased significantly over the years. This makes sense because the company is not capital intensive and does not require significant reinvestment in its infrastructure. Figure 5 shows the historical free cash flow on a log chart.

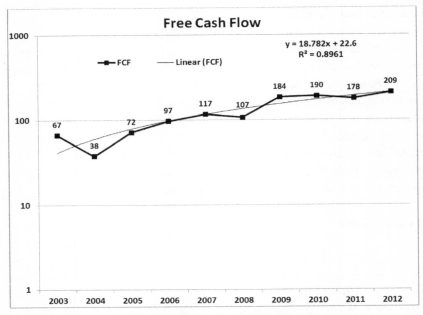

Figure 5: Historical FCF Trend

As shown in Figure 5, historical free cash flow has trended quite nicely at the growth rate of around 18% in the last 10 years.

Income Statement

The income statement indicates that the company is not in a razor thin margin, commodity business because net margins are above 21% in the 10-year period. The weighted average shares outstanding on a diluted basis trended down from 52 million in 2003 fiscal year-end to 46 million in 2012 fiscal year-end, as reported by Morningstar. This means that FDS has a reduction in share count of 11.5% via share repurchases.

Financial Ratios

Ratios are important to examine since they tell us about the performance of the business and how management is sustaining its competitive advantage. First, I'll discuss gross, operating, and net margins. Next, I'll discuss the remaining ratios of particular interest to investors such as operating cash flow and free cash flow (FCF) margins, FCF/Net Income ratio, shareholder yield, working capital efficiency, capital expense (CapEx) to sales ratio, return on equity (ROE), and cash return on invested capital (CROIC).

Gross, Operating, and Net Margins

Gross margins trended down from 70% to 65% in the last 10 years; however, management has been successful in maintaining operating margins above 31% and net margins above 21% in the last 10 years. Figure 6 shows the gross, operating and net margin trends.

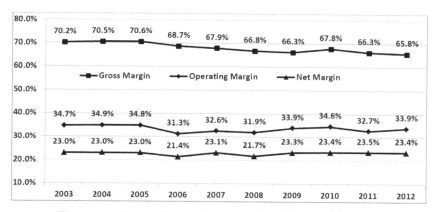

Figure 6: Gross, Operating, and Net Margin Trends

Despite the downtrend in gross margins, the operating and net margin trends indicate that management has control of costs.

Operating Cash Flow and Free Cash Flow Margins

FDS also enjoys high operating cash flow and free cash flow margins. Except for the Great Recession years, the operating cash flow margin and free cash flow margin are above 25% and 20%, respectively. Figure 7 shows the operating cash flow and free cash flow margins:

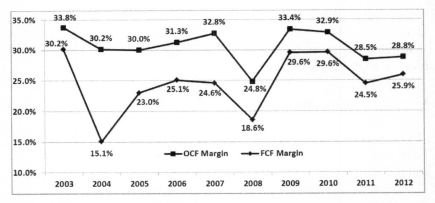

Figure 7: Operating Cash Flow and Free Cash Flow Margin Trends

Companies that enjoy these types of high cash flow margins will tend to accumulate a lot of cash on the balance sheet, as discussed previously. Prudent and rational allocation of cash is important to maintain competitiveness, and for management to continue to deliver high ROE and CROIC.

FCF/Net Income Ratio

Investors need to know the quality of earnings. The free cash flow to net income (FCF/Net Income) ratio is a litmus test that indicates the quality of earnings, i.e. it indicates the percent of net income that translates into free cash. Figure 8 shows the FCF/Net Income trend:

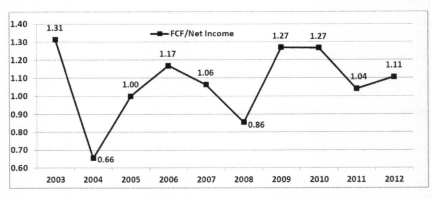

Figure 8: FCF/Net Income Trend

250

SEC filings indicate that the unusually low FCF/Net Income in 2004 is due to management deploying $26.9 million of the $37.8 million CapEx in the new Norwalk, Connecticut headquarters expansion. Particularly with leasehold improvements, furniture, and fixtures. There is no question that the Great Recession affected the cash flow generation of FDS in 2008 just as it would in any business that is tied to the financial industry. The lower FCF/Net Income in 2008 is due to an increase in accounts receivable, i.e. cash tied up in working capital. Aside from these two outlier years, it appears that FDS generates at least one dollar of free cash for each dollar of net income.

Shareholder Yield

The next ratio is shareholder yield, which is the ratio of return of capital to capital providers, divided by market capitalization. On the cash flow statement, we add the net repurchases of stock, dividend payouts, and net debt reductions. Since FDS has no debt, there is no net debt reduction to take into account. So, in this case, we add the net repurchase of stock and dividends paid. The result of which is divided by market capitalization. Figure 9 below shows the shareholder yield trend over the last 10 years:

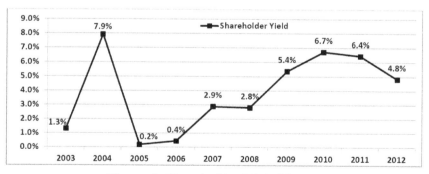

Figure 9: Shareholder Yield Trend

The unusually high shareholder yield ratio in 2004 is attributed to the fact that a co-founder indicated a need to sell two million shares as reported in a SEC filing. FDS elected to buy these co-founder shares as part of the share repurchase activity. The shareholder yield has trended up since 2005 and peaked in 2010, followed by a gradual decrease. It stands at 4.8% in fiscal 2012. This means that 4.8% of market capitalization was returned to shareholders in the form of stock repurchases and dividend payouts.

Working Capital Efficiency and CapEx-to-Sales Ratio

Next is the consideration of capital efficiency. There are two ratios that I look at; working capital efficiency and CapEx-to-sales ratio. For working capital efficiency we add the accounts receivable and inventory, then subtract accounts payable. The result is divided by sales. Note that the company does not have an inventory line item on the balance sheet, as discussed previously. CapEx-to-sales is the ratio that examines what percent of sales is allocated to capital expenses (CapEx) to grow the business or maintain competitiveness. Figure 10 shows these two capital efficiency ratios:

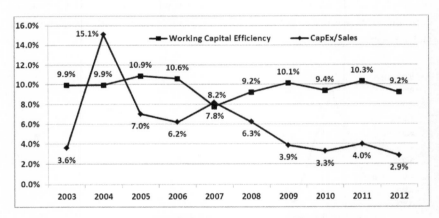

Figure 10: Capital Efficiency Ratios

The working capital efficiency trends indicate that it has fluctuated around 10% of sales, whereas the CapEx-to-sales ratio has trended down over the years. A downtrend in the working capital efficiency ratio indicates that there is less cash tied up in working capital as a percent of sales.

As stated previously, the company has been making acquisitions since 2006, thus it has allocated less CapEx for internal growth. Regardless, FDS's investment in its infrastructure to maintain competitiveness is not capital intensive, as can be seen by this low CapEx-to-sales ratio.

Return on Equity (ROE) and Cash Return on Invested Capital (CROIC)

The last two ratios are return on equity (ROE) and cash return on invested capital (CROIC) as shown in Figure 11:

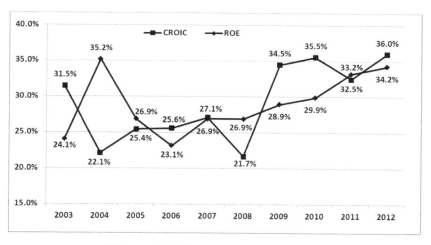

Figure 11: ROE and CROIC Trend

Since 2007, ROE has trended up with impressive results ending fiscal year 2012 with 34.2%. Examining DuPont components of ROE, net margin, asset turnover, and leverage, provides additional insights. The asset turnover ratio is fairly steady at around 1.11, while the asset to equity leverage ratio is also steady at around 1.28. This means that the key driver of ROE is the high net margin that stands around 23%, except for the Great Recession year, when net margin dipped to 21%. A high free cash flow generator that is not a capital-intensive business exhibits these types of favorable trends, especially when it is not in a commodity business.

Finally, CROIC is determined by first estimating invested capital. Total liabilities, less current liabilities added to equity is used as a proxy for invested capital, which is the denominator. Then the numerator is free cash flow (FCF), which is operating cash generated, less capital expenses. After that, CROIC is really simple; FCF divided by invested capital. As you can see from Figure 11, CROIC has trended up and ended 2012 at 36%, which is quite impressive despite the accumulation of cash on the balance sheet.

Summary

Excellent companies with proven business models that operate above cost of capital rarely trade at an attractive margin of safety relative to estimated intrinsic value. High net margins and management delivering high ROE and CROIC without long-term debt on a sustainable basis is an indication of FDS management's rational allocation of capital. In the 2003 to 2012 period, FDS has returned $1,139 million to shareholders in the form of net repurchase of stock and dividends. Existing shareholders should expect dividend growth to continue in the future. Value investors have to wait patiently for Mr. Market to provide temporary setbacks, and/or catalyst events for the price of FDS to head toward an attractive, or "fat pitch" level. When such infrequent opportunities occur with FDS, a high conviction bet can be taken by value investors.

Disclosure: Bakul Lalla is a shareholder of FDS.

NOTE: These case studies are not recommendations to buy or sell any security. They are presented for educational purposes only.

13.3 CASE STUDY #3:

Colgate-Palmolive Company:
Ticker Symbol: (CL)

Dr. Maulik Suthar, MD, Orange Holdings LLP,
Gandhinagar, Gujarat, India

Scott Thompson, MBA, Ameritrust Group
Sarasota, FL, USA

Time is the friend of the wonderful company and the enemy of the mediocre one. Before making an investment decision, seek understanding about the business, its products, sustainable competitive advantages, and competitors. Next, look for able and trustworthy managers who focus more on value than growth. Finally ask: Is there a bargain relative to its intrinsic value?

Before we make an investment decision, we must decide (Filter #1) if Colgate-Palmolive is a high quality business with good economics. Does Colgate-Palmolive have (Filter #2) enduring competitive advantages, and does Colgate-Palmolive have (Filter #3) honest and capable management? Finally, does Colgate-Palmolive make for an intelligent investment or intelligent speculation today? (Filter#4).

Filter #1: Circle of Competence: Is Colgate an understandable first class business?

In an era of high volatility, combined with many uncertainties, most investors are forced to focus on survival first (short-term) and growth later (long-term). Herbert Spencer's, "Survival of the fittest" concept is as relevant to Value Investing as it is to evolution theory. In extremely tough times, only the "fittest" can survive. Investors seek to identify businesses with resilient business economics, strong fundamentals, and healthy balance sheets. The Fast Moving Consumer Goods (FMCG) sector attracts attention from investors in times of uncertainty because demand for these products continues throughout the year. Products like shaving razors, detergents, toothpaste, soaps, etc., find consumers, no matter what the economic situation. Now let us think of this as a case for Colgate-Palmolive (NYSE: CL).

Founded in 1806, Colgate-Palmolive now holds a staggering 44.7% global market share with its flagship toothpaste line. Colgate's products are marketed in over 200 countries and territories. Colgate's brand strength in global markets allows it to command a large market share with high profit margins. Colgate continues to expand its global operations throughout Latin America, Africa, and Asia, while maintaining consistent sales growth in these regions.

Colgate-Palmolive is involved in production, distribution and provision of household, health care and personal products, such as soaps, detergents, and oral hygiene products, including toothpaste and toothbrushes. Its business is divided into two primary product segments; Oral, Personal and Home Care, and Pet Nutrition. Under its "Hill's" brand, it is also a manufacturer of veterinary products. It produces toothpaste, toothbrushes, mouth rinses, dental floss, and pharmaceutical products for dentists and other oral health professionals. Personal and Home Care items include; shower gels, shampoos, conditioners, deodorants, and antiperspirants, and liquid hand soaps; dishwashing liquids, household cleaners, oil soaps, and fabric conditioners. The Pet Nutrition division produces food for dogs and cats. These are sold to wholesale and retail distributors, as well as, to veterinarians and specialty pet retailers. (Filter #1) Understand the business.

Filter #2: Moats or Durable Competitive Advantage:

In terms of Opportunity Cost, is Colgate the best place to invest our money today? Or, are there better alternatives? How will Colgate compete going forward? Technologies change and new technologies can emerge. Keep in mind that a financial report is a reflection of the past and present. It may be used to project a future, but it may not account for factors yet unseen. Therefore, pay attention to competitive and market factors that may affect changes in profitability.

The social proof phenomenon, which derives from psychology, offers many advantages to scale. For example, global product distribution is hard to attain. Another advantage of Colgate, similar to Coca-Cola, is that it is available almost everywhere in the world. Suppose you have some toothpaste or soft drink to sell. Exactly how do you make it available all over the Earth? The worldwide distribution setup, which is slowly won by a big enterprise, gets to be a huge advantage. Similarly, after you achieve enough advantages of this type, it can become very difficult for competitors to dislodge you. Colgate's strong global distribution channel is integral to its strength. The company has established the largest distributed oral care brand in the world.

There is another kind of advantage of scale. In some businesses, the very nature of things is to sort of cascade toward the overwhelming dominance of one firm. The greater the number of product offerings, the more each resource is utilized, be it the distribution channel, the marketing or branding strengths. In this context, companies with a single product or just a few products are risky.

Number one, they have to continuously be wary of competitors coming in and weaning away market share. Therefore, they have to significantly increase advertising and marketing budgets. This is a double whammy for a company under pressure. On one hand, revenues are under pressure. On the other, costs go up and margins are squeezed. Also, due to this squeeze on profits, the business is often shy to invest in new products and expand its distribution network. In such businesses, future growth prospects get stunted.

Colgate offers a wide variety of products. Colgate has an oral care portfolio spread across different price points. Each product has a different value offering. The business has several offerings, like Colgate Dental Cream, Max Gel, and Advance Whitening, which cater to consumers as they upgrade and cross-sell. The business also has niche offerings like Colgate Sensitive for people who have sensitive teeth. On top of this, once there is an acquired brand loyalty, Colgate retains its customers.

FMCG companies' success is often attributed to their marketing and branding skills. The ability to continuously create successful brands, plus advertising, often spells success for a company. As they say, "nothing succeeds like success." Once a brand is successful, it is easier for a company to piggyback on its initial success to introduce more products and associate them with the known brand. Among the brands that have become household names are Colgate, Palmolive, Mennen, Speed Stick, Lady Speed Stick, Softsoap, Irish Spring, Protex, Sorriso, Kolynos, Elmex, Tom's of Maine, Ajax, Axion, Fabuloso, Soupline, Suavitel, Hill's Science Diet and Hill's Prescription Diet.

Another factor is pricing power. Despite of fear of losing customers during rising inflation, Colgate's brands have lower manufacturing costs. While the business manages to pass on a part of the rising cost to customers, they can also absorb some of the rising costs and retain their market share versus competitors. With a growth rate of over 15% over the past 5 years, it is a marketing multinational player.

Colgate has to spend a smaller amount of revenues for R&D compared with competitors operating within its sector, like Telecom, Pharma and Hi-tech. Colgate has less dependence on Innovation. Colgate saves a lot of money from its lack of heavy R&D expenses. This is a huge benefit for Colgate and its shareholders. Colgate maintains and grows its market share by introducing new product launches and variants. These new product introductions helped it tap into urban markets that change rapidly and continue demanding new, innovative products. New product launches allow Colgate to increase its global market share even larger. Colgate has also improved its product mix through higher sales of value-added products and better market realizations.

Colgate-Palmolive possesses significant barriers to entry that slows competitive threats. This helps to fend against competitive threats and it can increase shareholder profit. However, to retain the market share, Colgate needs to spend on advertising. It faces moderate competition from companies such as P&G, Avon, Clorox Company (CLX), Energizer Holdings (ENR), Henkel, Kimberly-Clark (KMB), L'Oreal, and Reckitt Benckiser. Thus, to retain its competitive advantage in the future, Colgate must keep spending on its brand, building through advertising and promotion. This will help increase sales volume and growth momentum.

In summary, Colgate's major advantages are the strength of its brand and its strong global distribution presence. Any competition in the oral care category will not pose a significant threat to Colgate in the short or medium term. Any new competitor would likely take market share from local brands rather than the market leader Colgate. Any serious competition would be met with an increase in advertising spending. Such a move could affect quarterly profitability and present an attractive bargain opportunity for the stock purchase. Colgate has great brand equity that should enable it to remain a market leader for decades to come.

Filter #3: Management

Look at the past record of management, its vision and its integrity. It is ultimately the management, who are the decision makers and therefore the guardians of your interests in the business. However, if management has a track record of being dishonest or slow to react to business and economic conditions, then the biggest distribution channel and the most diversified product portfolio may not give you your rightful share of the company's growth and profits.

Growth benefits investors only when the business can invest at incremental returns that are enticing. Each dollar used to finance growth should create over a dollar of long-term market value. In the case of a low-return business requiring incremental funds, growth hurts the investor. The wonderful companies sustain a competitive advantage, produce free cash flow, and use debt wisely.

Colgate successfully implements its global market strategy by offering rapid, cost-effective delivery of high-quality products to a diverse group of customers worldwide. It continues to focus on expanding its geographic reach. With the global economic downturn and decreasing consumer spending, this growth in corporate profits has been declining in the U.S. and globally.

The FMCG industry's reputation for being more recession resistant has led us to investigate potential investments in this industry. Colgate has demonstrated the ability to grow Revenues, Profits, Free Cash Flow, and NOPAT throughout this current, challenging environment. The expected growth rates for the overall company and its segments remain positive. Management feels comfortable predicting a 5-8% growth this year, even with the global economic slowdown.

Some of the strategic initiatives of Colgate's management are; "Focus on Consumers, the Profession and Our Customers, Effectiveness and Efficiency in Everything, Innovation and wherever applicable and improvement in Leadership."

Filter #4: Margin of Safety by a favorable Price/Value ratio.

Does Colgate-Palmolive make for an intelligent investment or intelligent speculation today? Let us do a rough estimation of intrinsic value per share.

The past 5-year trend of FCF (Free Cash Flow) pattern of CL indicates steady increases and no negative surprises. A positive cash flow is typically used for internal expansion, acquisitions, dividend payments, etc. A company that generates, rather than consumes cash is in much better shape to fund such activities on their own, rather than needing to borrow funds to do so.

We begin with $ 3,200,000,000 free cash flow, an estimated annual growth rate of 5% over years 1–10, then assuming a conservative 0% growth rate over years 11–15, with shares outstanding 467,700,000. We have chosen 12% as the discount rate on the highly conservative side.

Free Cash Flows (FCFs): Colgate-Palmolive Co. (CL)

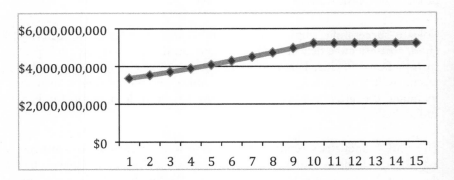

Our Discounted Cash Flow (DCF) analysis shows an estimated intrinsic value for Colgate (CL) of about $61.74 per share, compared with the Current Market Price (CMP) of Colgate, $119 per share (April 2013).

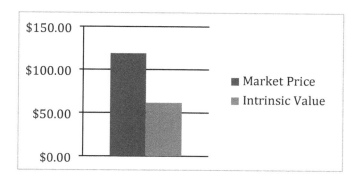

This implies a price-to-value ratio of 1.927, and a "Margin of Safety" (MOS) ratio of negative (–92.7%). If it were positive, a Margin Of Safety of more than 50% would be desirable to qualify Colgate as a deep value investing idea. However, the <u>negative MOS</u> is enough to refuse the idea of buying Colgate at its current valuation. Such a move would mean paying significantly above its intrinsic value.

Warren Buffett's Berkshire Hathaway has a much lower cost of borrowing, and float to invest. Does it make sense for them to buy? Starting with a base estimate of annual Free Cash Flow at a value of approximately $3,200,000,000 and the number of shares outstanding at 467,700,000 shares; we used a discount rate of 4%, an assumed FCF annual growth of 7% for year 1–10 years, and assume 0% growth from years 11–15. The resulting estimated intrinsic value per share (discounted back to the present) is approximately $120.75.

Free Cash Flows (FCFs): Colgate-Palmolive Co. (CL)

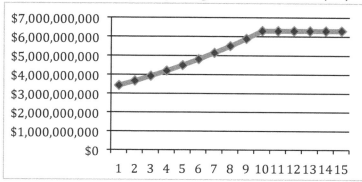

Under this scenario, Market Price = $119, and the estimated Intrinsic Value = $120.75. So, here the Margin of Safety (MOS) = 1.4%. The Price To Value (P/V) ratio = .986 and estimated bargain = $1.75. This is not enough of a bargain to entice Mr. Buffett. We simply place it here for your consideration and comparison.

Ratios:

Table: Valuations of Colgate-Palmolive vs. with Industry and S&P 500

	CL	Industry Avg	S&P 500	CL 5Y Avg*
Price/Earnings	23.23	20.3	16.6	19.0
Price/Book	25.2	4.5	2.3	17.9
Price/Sales	3.3	2.2	1.5	2.7
Price/Cash Flow	17.7	14.9	9.7	14.8
Dividend Yield %	2.2	2.5	2.3	2.3

Data as of April 17, 2013, *Price/Cash Flow uses 3-year average.

If we consider Colgate's P/E (price to earnings multiple) and market capitalization to sales ratio, the company is trading on par with its peers. Growth oriented businesses will most likely be trading at a premium to competitors, based on these two ratios. If so, then one has to gauge whether paying a premium to own its shares is justified. If the premium is unrealistically high, then it may not be wise to invest at that time. Valuations must justify the company's future earnings prospects.

People who just look at P/E don't appreciate; 1) Dividend history and hence the EPS, 2) Steady and incremental Free Cash Flow / Flat demand of products, even in a bad economy, 3) Debt free Balance sheet, 4) Strong pricing power because of strong brand value and quality, 5) World-class quality of Management.

Traditionally, FMCG companies have enjoyed high valuations, mainly because they are least impacted by changes in the macro-economic environment. Also, most businesses like HUL, Gillette, P&G, and Colgate enjoy premium valuations due to their multinational parents holding a majority stake in them, and their deep pockets.

Look at the business's cash flows and the working capital efficiencies. It will give you an idea of the company's bargaining power, as well as its ability to utilize its resources and supply chain. Also, look at the dividend paying track record. A healthy dividend payout, i.e., the ratio of dividends to earnings, is also a good indicator of the company's willingness to share wealth with small shareholders.

Profitability Analysis:

Colgate has experienced increasing revenue growth over the past 5 years. If this growth has come about due to continuous new product introductions, and growth in market share, it is an encouraging sign for Colgate-Palmolive.

· Five year annualized company revenue growth is 7%
· Five year annualized company earnings growth is 11%
· Five year annualized dividend growth rate is 13%.

Operating margin is a measurement of what portion of a business's revenue is left over after paying variable costs of production, such as raw materials, wages, and sales and marketing costs. A healthy operating margin is required for a company to be able to pay for its fixed costs, such as interest on debt. The higher the margin, the better it is for the company, as it indicates its operating efficiency.

Operating margin for Colgate is 22% and it appears stable for the past decade. The Net profit Margin is above 14 % and it is fairly consistent while the Industry average is only 10%. This shows that the economic moat of Colgate is sustainable. Gross Margin is 58% and has been stable for a decade. The companies that pass this criterion have strong positions within their respective industries and offer greater shareholder returns. A true test of the quality of a company is that they can sustain this margin.

Management Effectiveness:

For the past trailing 12 months (ttm), Return on Assets is 19.11% and Return on Equity (ttm) is 106.71%. ROE is higher because of the high amount of the leverage.

Colgate has grown its net profits at a CAGR of 16% in the past five years. Given a positive outlook for the oral care sector and the strong competitive position, Colgate expects profit growth to be 8% CAGR over the next three years.

PEG Ratio (5-yr expected) is 2.29.

To unearth more successful investments, deeper digging on the earnings headlines and a check-up on ROIC is essential. Businesses with consistently high ROIC are efficiently using capital. They can use their extra returns to buy back shares, further invest in their future success, or pay dividends to shareholders.

Return on capital invested (ROIC):

ROIC is an important tool to assess a company's potential to be a quality investment by determining how well the management is able to allocate capital to its operations for future growth. ROIC is perhaps the most important metric in value investing. By determining a company's ROIC, one can assess how well it's using the cash you entrust to it, and whether it's actually creating value for you. Simply put, ROIC divides a company's operating profit by the amount of investment it took to get that profit:

ROIC = Net operating profit after taxes / Invested capital

This one-size-fits-all calculation cuts out many of the legal accounting tricks (such as excessive debt) that managers use to boost earnings numbers, and provides you with an apples-to-apples way to evaluate businesses, even across industries. The higher the ROIC, the more efficiently the company uses capital.

Ultimately, we are looking for companies that can invest their money at rates that are higher than the cost of capital, and for most businesses those land between 8% to 12%. Ideally, we want to see ROIC greater than 12%. We are also seeking a history of increasing returns, or at least steady returns, that indicate the company's moat can withstand competitors' assaults.

Let's look at **Colgate-Palmolive** (NYSE: CL) and two of its industry peers to see how efficiently they use capital. Here are the ROIC figures for each company over several time periods:

	TTM	1 year ago	3 years ago	5 years ago
Colgate-Palmolive (NYSE: CL)	35.5%	32.6%	29.2%	22.9%
Clorox (NYSE: CLX)	20.6%	20.0%	22.7%	24.9%
Church & Dwight (NYSE: CHD)	11.5%	10.8%	9.4%	10.6%

Colgate-Palmolive offers us higher returns on invested capital, and displays the type of growth in returns we are looking for. The company's competitive position appears to be getting stronger, at least according to this metric.

Long-term Debt and Solvency Analysis:

Debt to Equity ratio is 2.39 and Debt to Capital ratio is 0.70. A highly leveraged business is the first to get hit during times of economic downturn, as companies still must pay interest costs, despite lower profitability. Instead, the company should have a low Debt/Equity ratio, which indicates a strong balance sheet. The Debt/Equity ratio should not be greater than 25%, or should be less than the average Debt/Equity for its industry. Total Debt/Equity of CL is not acceptable. One can find other, better businesses that do not have to borrow money to grow.

Interest Coverage ratio is 49.43. That is very high and hence it is not acceptable. Interest coverage ratio is used to determine how comfortably a company is placed in terms of payment of interest on outstanding debt. The interest coverage ratio is calculated by dividing a company's earnings before interest and taxes (EBIT) by its interest expense for a given period. The lower the ratio, the greater the risks.

Average shares outstanding:

Colgate-Palmolive (CL) has not been significantly increasing the number of shares outstanding within recent years, which is a good sign. CL currently has 467 million shares outstanding. This means the company is not taking any measures, with regards to the number of shares that will dilute or devalue the stock. The Altman Z-Score for Colgate-Palmolive (CL) is 7. This indicates that CL is in safe zone.

Risk profile of Colgate-Palmolive (CL)

A single product company: Colgate is a single product-type company with almost 90% of its sales from toothpastes. While the parent company has a rich product portfolio in personal products and foods, these have not been launched in India. Aside from toothpaste, other products like shower gel, hand wash and utensil washing paste are not making a substantial contribution to the bottom line. The reasons vary from being in a competitive segment to being in a nascent category. This dependence on one product, the equivalent of putting all eggs in one basket does not bode well for the company.

Strong emergence of local brands in Emerging markets: Colgate has suffered loss of market share due to increased competition. In the past decade, Colgate faced competition from private store brands of large retailers such as Wal-Mart and Target. Private label brands often sell at lower price points and earn higher margins because the retailers can control their production costs. Large retailers are closer to consumers. They have the point of sale data on consumer purchases, and are in a better position to understand consumer behavior.

These strengths contribute to better private label product development, which directly compete with Colgate products. Retailers also promote their own brands as they earn higher margins on them. However, Colgate continues to maintain a 44.7% market share in toothpaste and a strong brand name, which will make it difficult for private labels to erode Colgate's market leadership.

Margin pressure: Though demand is expected to remain on a firm footing, certain personal care products and branded items could witness a fall in consumer interest. Besides, high prices of key inputs remain a cause for concern for all FMCG companies. The limited pricing power for most products in this industry is an impediment in times of inflation.

However, any drop in the prices of key raw materials in the near future or additional price hikes will boost the profitability for FMCG companies. The prices of major raw materials continue to be at high levels. Margin pressure is inevitable, despite the focus on value added or premium products, where realizations are much higher than core products. Thanks to competition, advertising is vital for the company and therefore is required to spend more on promotion.

Currency fluctuation: The relative strength of the dollar also affects the risk profile. Although the company is based in the U.S., Colgate-Palmolive generates more than two thirds of its revenue outside USA. Because of this, the company is very sensitive to the strength of the dollar, with a weaker dollar generally boosting sales. Colgate has broad exposure to foreign currencies and actively hedges a large portion of these to avoid wide swings in earnings from currency fluctuations. Although this heading limits the potential upside of a weakening dollar, it also insulates the company from drastic upswings in the dollar's strength.

Catalysts:

Going forward, are there any transformational catalysts or condition indicators imaginable on the horizon? Yes, there are. Some of the catalysts driving future profit growth are:

- Rapid increases in demand from emerging markets. Emerging markets across the globe present strong growth opportunities for Colgate-Palmolive. As populations grow wealthier in emerging markets such as Brazil, Russia, India and China, consumers are becoming ever more sophisticated shoppers. Colgate-Palmolive's strong international brand presence means that it is much more highly exposed to emerging markets than its competitors. Generally, this exposure benefits Colgate. Emerging markets can grow at three to four times the rate of developed markets such as the U.S., Western Europe, and Japan, which means more profit opportunities and sales growth for Colgate.
- Its strong and improving product portfolio gives it a competitive advantage in commanding shelf space.
- A shift towards better margin products in the oral, personal and pet care categories.
- A shift towards better margin products in the oral, personal and pet care categories.
- An ongoing restructuring program that emphasizes; 1) improving gross and operating profits by streamlining its global supply chain, and also its manufacturing facilities by reducing headcount, 2) stepped up marketing effort to drive volume, and 3) building global market share.

The Final Verdict:

Does Colgate make for an intelligent investment or intelligent speculation today? The answer is Colgate-Palmolive (CL) is a great company at a mediocre price. The greatest investment opportunities arise when wonderful businesses are on the operating table, and suffering from a temporary solvable problem. Over the long-term, I think this investment looks promising, but we would prefer to see the company with a stock valuation closer to $60 or even in the $50's. The high level of debt is scary enough for value investors. For a company like Colgate-Palmolive, the debt to equity ratio must be less than 0.5.

Summary:

Colgate will benefit from; 1) consumer upgrades, 2) high market growth opportunity, 3) a strong distribution network, and 4) powerful brand equity. Colgate has been able to stay convincingly ahead of the market thanks to its ability to segment market categories (including toothbrushes and mouthwashes) in which product differentiation is difficult to achieve.

Colgate-Palmolive is a stable, growing company with impressive international sales in a highly competitive and recession-resistant industry. It has an excellent market share of oral and personal care products, as well as pet nutrition products. The talk in the FMCG sector is all about growth and margins. Predictably so, as the future prospects of the sector hinges solely on these factors. The margins have been under pressure over the past year due to rising raw material costs, oil prices and so on, and it could come increasingly under pressure in the future. If you have already invested in the sector, it makes sense to hold on to your shares, given the fact that markets are likely to remain uncertain in the near term. Most FMCG stocks are blue-chip businesses with good corporate governance, management, and long-term track records.

Colgate offers high quality basic products, but it faces continual risk from foreign exchange rates, commodity costs, and cheaper product alternatives, as well as strong competition from other top brands. Approximately 70% of sales come from outside of the U.S. despite this being a U.S. based business. Its products boast high market shares in its markets, and they are attractively packaged to promote further brand growth. Although we like the business, it carries higher debt levels, and is trading at a premium to intrinsic value.

CHAPTER FOURTEEN:

Macroeconomic & Geopolitical

14.1 Overview:

Macroeconomic and geopolitical events can trigger catalyst events that affect stock prices. Warren does not focus much on macro events. He focuses more on individual businesses. Through his voracious reading habits, Warren maintains a firm grasp on how the world works.

Warren spends about seven hours reading every day. Warren's daily reading includes: six newspapers, stacks of annual reports, 10-K, 10-Q, 13-F statements, financial statements, and other SEC filings. Warren was asked how he knows so much about the annual reports of thousands of businesses. Warren just smiled and said, "Start with the A's!"

According to the World Federation of Exchanges, there were 8,823 publicly traded stocks listed on US exchanges in October-1997. However, 15 years later, in October-2012, this number had decreased to only 4,943 publicly traded stocks (listed on American NYSE and NASDAQ exchanges). This shows a decline of 3,880 publicly traded stocks de-listed from American exchanges over the 15-year period from 1997 to 2012.

Fortunately for today's investors, 4,943 stocks (in 2012) are much more manageable to analyze than 8,823 stocks (in 1997) as traded on U.S. exchanges (according to the World Federal of Exchanges). This also reduces the number of potential investments available for investors to consider. Value investors must make certain their valuations and analyses are accurate, especially when investing other peoples' money.

14.2 Macroeconomic & Geopolitical:

If you discover a macroeconomic event about to occur, ask yourself which sector of businesses is it most likely to affect? Macroeconomic and geopolitical catalysts are only two of many potential catalysts that can affect stock prices. Consider performing valuations in advance for many businesses. Make sure your valuations are accurate, so you can be prepared to take swift action when opportunity arises.

"Be greedy when others are fearful. Be fearful when others are greedy." Ben Graham

Many of the best opportunities are only open for a limited time, so be prepared in advance to act decisively when the need arises. History shows that Warren made many of his biggest investment decisions during periods when their stock prices were trading near record lows. During these periods when other investors are paralyzed with fear (or wiped out by margin calls), Warren boldly and decisively invests his capital wisely.

The most successful value investors read multiple annual reports, financial statements, research business fundamentals, estimate valuations, and identify the best businesses within each sector and industry.

Investors like Kyle Bass (Hayman Capital) focus more on macroeconomic events, such as sovereign debt levels as a multiple of sovereign tax revenues. In 2013, Hayman Capital tracked Japan's central bank monetary policy, which had printed its yen currency into the quadrillions. Conversely, Warren focuses more on individual businesses. Decide where you will focus your energy, and which investment strategy is right for you.

Warren says the most successful value investors possess an ability to "see around corners." In other words, these investors can extrapolate today's data to estimate likely future outcomes. Investors make money looking through the windshield (future), not in the rearview mirror (past).

After 60 years of reading and acquiring knowledge, Warren has become somewhat of a human encyclopedia, with amazing knowledge and recall of vast amounts of information, cross-referenced at will.

Warren focuses on individual businesses. However, it's clear he also understands businesses in the context of their environments of market, sector, industry, and competition. Ask yourself: How many annual reports do I read per day? How many financial newspapers? Am I aware of market conditions across several sectors and industries? Which businesses, sectors, or industries are undervalued? Which are overvalued? Where are the best opportunities? Like Warren, can you see around corners?

CHAPTER FIFTEEN:

Parables of Investment Wisdom

By Scott Thompson

Over the past several years I have enjoyed compiling the following list of investment parables. They can be used as helpful tools to guide you to make better life decisions. *(Arranged alphabetically)*

15.1 Parables of Investment Wisdom:

"A great investment is not a bargain at any price."

"A quantitative approach to financial analysis can help us identify nuances of the qualitative."

"Action, not words, is the true test."

"After you create an expectation, live up to it."

"Allow your money to work for you, or you will always be working for your money."

"Anyone can invest in assets, but to optimally allocate assets to their highest and best use consistently, requires skill not luck."

"Are you motivated by internal or external factors?"

"Art often refers to qualitative, whereas science often refers to quantitative. Therefore, value investing is both an art and a science."

"At some price a bargain is no longer a bargain."

"Be an investor, not a consumer."

"Be as eager to pay off debt as you are to acquire it."

"Become the best version of yourself, not somebody else."

"Before allocating capital, always consider opportunity cost."

"Beware of the low interest rate trap. Rates can unexpectedly increase faster than you can remain solvent."

"Buy shares of high-quality businesses at bargain prices when they are out of favor. Avoid value traps."

"Calculate the certainty of success before you invest your money."

"Capital is finite. Invest it wisely."

"Capitalism is not the problem. Interventionism is the problem. In true free-market capitalism, gains are privatized and losses are privatized. However, when governments intervene, gains are privatized, but losses become socialized. This is not capitalism. This is interventionism."

"Coal and diamonds both start off the same, but diamonds emerge after enduring periods of intense heat and pressure."

"Compound interest is a wonderful thing if you're receiving it, and potentially devastating if you're paying it."

"Control your expenditures."

"Debt is a form of slavery."

"Decisions have consequences. Before you invest, consider both intended and unintended consequences."

"Determine what the business is worth, not what the stock price is today."

"Develop a centered and unshakeable core."

"Do things now because you want to, not at the very last minute when you are forced to."

"Do you learn from your mistakes, or just repeat the same ones over and over again?"

"Doing smart things can make investors money, but not doing dumb things can make investors even more money."

"Don't be jealous of another's success. Instead learn what makes them successful and incorporate those qualities into yourself."

"Don't confuse activity with accomplishment."

"Don't fight every battle... only those you can win."

"Don't make commitments you can't deliver."

"Don't misperceive bumps in the road as insurmountable obstacles."

"Don't spend money you think you will receive in the future until you actually receive it, because quite often, future money never arrives."

"Earn infinitely, spend finitely."

"Earning it, is more fun than spending it."

"Eliminate distractions."

"Everyone has opinions about investing– stick with facts, not opinions."

"Everyone says, 'Buy low, sell high,' but few possess the discipline to actually achieve it."

"Evolve your thinking from employee to entrepreneur."

"Financial education is important, and it is a detriment to society that schools do not teach it."

"Fiscal discipline includes denying yourself depreciating assets in the short-term, for appreciating assets in the long-term."

"Focus more on the long-term than short-term."

"Focus on value, not price."

"For many people, credit cards are an irresistible way to trade the future for the present."

"Friends call just because. Opportunists call when they need something."

"Gamblers do it for the thrill. Value investors do it for the returns."

"Good financial habits are important to establish early. After a while momentum just feeds on itself."

"Good intentions are no substitute for taking action."

"Good people with good intentions often fail to consider unintended consequences."

"Great investing includes great valuations."

"Have the discipline to say No."

"I choose humility over pride. I choose confidence over arrogance. I choose philanthropy over money. I choose to be a voice for those who don't have one, and through this I have found my own voice."

"I do not always like reality, but it is best to face the truth head on and see it for what it truly is."

"I don't speculate in ideas or start-ups. I invest in established businesses."

"I find my investments. My investments don't find me."

"I grow financial oak trees. I just plant acorns and wait."

"I tend to be conservative in my intrinsic valuations. I'd rather underestimate, than overestimate."

"I'd rather walk away than overpay."

"I'm neither a pessimist nor an optimist. I get paid to be a realist."

"Identify value where others do not."

"Idiocy knows no boundaries. Genius does."

"If principles change, they are not principles."

"If facts make you mad, maybe your opinion is wrong."

"If the water level of a lake drops significantly does the value of your boat decrease? No. Similarly, although stock market prices fluctuate wildly, underlying asset value remains relatively stable."

"If you can't value the underlying business you shouldn't buy its stock."

"If you can't value a business, find someone who can."

"If you're in debt, you pay interest. If you invest, you receive interest. Which is more sustainable?"

"In a bidding war, the winner is the loser."

"In a free market, consumers vote with their money."

"Invest in appreciating assets, instead of spending on depreciating assets."

"In investing, focus on facts not opinions."

"In life, know the difference between friends and opportunists."

"In order to become a value investor, you must learn to estimate the value of the underlying business."

"Inexperienced investors hope for best-case scenarios, but worst-case scenarios often happen. Hope is not a strategy."

"Inner scoreboard is humility. Outer scoreboard is arrogance."

"Integrity is keeping your promise long after the emotion of the moment has passed, in which you made your promise."

"Investing it wisely is more fun than spending it on depreciating assets."

"Investment capital is finite. Allocate it wisely."

"Investors make money through the windshield not the rear-view mirror."

"It wasn't raining when Noah built the ark."

"It's amazing how many speculate based on emotion, instead of facts."

"It's foolish to kick the can down the road, because eventually the future becomes now."

"It's no use trying to apply logic where there is none."

"It's not just the smart things you do, but the dumb things you don't do that make you a successful value investor."

"It is easier to stay out of debt, than to get out of debt."

"It is hard to go broke when you don't owe any money."

"Know what you seek, before you begin your search."

"Know what you're actually investing in, before you invest in it."

"Learn from the lessons of history, or be doomed to repeat the past."

"Let go of who you've become, and become who you're meant to be!"

"Let integrity define you, not broken promises."

"Life changes, but principles do not."

"Life is a series of problem-solving opportunities."

"Live below your means and your wealth will multiply."

"Many erroneously believe stocks are somehow magically exempt from the laws of valuation."

"Many erroneously make investment decisions based on what others do, not on the merits of the investment."

"Many would like to receive the reward, but few are willing to do the hard work required."

"Markets are inefficient in the short-term and efficient in the long term."

"Most financial advisors are better asset gatherers than asset allocators."

"Most speculate based on emotion– not analysis or fact."

"Most gamblers and speculators lose money, while most value investors earn money."

"My favorite chapter in the Bible is Proverbs. Choose wisdom first."

"My focus is like a laser and unwavering."

"My grandfather was a farmer who understood value. He'd never overpay for a tractor, and I'd never overpay for a stock."

"Never invest in anything you don't understand."

"Never risk anything important to you for something unimportant to you. You will likely end up with neither."

"Never trade something you need for something you want."

"Nothing is a bargain at any price."

"Nuances of qualitative factors become detectable during quantitative analysis."

"Pay down your highest interest debt first."

"People spend more time planning their vacation, than their retirement."

"People tend to keep their bad stocks and get rid of their good ones. If stocks were friends, wouldn't it better to keep the good ones and get rid of the bad ones?"

"Philanthropy has less to do with money, and more to do with service to your community."

"Philanthropy is the love of others expressed by donations of time, service, volunteering, money, or anything of value."

"Prepare for opportunity before it arrives."

"Provide value first. After you help people get what they want, then you get what you want."

"Quantify price-to-value. At what price is a bargain no longer a bargain?"

"Qualitative, quantitative, and catalyst."

"Respond, don't react."

"Results, not excuses."

"Risk is not volatility. Risk is the possibility of losing money."

"Rule #1 of real estate investing is: Never invest in a property you can't drive past every day."

"See things how they are, not how you wish them to be."

"Seeds of success or failure are in your own thinking."

"Sharpen your focus until its undeterred, like an arrow flying straight to its target."

"Show restraint. Just because you can, doesn't always mean you must."

"So much beneficial wisdom falls on deaf ears."

"Someday may never come, so make someday today."

"Step into your destiny."

"Stocks are not lottery tickets. Instead, stocks are fractional ownership shares of operating businesses."

"Stop competing, and run your own race."

"Stop spending. Start saving."

"Success has more to do with happiness than money."

"Tell people the truth, even if it's what they don't want to hear."

"The best research is your own."

"The best things in life cannot be measured monetarily."

"The best way to get a referral is to give one."

"The boundaries of poverty are furthest away from the debt-free."

"The brain is like software. You can program it any way you choose."

"The entire premise of value investing is to buy high-quality assets below their intrinsic value and sell them near their intrinsic value."

"The only two prices that matter are the day you buy a stock and the day you sell it. The volatility in between is inconsequential."

"The private sector is a better allocator of capital than the government."

"The simple objective is to buy low and sell high, but few investors actually achieve this."

"The stock market is where people don't buy when things go on sale."

"The wealthiest people are those who've learned to delay gratification."

"The world cannot stop a motivated mind."

"There are no shortcuts. To have staying power, you must do the work."

"There are three ways to invest: overvalued, fairly-valued, and undervalued. Value investors choose undervalued."

"There is just no need to accept extraordinary risk, to earn extraordinary returns."

"Think long-term, not short-term."

"Trying to borrow your way out of debt is like trying to drink your way out of alcoholism."

"Under-promise and over-deliver."

"Unless you change the path you're on, you'll likely end up exactly where you're headed."

"Use the quantitative to help reveal the qualitative."

"Using lower discount rates, especially those below the cost of capital (WACC), can falsely increase the appearance of Intrinsic Value."

"Value investors don't try to predict the future. Instead, we invest in high-quality business with earnings we believe will continue into the future."

"Value investors make investment decisions based on what's optimal, instead of what's available."

"Value investors profit from dislocations between price and value caused by sellers who do not know how to properly value assets they are selling."

"Value investors think the other 95% of investors are contrarians."

"Wall Street makes money off clients. We make money for clients."

"Wall Street is more concerned with correlation than valuation."

"Watching small financial acorns grow into large financial oak trees is not exciting, but it makes a lot of money."

"We all have time for our priorities."

"What you input into your mind is what you output."

"What you think in private, you eventually become in public."

"When analyzing financial data, one year is not a trend."

"When analyzing potential investments, it is not what the entire business earns, it is what the investor earns."

"When it comes to investing, possessing a calm rational temperament is just as important as selecting the right securities."

"Why do people spend as much as they earn, no matter how much their income increases?"

"You can't make it what it isn't, but you can accept it for what it is."

"You cannot borrow your way out of debt."

"You don't make money on what you meant to invest in, only on what you did invest in."

"You never fail unless you stop trying."

15.2 Best Practices of Buffett and Munger:

Warren Buffett and Charlie Munger have created one of the best investment practices, which have benefited many investors. Here's how they worded it in the 1977 and 1989 letters to shareholders.

1977: "Charlie and I look for: businesses we understand; favorable long-term economics; able and trustworthy management; and a sensible price."
[i] Berkshire Chairman's Letter to Shareholders, 1977,
http://www.berkshirehathaway.com/letters/1977.html

1989: "When buying companies or common stocks, we look for understandable 1st class businesses with enduring competitive advantages, accompanied by first-class managements, available at a bargain price."
[ii] Berkshire Chairman's Letter to Shareholders, 1989,
http://www.berkshirehathaway.com/letters/1989.html

Berkshire Hathaway's 1977 annual letter to shareholders is the earliest letter mentioning Buffett and Munger's Four-Filters, first presented as:

We select our marketable equity securities in much the same way we would evaluate a business for acquisition in its entirety. We want a business to be: (1) one that we can understand, (2) with favorable long-term prospects, (3) operated by honest and competent people, and (4) available at a very attractive price.

After Charlie and Warren overcame the hurdle of recognizing businesses that could be bargains based on quantitative measures that would have horrified Ben Graham, they started thinking about better businesses. Their results show the bulk of their billions earned came from investing in better businesses. Munger said: "We came to this notion of finding a mispriced bet and loading up when we were very confident that we were right. So we're way less diversified, and I think our system is miles better."

[i] "A Lesson on Elementary, Worldly Wisdom As It Relates To Investment Management & Business." Charles Munger, USC Business School, 1994.

CHAPTER SIXTEEN:

Responsible Philanthropy

"Philanthropy is the love of others expressed by donations of time, service, volunteering, money, or anything of value." Scott Thompson

16.1 Overview:

Wealth in circulation spurs prosperity at many levels. Consumption and capital investments are a means of fostering growth, but donations of resources are another. Contributions of educational supplies, money, time and physical brawn change the world. No one ever improves his wealth alone; rather people interlink arms to share resources with each other. Wealth and donated resources are the means by which we offer nourishment – at many levels – to one another in order to foster growth. It's resource exchange, rather than the welfare state invoked in government hand-outs, and is the way to improve the quality of life across the globe.

Philanthropy, which means, "love of others," is a prescribed avenue for sharing donations of money, materials, time, services, talents, etc. to help others. By participating in philanthropy, individuals also participate in the cycle of wealth and prosperity that generates larger and larger concentric circles of resources. Your actions will create a ripple effect that continues to flow into the larger stream of resources that make-up humanity, and return to you seven-fold – though possibly in different forms.

The tutoring you provide to a disadvantaged youth may lead to the vaccination a young girl receives in Ghana after that youth you tutored grows-up, becomes a doctor and donates his services. Many connections are facilitated through philanthropy and many positive actions started in motion, remain in motion. It's the wish of this author that you consider using your wealth to empower others. Imagine the societal benefits that can be achieved by the cumulative wealth set into motion by thousands of philanthropists taking an active interest in the empowerment of others.

Be a conduit to guide people toward increased esteem, confidence, and self-determination. Seek organizations that help others help themselves. Avoid working with organizations that "enable" recipients to remain mired in their dysfunction. It does little good to offer funds to substance abusers, as the old SSI system did, because added cash flow to abusers does nothing to better their plight. Instead, they require a transformation of heart and conscience and the ability to reconcile their past and bolster resilience. In short, they require your support so they can learn how to believe and invest in themselves. Donations of services and time can often be the catalyst needed to transform peoples' lives into lives they're proud of living. That which you support, expands and amplifies. Perform your research in advance to be sure your resources are well allocated.

Imagine the possibilities and consider organizations, regardless of size, that foster real growth. Rather than donating funds, you may invest your time, promoting confidence in people with whom you volunteer. Perhaps, you will be an inspiration in their lives because you believe in them. Or perhaps they will be an inspiration to you.

As they change themselves, they change the world. One person at a time, our world is transformed. Many have risen from drug abuse, emotional degradation, and poverty because someone believed in them and gave them the resources to learn to care for themselves. Possible avenues for you to consider might be tutoring disadvantaged children, donating clothing, giving funds to buy livestock for start-up farms, digging wells, donating educational supplies, teaching villagers about soil regeneration, etc. The key is to investigate the stream into which your resources will flow, and seek those that are in positive motion. Know the difference between good intentions and effective results.

16.2 Warren Buffett's Philanthropy:

In 2006, Warren Buffett announced his charitable donation of giving away 99% of his fortune. The recipients were five foundations: The Bill & Melinda Gates Foundation received the bulk of Warren's philanthropic gift; The Suzan Thompson Foundation received $5 billion; and the foundations of each of Warren's three adult children received $1 billion each. Warren's philanthropic gift remains the largest in the history of the world. Warren's gift requires either Bill or Melinda Gates to remain active within the foundation. One hundred percent of Warren's philanthropic donation must be given away within Bill and Melinda's lifetime.

Warren Buffett said that he wants his wealth to return to the same society that allowed him to create it. It remains to be seen how these five foundations will allocate the billions he worked hard to accumulate.

16.3 Planned Giving:

In the USA, non-profit organizations are often classified under the 501-c3 heading under current IRS tax code (as of 2013). These organizations are exempt from paying taxes, and donations to these organizations are often 100% tax-deductible. Philanthropists often experience unintended consequences. Strive to be a responsible philanthropist. Try to see as far into the future as possible, and perform due diligence before you donate. Research the organization in advance, because after your check gets cashed, it is gone. *View the Thompson models of philanthropy (below). We recommend the 1st model (on left), to reduce the potential of misallocated capital.*

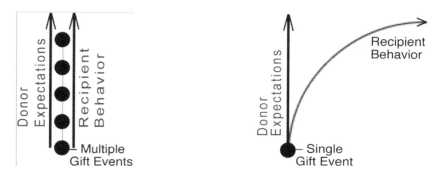

Philanthropists should consider not gifting their entire donation all at once. This may create opportunities for the recipient to misallocate the donation without accountability or consequences.

Instead, consider establishing "milestones" in advance of the donations against which progress can be measured. Recipients are expected to use the resources wisely in order to qualify for the next portion of your donation. This increases accountability, and decreases the possibility donations could be misused.

Most people are not good allocators of capital. Even so-called financial experts who have studied finance their entire lives are not always good allocators of capital. So why would those in charge of a non-profit organization, who have never studied finance and who suddenly receive a large philanthropic donation, be good allocators of capital? They often are not. This emphasizes the importance of researching recipient organizations before committing donations.

Some argue that efficiently allocating capital is not important in non-profit organizations. Many in the "non-profit" world make emotional arguments instead of financially sound arguments to justify their allocation of capital. Potential donors should observe how non-profit organizations allocate their capital, and after investigating this, decide whether to donate.

Interestingly, many "non-profits" are some the most profitable businesses. While they pay no taxes, their executives earn in excess of six-figure salaries, higher than those in for-profit businesses! Avoid non-profits that enrich their executives, managers, and board members with fat salaries instead of helping the causes they claim to support. Perform your own research. Seek only those ethical organizations that do the most good for the most people, by efficiently allocating their finite capital. For more info, visit: www.CharityNavigator.org .You may be surprised at what you find.

Avoid non-profits who intentionally play on the heartstrings of donors to solicit donations. Many donors are not wise capital allocators and may be lured by the emotion of the moment. Instead, take some time to carefully evaluate various non-profit organizations. Get to know the organizations, meet the executive board, tour the facility, etc. This will help you avoid situations where your donation has already been given, but you later learn of serious misallocations of capital by the recipient organization. Remember the goal of philanthropy is to help those in need, not enrich the management team. Ask which percent of each dollar donated goes to administrative costs, and which percent actually goes to those in need?

16.4 Philanthropic Due Diligence:

Due diligence is the process of performing an investigation into the recipient organization before making a potential philanthropic donation. Performing a sound due diligence process first, can minimize and prevent misallocations of capital. These ten due diligence steps will help guide new philanthropists to stay on the path of informed, responsible philanthropy.

1. Donate only to organizations verified as having IRS 501-c3 tax-exempt status (USA only). Organizations outside the USA will not have this designation, and will require further due diligence to verify their validity as a genuine charitable organization.

2. How can philanthropists be confident nearly 100% of their donations will actually reach those in need, and not be squandered? Quantify in advance the percentage that will go to the recipient organization's operations, and which percentage will go directly to those in need. For instance, will 10% go to recipient organization's management salaries and 90% to those in need? Or other way around? Avoid organizations with exorbitant administrative costs. Make sure at least 90% of your donations will actually be received by those in need.

3. Determine in advance which persons within the recipient organization are ultimately accountable to how your donation will be allocated. Follow up.

4. Which macro-economic, geo-political, and systemic factors could adversely affect whether donations actually reach those in need? For instance, lack of infrastructure, roads, reliable transportation, clean water, food, medicines, vaccines, education, schools, teachers, cooperation of national and local government agencies, etc. Discuss and design contingency plans. For example, if you plan to build schools, what if students are starving, have no water, and cannot concentrate on their school lessons? Visit the destination. Listen to the people. Learn first, before taking action.

5. Identify measurable milestones in advance, clearly defining success or failure. Has the recipient organization been a good steward of past donations? Can they verify their responsible stewardship of past donations, or is the opposite true?

6. No lump sums should be given up front. Instead, donations should be gifted into multiple portions over time, after the recipient organization demonstrates they have clearly achieved predetermined milestones. Define milestones in advance in writing, and have both parties sign the agreement.

7. What is the penalty if milestones are not achieved, or if donations become mismanaged, embezzled, diverted, or misallocated to areas other than the donor intended?

8. Are other philanthropists currently considering gifting to the same recipient organization or cause? Which ones? How much is their donation? Will too many resources be allocated to the same need? Should donations be allocated to other needs? Which ones? Ask questions of your recipient organization. Listen and learn first, before donating.

9. Specify how the recipient organization will benefit from your proposed philanthropic donation.

10. Have fun. Enjoy the process. Philanthropy should be fun. Make friends. Avoid opportunists. Know the difference.

16.5 Philanthropic Colonialism:

Philanthropic Colonialism occurs when philanthropists naively enter foreign countries where much help is needed, then impose ill-chosen "solutions" without first learning the nature of the underlying problem. These philanthropic colonialists have a "give, conquer and leave" mentality, and do not take time to first listen and learn from the local recipient community. Unintended consequences can arise caused by duplication of resources by philanthropists and NGOs (Non-Government Organizations) making donations to the same cause. These situations can be avoided if philanthropists spend a little more time researching and interacting with the local recipients in advance of their philanthropic gift.

Blindly throwing money at a problem is never as effective as listening, learning, understanding the problem, and arriving at a solution together with the help of the local community. In philanthropic colonialism, the act of "donating" makes the philanthropist feel good, but their donation will not be near as effective if they were to spend the necessary time with the local community leaders, governments, to gain a clearer sense of the actual problem and most effective ways to solve it.

The field of philanthropy needs more thoughtful donors, instead of well-intended donors whose donations are not as effective. If the goal of philanthropy is to help as many recipients as possible per dollar donated, then it is imperative philanthropists perform necessary research and due diligence to increase the effectiveness of their donations.

Therefore, it is incumbent upon philanthropists to develop responsible giving strategies. When it comes to giving money away, there will obviously be no shortage of open hands! However, if you apply these concepts of responsible philanthropy, you will achieve more good helping more people with your finite resources.

16.6 Volunteering:

Mother Teresa wisely said that volunteering is the greatest gift you could ever give yourself. One of my favorite Mother Teresa quotes is, *"We think sometimes that poverty is only being hungry, naked and homeless. The poverty of being unwanted, unloved and uncared for is the greatest poverty. We must start in our own homes to remedy this kind of poverty."*

I've enjoyed volunteering thousands of hours with amazing people and their wonderful families. I've spent so much time with these wonderful people that they've made me feel like part of their families. Over the years of volunteering, I've attended numerous weddings, dinners, events, funerals, graduation parties, cookouts, and fundraising events. Volunteering is a great way to serve your community, meet new people, and make a difference in the lives of others.

I've enjoyed volunteer coaching the Minnesota Magic wheelchair power soccer team who won the #1 United States Power Soccer Association (USPSA) national championship 3 years in-a-row, 2010, 2011, and 2012. It has been an honor to spend time with such amazing athletes and parents! For more info or to make a donation visit: www.MnMagic.org

16.7 Scholarships:

Scholarships are an effective way to empower others through education. Great leaders recognize the importance of education. Frederick Douglass affirmed this and believed education is the key for people to improve their lives. In this spirit, I created a diversity scholarship to benefit students from diverse ethnic backgrounds who otherwise could not afford to attend college. My parents also believe in education and are inspirational.

Education is important to me. My mother was a teacher in public schools, and also taught Title I education to students who needed extra help learning to read. Over her career, my mother taught hundreds of young children from diverse backgrounds how to read.

Later in life, I remember many of her former students approaching her in the supermarket, overcome with emotion, expressing how she helped them learn to read after other teachers had given-up on them. They expressed how my mother made a difference in their lives, and how well they are doing now. It would mean a lot to me if my scholarships also made a difference by having a lasting impact in the lives of others.

"It's not what you get. It's what you give." Scott Thompson

In closing, in the words of Marianne Williamson, "Our deepest fear is not that we are inadequate. Our deepest fear is that we are powerful beyond measure. It is our light, not our darkness that most frightens us. We ask ourselves, who am I to be brilliant, gorgeous, talented, fabulous? Actually, who are you *not* to be? You are a child of God. Your playing small does not serve the world. There is nothing enlightened about shrinking so that other people won't feel insecure around you. We are all meant to shine, as children do. We were born to make manifest the glory of God that is within us. It's not just in some of us; it's in everyone. And as we let our own light shine, we unconsciously give other people permission to do the same. As we are liberated from our own fear, our presence automatically liberates others."

"The best things in life cannot be measured monetarily." Scott Thompson

BIO:

Scott Thompson, MBA is Chairman and CEO of Ameritrust Group, and was previously managing director of Intrinsic Value Capital. Scott is a disciple of value investors Warren Buffett, Charlie Munger, Ben Graham, and Phil Fisher. Scott implements rigorous quantitative and qualitative value investing strategies, minimizes risk, and is an expert at identifying undervalued assets. For more info visit: AmeritrustCorp.com

Scott graduated from Northern Illinois University in 1991 with his Bachelor of Science Degree. Then, graduated summa cum laude from Aspen University with his MBA, earning the "Graduate Student of the Year" award. After college, he worked with several Fortune-500 companies including Merrill Lynch/Bank of America and served as Vice President of an investment bank.

Like Buffett, Scott also believes in philanthropy, and has donated financially as well as thousands of volunteer hours to help those in need. Scott serves on numerous boards and charity organizations, including Allina Health's "Courage Kenny Rehabilitation Institute," which is the 5th largest healthcare rehabilitation organization in the United States. He has organized and attended large charity events across the country with friend Peter Buffett (author, musician, philanthropist, and son of billionaire investor Warren Buffett). Scott enjoys authoring books, reading, and speaking at investor seminars, book-signing events, and value investing conferences worldwide. His team can be reached at: info@ProValueSource.com

Peter Buffett, Scott Thompson, Warren Buffett
(Founder: Berkshire Hathaway)

Scott Thompson, Bill Gates, III
(Founder: Microsoft)

May-2014: FOX BUSINESS NEWS mentions Scott Thompson's book during 1-hour interview with billionaires: Bill Gates, Warren Buffett, and Charlie Munger, by news anchor Liz Claman after Berkshire Hathaway shareholder meeting.
https://www.youtube.com/watch?v=i6-_8rrVkTo

"Minnesota Magic" #1 national wheelchair power soccer team

Scott Thompson volunteer coached the "Minnesota Magic" wheelchair power soccer team since 2008. MN Magic won 1st place in the national USPSA tournament in 2010, 2011, and 2012. Several of the wheelchair athletes Scott coached are now on Team USA. For more info or to make a tax-deductible donation, visit: http://www.MnMagic.org

The "Scott Thompson and Dr. Yang Dao" Diversity Scholarship

Scott Thompson founded a diversity college scholarship with President of Century College, Executive Director of the Century Foundation, and top political leaders of Southeast Asian community. Dr. Yang Dao is the 1st Hmong person in this history of the world to earn his Ph.D.

The "Scott Thompson and Dr. Yang Dao" Scholarship encourages diversity and benefits students from diverse ethnic backgrounds to attend college who otherwise could not afford to attend college.
http://www.Century.edu

Scott has volunteered with Courage Kenny since 2008, and has surpassed a milestone of over 1,500+ volunteer hours empowering children with disabilities!

Scott Thompson serves on the Development Board of Allina Health's Courage Kenny Rehabilitation Institute (formerly Courage Center / Sister Kenny); which is the 5th largest rehabilitation healthcare organization in the entire United States. http://www.CourageCenter.org

REFERENCE:

An Owner's Manual to Berkshire Hathaway's shareholders

In June 1996, Berkshire's Chairman, Warren E. Buffett, issued a booklet entitled **"An Owner's Manual©"** to Berkshire's Class A and Class B shareholders. The purpose of the manual was to explain Berkshire's broad economic principles of operation. An updated version is reproduced on this and the following pages.

OWNER-RELATED BUSINESS PRINCIPLES

At the time of the Blue Chip merger in 1983, I set down 13 owner-related business principles that I thought would help new shareholders understand our managerial approach. As is appropriate for "principles," all 13 remain alive and well today, and they are stated here in italics.

1. *Although our form is corporate, our attitude is partnership. Charlie Munger and I think of our shareholders as owner-partners, and of ourselves as managing partners. (Because of the size of our shareholdings we are also, for better or worse, controlling partners.) We do not view the company itself as the ultimate owner of our business assets but instead view the company as a conduit through which our shareholders own the assets.*   Charlie and I hope that you do not think of yourself as merely owning a piece of paper whose price wiggles around daily and that is a candidate for sale when some economic or political event makes you nervous. We hope you instead visualize yourself as a part owner of a business that you expect to stay with indefinitely, much as you might if you owned a farm or apartment house in partnership with members of your family. For our part, we do not view Berkshire shareholders as faceless members of an ever-shifting crowd, but rather as co-venturers who have entrusted their funds to us for what may well turn out to be the remainder of their lives.   The evidence suggests that most Berkshire shareholders have indeed embraced this long-term partnership concept. The annual percentage turnover in Berkshire's shares is a fraction of that occurring in the stocks of other major American corporations, even when the shares I own are excluded from the calculation.   In effect, our shareholders behave in respect to their Berkshire stock much as Berkshire itself behaves in respect to companies in which it has an investment. As owners of, say, Coca-Cola or American Express

shares, we think of Berkshire as being a non- managing partner in two extraordinary businesses, in which we measure our success by the long-term progress of the companies rather than by the month-to-month movements of their stocks. In fact, we would not care in the least if several years went by in which there was no trading, or quotation of prices, in the stocks of those companies. If we have good long-term expectations, short-term price changes are meaningless for us except to the extent they offer us an opportunity to increase our ownership at an attractive price.

2. *In line with Berkshire's owner-orientation, most of our directors have a major portion of their net worth invested in the company. We eat our own cooking.*

   Charlie's family has 80% or more of its net worth in Berkshire shares; I have more than 98%. In addition, many of my relatives – my sisters and cousins, for example – keep a huge portion of their net worth in Berkshire stock. Charlie and I feel totally comfortable with this eggs-in-one-basket situation because Berkshire itself owns a wide variety of truly extraordinary businesses. Indeed, we believe that Berkshire is close to being unique in the quality and diversity of the businesses in which it owns either a controlling interest or a minority interest of significance. Charlie and I cannot promise you results. But we can guarantee that your financial fortunes will move in lockstep with ours for whatever period of time you elect to be our partner. We have no interest in large salaries or options or other means of gaining an "edge" over you. We want to make money only when our partners do and in exactly the same proportion. Moreover, when I do something dumb, I want you to be able to derive some solace from the fact my financial suffering is proportional to yours.

3. *Our long-term economic goal (subject to some qualifications mentioned later) is to maximize Berkshire's average annual rate of gain in intrinsic business value on a per-share basis. We do not measure the economic significance or performance of Berkshire by its size; we measure by per-share progress. We are certain that the rate of per-share progress will diminish in the future – a greatly enlarged capital base will see to that. But we will be disappointed if our rate does not exceed that of the average large American corporation.*

4. *Our preference would be to reach our goal by directly owning a diversified group of businesses that generate cash and consistently earn above-average returns on capital. Our second choice is to own parts of similar businesses, attained primarily through purchases of marketable common stocks by our insurance subsidiaries. The price and availability of businesses and the need for insurance capital determine any given year's capital allocation.*

Berkshire Hathaway's Performance vs. S&P 500

Berkshire's Corporate Performance vs. the S&P 500

Year	Annual Percentage Change in Per-Share Book Value of Berkshire (1)	in S&P 500 with Dividends Included (2)	Relative Results (1)-(2)
1965	23.8	10.0	13.8
1966	20.3	(11.7)	32.0
1967	11.0	30.9	(19.9)
1968	19.0	11.0	8.0
1969	16.2	(8.4)	24.6
1970	12.0	3.9	8.1
1971	16.4	14.6	1.8
1972	21.7	18.9	2.8
1973	4.7	(14.8)	19.5
1974	5.5	(26.4)	31.9
1975	21.9	37.2	(15.3)
1976	59.3	23.6	35.7
1977	31.9	(7.4)	39.3
1978	24.0	6.4	17.6
1979	35.7	18.2	17.5
1980	19.3	32.3	(13.0)
1981	31.4	(5.0)	36.4
1982	40.0	21.4	18.6
1983	32.3	22.4	9.9
1984	13.6	6.1	7.5
1985	48.2	31.6	16.6
1986	26.1	18.6	7.5
1987	19.5	5.1	14.4
1988	20.1	16.6	3.5
1989	44.4	31.7	12.7
1990	7.4	(3.1)	10.5
1991	39.6	30.5	9.1
1992	20.3	7.6	12.7
1993	14.3	10.1	4.2
1994	13.9	1.3	12.6
1995	43.1	37.6	5.5
1996	31.8	23.0	8.8
1997	34.1	33.4	0.7
1998	48.3	28.6	19.7
1999	0.5	21.0	(20.5)
2000	6.5	(9.1)	15.6
2001	(6.2)	(11.9)	5.7
2002	10.0	(22.1)	32.1
2003	21.0	28.7	(7.7)
2004	10.5	10.9	(0.4)
2005	6.4	4.9	1.5
2006	18.4	15.8	2.6
2007	11.0	5.5	5.5
2008	(9.6)	(37.0)	27.4
2009	19.8	26.5	(6.7)
2010	13.0	15.1	(2.1)
2011	4.6	2.1	2.5
2012	14.4	16.0	(1.6)
2013	18.2	32.4	(14.2)
Compounded Annual Gain – 1965-2013	19.7%	9.8%	9.9
Overall Gain – 1964-2013	693,518%	9,841%	

Notes: Data are for calendar years with these exceptions: 1965 and 1966, year ended 9/30; 1967, 15 months ended 12/31. Starting in 1979, accounting rules required insurance companies to value the equity securities they hold at market rather than at the lower of cost or market, which was previously the requirement. In this table, Berkshire's results through 1978 have been restated to conform to the changed rules. In all other respects, the results are calculated using the numbers originally reported. The S&P 500 numbers are **pre-tax** whereas the Berkshire numbers are **after-tax**. If a corporation such as Berkshire were simply to have owned the S&P 500 and accrued the appropriate taxes, its results would have lagged the S&P 500 in years when that index showed a positive return, but would have exceeded the S&P 500 in years when the index showed a negative return. Over the years, the tax costs would have caused the aggregate lag to be substantial.

Chart: Effective Yield of a Bargain Purchase after 10-years

Contributed by Bakul Lalla (Lalla, 2010)

Once you have a suitable investment candidate that fulfills the first three filters, estimate the intrinsic value. Margin of safety = Intrinsic Value minus Market Price. Convert this into percentage form like this: (1 - Market Price/Intrinsic Value) * 100

Using your estimated percent margin of safety relative to market price, look to where the margin of safety intersects with a reasonable growth rate to find an estimate for an effective annual yield after ten years.

Thanks to John Kish, here is the same idea in a formula form:

If you know the Future Value, FV, and the period is fixed at 10 years, the annual rate of return would be: ((FV/(purchase price)) ^ (1/10))-1.

If you are treating FV as 1 (full value), then purchase price is (1 - % bargain). So the full formula for the annual return for a bargain returning to fair value over 10 years is ((1/(1-%bargain))^.1)-1. Therefore, a 50% bargain returns a little over 7% annually over ten years: ((1/.5)^.1)-1 = 7.17%

If you know that the growth of the company's free cash flow is at a rate of 7% over that same period, then 7 + 7.17 = 14.17% is the "extra kicker" obtained from the quality bargain purchase.

Growth

Margin of Safety	3%	4%	5%	6%	7%	8%	9%	10%	11%	12%	13%	14%	15%	16%	17%	18%	19%	20%
5%	3.53%	4.53%	5.54%	6.55%	7.55%	8.56%	9.56%	10.57%	11.57%	12.58%	13.58%	14.59%	15.59%	16.60%	17.60%	18.61%	19.61%	20.62%
10%	4.09%	5.10%	6.11%	7.12%	8.13%	9.14%	10.15%	11.17%	12.18%	13.19%	14.20%	15.21%	16.22%	17.23%	18.24%	19.25%	20.26%	21.27%
15%	4.69%	5.70%	6.72%	7.74%	8.75%	9.77%	10.79%	11.80%	12.82%	13.84%	14.85%	15.87%	16.88%	17.90%	18.92%	19.93%	20.95%	21.97%
20%	5.32%	6.35%	7.37%	8.39%	9.41%	10.44%	11.46%	12.48%	13.50%	14.53%	15.55%	16.57%	17.59%	18.62%	19.64%	20.66%	21.69%	22.71%
25%	6.01%	7.04%	8.06%	9.09%	10.12%	11.15%	12.18%	13.21%	14.24%	15.27%	16.30%	17.33%	18.36%	19.39%	20.41%	21.44%	22.47%	23.50%
30%	6.74%	7.78%	8.81%	9.85%	10.89%	11.92%	12.96%	13.99%	15.03%	16.07%	17.10%	18.14%	19.18%	20.21%	21.25%	22.28%	23.32%	24.36%
35%	7.53%	8.58%	9.62%	10.67%	11.71%	12.75%	13.80%	14.84%	15.89%	16.93%	17.97%	19.02%	20.06%	21.11%	22.15%	23.19%	24.24%	25.28%
40%	8.40%	9.45%	10.50%	11.56%	12.61%	13.66%	14.71%	15.77%	16.82%	17.87%	18.92%	19.97%	21.03%	22.08%	23.13%	24.18%	25.24%	26.29%
45%	9.35%	10.41%	11.47%	12.53%	13.59%	14.65%	15.72%	16.78%	17.84%	18.90%	19.96%	21.02%	22.08%	23.15%	24.21%	25.27%	26.33%	27.39%
50%	10.39%	11.46%	12.54%	13.61%	14.68%	15.75%	16.82%	17.90%	18.97%	20.04%	21.11%	22.18%	23.25%	24.33%	25.40%	26.47%	27.54%	28.61%
55%	11.56%	12.65%	13.73%	14.81%	15.89%	16.98%	18.06%	19.14%	20.23%	21.31%	22.39%	23.48%	24.56%	25.64%	26.73%	27.81%	28.89%	29.98%
60%	12.88%	13.98%	15.08%	16.17%	17.27%	18.36%	19.46%	20.56%	21.65%	22.75%	23.84%	24.94%	26.04%	27.13%	28.23%	29.32%	30.42%	31.51%
65%	14.40%	15.51%	16.62%	17.73%	18.84%	19.95%	21.07%	22.18%	23.29%	24.40%	25.51%	26.62%	27.73%	28.84%	29.95%	31.06%	32.17%	33.28%
70%	16.18%	17.31%	18.43%	19.56%	20.69%	21.82%	22.95%	24.07%	25.20%	26.33%	27.46%	28.59%	29.71%	30.84%	31.97%	33.10%	34.23%	35.35%
75%	18.32%	19.46%	20.61%	21.76%	22.91%	24.06%	25.21%	26.36%	27.51%	28.65%	29.80%	30.95%	32.10%	33.25%	34.40%	35.55%	36.70%	37.84%
80%	20.99%	22.16%	23.33%	24.51%	25.68%	26.86%	28.03%	29.21%	30.38%	31.56%	32.73%	33.91%	35.08%	36.26%	37.43%	38.61%	39.78%	40.95%
85%	24.52%	25.73%	26.93%	28.14%	29.35%	30.56%	31.77%	32.98%	34.19%	35.40%	36.61%	37.81%	39.02%	40.23%	41.44%	42.65%	43.86%	45.07%
90%	29.67%	30.93%	32.19%	33.45%	34.71%	35.96%	37.22%	38.48%	39.74%	41.00%	42.26%	43.52%	44.78%	46.04%	47.29%	48.55%	49.81%	51.07%

Warren Buffett's Coca-Cola Magic

Contributed by Bud Labitan

While I was happy with our book "1988 Valuation of Coca-Cola: Estimated Intrinsic Value," I felt like we did not fully explain the importance, value and power of that bargain purchase.

I would think, "How can this be? My investing heroes, Warren Buffett and Charlie Munger" always smile and resist cries from shareholders to sell the Coca-Cola (KO) shares. What I rediscovered is that the magic of Warren Buffett's and Charlie Munger's 1988 purchase of Coca-Cola stock is: YIELD ON COST.

Think of "yield on cost" as "yield relative to my cost" or "the yield received per-share cost" or "yield / per-share cost." It can be described as "yield ÷ cost per share."

My initial thinking went something like this: Think of it as getting an average gain of a $570 million dividend every single year from that principal investment cost of $1.299 billion in Coca-Cola. If you multiply $570 million x 24 years, we get $13.15 billion. Add this $13.15 billion to the $1.29 billion principal, and we get very, very close to the current value of $14.44 billion in BRK's ownership of Coca-Cola.

Look at their cost of $1.299 billion, 0.44 rate of average annual return, and 0.57, which represents my assumption of $570 million. Multiply 0.57 x 23 (23 because of end-of-year adjustment), plus one-half of year of approximately 0.29, so 1.299 + 13.43 = $14.73 billion, and it is darn close.

I found an old 2010 article that said: When Buffett began purchasing stock in Coca Cola in 1988, many Wall Street analysts were skeptical because it seemed only a matter of time before other beverage companies would take away its market share. In addition, Coca-Cola had reported earnings down 2 percent from the previous year, and had an unimpressive P/E ratio of between 14 to 19. At the time, shares of KO were worth between $35 and $45. As of September 2010, Buffett's unrealized gains on

KO were $10.4 billion. This comes out to a 766 percent increase in value. This is one of Buffett's greatest investing triumphs.

Using the same simple logic... When $2 grows into $6, no matter the duration, we say 6/2=3 and 3*100 = a 300% increase in value, no matter if it takes 1 or 900 years. In this simple math, duration is irrelevant.

By 2013, KO stock has split 4 times and BRK has 400 million shares with a cost basis of $1.299 billion, and a market value of $14.5 billion. Forget for a moment that it took about 24.5 years to get here. Furthermore, suspend the idea of splits because we know the cost and the present dollar value that is already split-adjusted.

When $1.299 billion grows to $14.500 billion, we say 14.500/1.299=11.16 and *100 is a 1,116% increase in value. Again, in simple math, how much can we allocate to each year? Let us use a simple average and make it even. Now, a simple rough average of 1116/24.5 years=45.55% approximate gain per year, and this does not even count the value of the dividends.

(Next, I get a little theoretical.) Let us add in the probably low but fair figure of $5 billion for all the dividends (with no major time value of money adjustments). When $1.299 grows to $19.500, we say 19.500/1.299=15.01 and *100 is a 1,501% increase in value. Now, a simple rough average of 1501/24.5 years=61.27% gain in value (on top of the $1.29 billion) per year, or around $570 million each year.

Now, I felt like I was getting close to why Buffett's 1988 bargain purchase of KO is so powerful and important. Rather than looking at the compounding of value over time, you are looking at the average annual increase in value against the original $1.299 billion invested. So, if I think of the original stock purchase as buying a bond instead, that "bond" continuously pays increasing interest rate over time. Buffett has basically bought a bond for $1.299 billion that has paid on average coupon of 61.27% annually. Said Richard Griebe, "This is a feat that would make gangsters jealous !"

I kept searching the Internet for this "yield" concept that I was looking for. I was looking for Buffett's effective yield per share compared to my yield per share. I stumbled upon the bond concept of YIELD ON COST. That is it! Yield per "share cost."

Did I realize that 1.299 billion/400 million shares = Buffett's $3.25 per share cost per share of KO? Did you?

From the website Investopedia, Yield on cost (YOC) is defined as: "The annual dividend rate of a security divided by the average cost basis of the investments. It shows the dividend yield of the original investment. If the number of shares owned by the investor does not change, the yield on cost will increase if the company increases the dividend it pays to shareholders; otherwise it will remain the same."

To calculate yield on cost for a stock, an investor must divide the stock's annual dividend by the average cost basis per share and multiple the resulting number by 100 (to get a percentage). For example, an investor who purchased 10 shares of stock at $15 and 20 shares at $18 would have an average cost basis of $17 per share ($15*10 + $18*20)/(10 + 20). If the annual dividend is $0.90 per share, the yield on cost would be 5.29% ($0.90/$17 * 100).

Using this information, and knowing that Buffett's cost per share of KO is $3.25, can I calculate his yield on cost for 2012? The 2012 dividends per share were: March 13, 2013 $0.28, Nov. 28, 2012 $0.26, Sept. 12, 2012 $0.26, June 13, 2012 $0.26, March 13, 2012 $0.26, and the sum is $1.30

So, $1.30 / $3.25 = 0.40 and 0.40 * 100 = 40%. Buffett and Berkshire Hathaway received a 40% yield on cost just for the year 2012 dividends alone!

Alternatively, and again thinking in bond-like thoughts, if we believe the $570 million average return per year on top of the $1.299 billion principal. $570 million / 400 million shares is 1.43, and that is like a gain of 43% each year over the initial investment.

Prediction: Since 45% + 40% = 85%, I predict that the total yearly return will soon surpass the initial $1.29 billion cost basis of this Coca-Cola investment.

BIBLIOGRAPHY:

Buffett, W. (1956-1969). *Buffett Partnership Letters*. Omaha: Warren Buffett.

Buffett, W. (1977-2012). *Annual Letter to the Shareholders of Berkshire Hathaway, Inc.* Omaha: Berkshire Hathaway, Inc.

Buffett, W. (1988). *Phil Fisher, mentioned in the Berkshire Chairman's Letter to Shareholders*. Omaha: Berkshire Hathaway Inc.

Buffett, W. (1996). *Phil Carret was mentioned at the 1996 Buffett Letter to Shareholders*. 1996.

Buffett, W. (1998). *From a talk given at the University of Florida, quoted in the Miami Herald (December 27, 1998)*. Miami: University of Florida.

Buffett, W. E. (1984). *The Superinvestors of Graham-and-Doddsville*. Hermes.

Graham, B. (1949). *The Intelligent Investor*. New York.

Greenwald, B. (2001). *Value Investing: From Graham to Buffett and Beyond*. Wiley Finance.

Kaufman, P. D. (2005). *(The Psychology of Human Misjudgment Revised Speech by Charles T. Munger), Poor Charlie's Almanack*. Virginia Beach, VA: PCA Publication, LLC.

Labitan, B. (2010). *The Four Filters Invention of Warren Buffett and Charlie Munger*. Chicago: Acalmix.

Labitan, B. (2012). *MOATS: Competitive Advantages of Buffett and Munger Businesses*. Chicago: Acalmix.

Labitan/Thompson. (2013). *1988 Valuation of Coca-Cola*. Chicago: Acalmix.

Lalla, B. (2010). *The Lalla Effective Yield After 10 Years Table, Based on a discussion we had about the effect of a 50% bargain on a steady 7% earning company. Mr. Bakul Lalla expanded this idea and he was generous in donating this table.* . Bakul Lalla.

Munger, C. T. (1994). *A Lesson on Elementary, Worldly Wisdom As It Relates To Investment Management & Business.* Los Angeles: USC Business School.

Munger, C. T. (1994). *A Lesson on Elementary, Worldly Wisdom As It Relates To Investment Management & Business. A 1994 Speech.* Los Angeles: USC Business School.

Munger, C. T. (2001). *Charlie Munger Talk at Harvard Law School.* Boston: Harvard Law School.

Williams, John Burr (1938). *The Theory of Investment Value* . Cambridge: Harvard.

Lightning Source UK Ltd.
Milton Keynes UK
UKHW042238060919
349227UK00001B/21/P